Islam and Natural Law

The Department of Research and Publications at the Islamic College for Advanced Studies (ICAS) is an academic and cultural centre, concerned with general issues of Islamic thought. The idea of an Islamic institution of higher learning grounded on Islamic normative values and historical heritage, yet fully capable of responding to, and guiding Muslims in meeting the demands of modern Western epistemological, cultural, socio-political and economic ideas, are based on years of experience and contemplation, all of which now form conceptual history of ICAS. The Department provides a meeting point for the Western and Islamic worlds of learning. At ICAS it contributes to the multi-disciplinary and cross-disciplinary study of the contemporary world. Beyond ICAS, its role is strengthened by developing international academic contacts. It is an intellectual forum working from an Islamic perspective to promote and support research projects, organise intellectual and cultural seminars and publish scholarly works. It tries to establish a distinct intellectual trend in Islamic thought which relates to the vivid legacy of the Muslim nation and its continuous efforts for intellectual and methodological reform. This involves a large number of researchers and scholars from various parts of the world.

ICAS' publications fall into the following categories: *Theology, Philosophy, Mysticism, Islamic Legal Theory and Islamic Law, hermeneutics and Qur'anic studies, Hadith methodology, Social Sciences, and Languages.*

Since ICAS is an academic college promoting intellectual debate, and scholarship, the views expressed in the books published will always reflect independent views and diverse approaches to the problems being dealt with.

ICAS Press

A. Ezzati

Islam and Natural Law

ICAS Press

British Library Cataloguing-in-Publication Data
A catalogue record for this book is available from the
British Library

ISBN 1 904063 05 5 (pb)

This edition first published 2002

Published by
Islamic College for Advanced Studies Press (ICAS)
133 High Road, Willesden, London NW10 2SW

Contents

Preface

Islam introduces itself as the religion of inclusive and absolute monotheism mainly, though not inclusively, on the basis of human primordial nature and reason. It naturally, thus, suggests that the doctrine of inclusive monotheism establishes inclusive unity, balance and harmony in the entire creation, universe, nature, humanity and the different dimensions of life of individuals and the human community.

The obvious consequence of this doctrine is that Islam supports a holistic approach towards the entire creation including man, taking into consideration directly and indirectly all his physical, rational, emotional, spiritual, natural, ethical and other needs. In Islam the rational and emotional/spiritual needs of man do not have to be considered at the expense of the other needs. Nature, natural laws, universal order and human natural rights do not contradict man's spiritual, ethical and religious needs and order. Heart does not contradict mind, faith is not in opposition to logical and rational beliefs and there is no conflict between man and nature, body, soul and spirit, faith and the needs of man.

Man is a major part of the entire creation, a harmonious unit, and should be in harmony with the order of nature and the entire universe. Mankind being what it is, a complex mixture of rational–emotional, physical–spiritual, individual–social and other dimensions and needs, must be taken into consideration as a whole and in harmony with the universe by any religion and system of belief that claims universality. A faith and a religion cannot afford to be only emotional or only rational and cannot put man against nature/universe and put man's heart against his reason or vice versa. Religions are supposed to establish harmony and provide man with peace of mind and a peaceful life and not tension and conflict. The peace and harmony within man cannot be established without establishing harmony between man and the universe. This inclusive harmony cannot be achieved without a sound spiritual and ethical basis. In the West and Western-oriented world this may be achieved through natural law and natural law ethics and in the Muslim world through Islam, which sanctions and supports the concept of natural law and human rights. It is with this perspective that nature, its order and the entire creation and universe and man, human nature along with his multi-dimensional needs, is taken into consideration in Islam as a universal religion. This is possible only if the entire creation is taken into consideration in the light of its own unity and the unity of its Creator and if only God, and not man, science, society, nature or a multiplicity of them, is the Creator. This is possible only if these beliefs, concepts and doctrine are founded on a solid basis with absolute characteristics and properties.

Islam approaches this issue by suggesting that the standard of man's behaviour towards God, himself, his fellow human beings, his fellow creatures, nature, the orders and laws of nature and the entire creation and universe is directly and indirectly defined by Allah (swt) and the moral/ethical code of his behaviour is set by Allah (swt) either directly or otherwise, in accordance and in harmony with nature and human primordial nature. Man's responsibility for fulfilling divine duties is based on man's divine potential and properties to appreciate this responsibility. It is in this light that man's rational, physical, emotional, and spiritual potential and his primordial nature are regarded as divine gifts and thus human reason is regarded as the divine agent working to lead man to his inclusive perfection and wholesome salvation, happiness and felicity. This enables his feelings and emotions, heart and faith to be in full harmony with his mind and reason and leads man to feel that he is in harmony with nature and the entire creation, thus realizing the harmony of religious commands and the moral/ethical principles, on one side, and the harmony of man, and man's primordial nature, and nature, laws of nature, the entire creation, on the other. Accordingly, man's rights and responsibilities should be based on his inclusive, harmonious and comprehensive world view and be in harmony with the rights of the entire creation, his primordial nature, and his inclusive needs and potentials.

To explain these points and other related issues, this book has been prepared. The first chapter of the book deals with the question of natural law and human rights in the West. The second chapter deals with the position of natural law and human rights in Islam in general. The third chapter deals with human *fitrah* or human primordial nature as one of the foundations and sources of natural law, human rights and absolute ethical principles. The fourth chapter deals with the major features and principles of Islamic rationality and introduces Islamic rationality as the major source and philosophy of natural law and human rights in general and in Islam in particular. The fifth chapter sheds some light on Islamic rationality as the source of the Islamic concept of natural law and human rights in Islam, in some detail. And finally the question of human rights is dealt with in the light of the United Nations Universal Declaration of Human Rights (UDHR), Islamic concept of human rights and the Constitution of the Islamic Republic of Iran (IRI). To be fair to readers, we must point out that there are different approaches to understanding Islam and that the approach adopted in this book should not be regarded as the only approach and exclusive of the others. We regard this work as a humble contribution to the study of certain aspects of Islam.

During the last two centuries, an Islamic movement has taken shape with the intention of modernizing Islam and the Muslim community. This may be viewed as a reaction to the traditional approach to Islam. But it could also be a movement with the sincere intention of facing the challenges of modern life and answering its new problems and questions. Recently a counter-movement against the modernist movement has taken place too. There are thus conflicting approaches to Islam due to many factors. In this work we have tried our best, as far as possible, to avoid conflict and tension. But the question of human rights, in its contemporary form, is a question of the modern era. However, just because it is a new question it does not mean that there are no traditional and religious answers and explanations for it.

As there is some overlapping of various aspects of certain issues dealt with here, repetition could not be avoided. I hope that the readers will forgive the repetition for it has served a purpose.

We admit that one of the major problems we have encountered has been that of Islamic terminology. The field of Islamic terminology in English is full of difficulties. To avoid these difficulties we have almost always included the actual Arabic Islamic terms in the text.

One

Natural Law and Human Rights in the West

Law and morality, and their relationship, in one form or another, have been the concern of humanity throughout history. The fact that legal and moral norms sometimes contradict each other and also the fact that both legal and moral norms vary from one community, one historical period and one set of circumstances to another lie in part behind a persistent search and theme in the philosophy of law and ethics: the search for unchanging and absolute legal and ethical norms that are universally valid. This is why there has been a continuous attempt to base these norms on universally observed and recognized facts about nature in general and human nature in particular. The attempt to base these norms on some such category of facts has for two millennia been associated with the concept and doctrine of 'natural law'.

Throughout the history of the concept, from Greek antiquity, there have been disagreements over the meaning of natural law. There have also been many versions of natural law. However, it has always been possible to trace a mainstream of natural law thought and concept throughout the history of law, politics and ethics. Nature, natural, laws of nature, natural law and a group of words and concepts derived from them and associated with them have at all times filled a great place in the thought of man and taken a strong hold on the mind and feelings of mankind. Probably this is why it is very difficult to introduce a universally accepted definition of these terms and concepts. The doctrine of natural law thus has been the subject of different interpretations and has enjoyed different commentaries, explanations and justifications. St Thomas Aquinas (1225–74) for example, believed that

> the precepts of natural law are universal and self-evident both in themselves and also in relation to us.' Certain order is found in those things that are self-evident and apprehended universally which is natural law. 'Being' is the first thing, which is apprehended. 'Good' also falls under the apprehension of the practical reason. Thus, the first principle in the practical reason is one founded on the notion of good, viz., *good is that which all things seek*

> *after and is to be done.* All other precepts of natural law are based upon this, so that whatever the practical reason naturally apprehends as man's good (or evil) belongs to the precepts of the natural law as something to be done or avoided. To the natural law belong all those things to which man is inclined naturally.
>
> We shall explain Aquinas's thoughts about natural law later.

There have been many different interpretations of natural law from the very beginning of its history. These interpretations increased in the Middle Ages and in modern times. In fact, it is more appropriate to speak of a family of the concept of natural law. Due partly to the different interpretations of natural law, there also exists a family of concepts of human rights. These differing concepts of human rights shared the same history with roots in Stoic philosophy and Roman legal concept of natural law but they differed in the interpretation of both natural law and human rights. However, it has always been possible to trace the mainstream of natural law thought throughout its history and development.

The concept and theory of natural law covers *inter alia* the fields of ethics, politics, law and philosophy of law. Law has been a significant topic for philosophical discussion for a long time, since its beginnings. One of the major theories in this field is the concept of natural law. Attempts to discover the principles of cosmic order, and to discover or secure the principles of order in human communities, have been the wellsprings and source of inquiry into law. Such inquiry has probed the nature and being of law and its virtues. A dialectic of reason and will is to be found in philosophical speculation about the underpinning principles of law. On the one side, there is the idea that the cosmos itself, and human society too, contain immanent principles of rational or reasonable order, and this order must be capable of being discovered or apprehended by rational (or 'reasonable') beings. On the other side, there is the view that order, especially in society and in human conduct, is not found but made, not disclosed to reason but asserted by acts of will and by authorities. Either there is a law of reason and nature or there is a law by command of the sovereign; either the legal virtues are intrinsical or ought to be cultivated by lawgivers, judges or engaged citizens. The proponents of natural law support the first theory.

The proponents of natural law claim that it is a system of norms and also a system which offers to explain and defend certain claims made in the discourse of moral argument, politics and law. They suggest that certain choices, actions, dispositions and behaviours are regarded as absolutely 'inhuman', 'unnaturally cruel', 'perverse', or 'unreasonable'. They also suggest that certain proposals, policies, conducts, rules and customs may be described as violations of natural law and human rights, and crimes against humanity. They also claim that certain actions, behaviours and choices are good and deserve praise and rewards. The natural law theory offers to explain why claims of this sort can be rationally and inherently warranted and true by locating such claims in the context of a general theory of good and evil in human life which can be called a general theory of right and wrong and lawful or unlawful in human nature, choices and actions. Natural law is thus concerned both with normative propositions, identifying right and wrong, obligatory and forbidden, and also with non-normative propositions about the objectivity and epistemological/cognitive requirements of the normative propositions.

It should be pointed out that these normative propositions, suggested by natural law, are not necessarily derived from 'nature' or inspected in the 'nature of things', nor are they deduced from 'natural sciences'. They are not necessarily concerned either with a 'state of nature', in the sense of some golden age or state of affairs prior to the formation of human societies or political communities. Natural law is natural because it is a system that challenges the systems which are not natural to man, such as positivism and scepticism.The term 'natural' in this context ethically signifies any one or more of the following:

a. The relevant standards are not 'positive', i.e. they are pre-determined prior to any positing by individual decision or group choice or convention.
b. The relevant standards are higher than posited laws, conventions and practices, i.e. they provide the premises for critical evaluation and endorsement or justified rejection of or disobedience to such laws, conventions or practices.
c. The relevant standards conform to the most demanding requirements of critical reason and are objective, in the sense that a person who fails to accept them as standards for judgement is in error.
d. Adherence to the relevant standards tends systematically to promote human welfare, the fulfilment of the potential of human individuals and communities.

Natural law is both a system of law/philosophy of law and a system of philosophy. It is a system of law because

a. it issues and discovers norms of obligations and prohibitions, which are divinely and rationally good and evil;
b. choices otherwise than in accordance with them are unreasonable, unnatural and evil and thus illegal/unlawful;

c. it provides jurisprudential explanations and thus introduces a legal system and a system of philosophy of law;
d. these moral precepts divinely commanded are commanded because they are fitting and obligatory, not fitting or obligatory because commanded (or that the source of their obligation is rather divine wisdom than divine will);
e. the term 'law' in the phrase 'natural law' refers to standards of right choosing, standards which are normative, i.e. rationally directed and 'obligatory', because they are true and choice otherwise than in accordance with them is unreasonable;[1]
f. in the contemporary period, some of these rules of natural law, in the forms of human rights, have been given legal status and enforcement by the UN, international conventions and governments.

The concept and theory of natural law will be explained further in the course of the history of natural law.

Natural law in philosophy is a system of right or justice held to be common to all humankind and derived from nature rather than from the rules and the will of society, or positive law. For the advocates of natural law theory such as Grotius, Pufendorf and Locke the idea of justice is closely linked with an assumed law of nature that is grounded in the physical and psychic constitution of man. The classic theory of natural law, as Hart puts it, is that there are certain principles of human conduct, awaiting discovery by human reason, with which man-made law must conform if it is to be valid. [2]

There are many questions regarding the issue of natural law. First there is the question whether there are absolute ethical values (ethical objectivism) or there are not (ethical subjectivism). According to the proponents of the second view, the so-called ethical judgements are formed by various circumstances. The proponents of natural law may be regarded as supporters of ethical objectivity. The proponents of ethical subjectivity are of many shades and schools, some of which will be dealt with at the end of this chapter. As for the question of how these absolute ethical values are to be recognized, the answer varies according to different philosophers and schools of ethics. It has been suggested that it is now clear that at least on some major and important points and principles, almost all societies are in agreement (universality). Proponents of natural law support this view. Some philosophers, such as Rousseau and Hume, believed that the origins and source of ethics were to be found in certain natural feelings or sentiments whereas others such as Kant rejected utterly the link between ethics and feelings and instead suggested that ethical values and their origins are given by reason alone. There are also some who suggest that both reason and feelings provide the origins of ethics, human rights and the authority of natural law. The majority of Muslim scholars support this view.

Once we have found and formed a view about what things are good and how to recognize them we have to find an answer to the question as to how to judge actions as right or wrong (application of ethical principles). There are three major alternatives here:

1. Judge them on the basis of their compliance with ethical principles and values irrespective of their consequences. The proponents of natural law ethics support this view. Aquinas, Kant and others who insisted on the absolute nature of ethical values and duty supported this view.
2. The consequentialists in general and utilitarians in particular, on the other side, support the view that circumstances and consequences should be the basis of the judgement.
3. The third alternative, however, is the attempt to bridge the gap between the first two alternatives. This third alternative suggests that while we accept the view that there are absolute ethical principles and values irrespective of their consequences we must acknowledge the need for exceptions of absolute ethical values according to exceptional circumstances and conditions.[3]

The History of Natural Law

Antiquity

The concept of natural law has been dealt with from three different view points and has gone through many distinct phases: the intellectual/philosophical, the moral/ethical and the legal/political. In philosophy natural law is a system of orders; the order of nature and the order of human behaviour which consist mainly of rights and principles held to be common to all humankind and derived from the nature of man rather than from the rules of society, positivist law or any other sources. The concept in its philosophical dimension has roots in ancient Greek thought even before different schools of Greek philosophy arose. For the Greeks the universe was an order or cosmos (cosmos: unity) with life and intelligence whose parts participated in the life and intelligibility of the whole.[4] Aristotelian 'theorists of nature' called the first Greek philosophers, the Ionians.

The natural law, from its inception and beginning, consisted of two main sets of orders: the order of the universe and nature and the order and norms of human behaviour, because man is regarded as an inseparable part of nature. The ancient Greeks explained these orders in one way or another. The Ionians, Socrates, Pythagoras, Plato, Aristotle and the Stoics all, in one form or another, recognized the order of the universe and nature. According to Pythagoras, what provided order in the realm of nature was mathematical – not just any mathematical pattern but a pattern based on harmony or more precisely on musical harmony and it was thus both quantitative and qualitative order. Plato, like Pythagoras, emphasized the significance of this pattern and order, especially geometric order. Plato explained the order of nature in terms of forms, which are the only real intelligible entities. Aristotle did not really reject Plato's idea of forms. He refused only to accept their reality independent of matter. His forms are God's thought and they reveal the way God 'thinks'. He conceived all changes not only according to order but also teleologically. Both Plato and Aristotle accepted that the cosmos is ruled by one supreme principle. He, like a craftsman, has moulded the world and created its order, as stated by Plato in *Philebus and Timaeus.*[5]

The major difference between the two here is that Plato considered the 'craftsman' of nature to be transcendent and Aristotle considered it to be immanent. One may thus suggest that the ancient Greek philosophers generally associated these orders of nature with divinity. One can say that Aristotelian forms are God's thought and reveal the way God thinks. Aristotle also states that the wisdom of God pervades the whole of nature and that the process of nature is produced by the love of God. Even inert impulses of nature move towards God by virtue of this love. This is why Greek philosophical explanations were integrated by schools of philosophy within Abrahamic, especially Islamic, monotheism. (This point has been expressed in Islamic literature as God's bounty or *lotf*) Aristotle conceived all changes in the world to be not only according to order but also teleological and introduced God as the first and the final cause who was Himself the unmoved Mover. The conclusion here is that the most important feature of the cosmos accepted by most Greeks was that it is a hierarchical ordered whole that is intelligible. This is close to a metaphysical, spiritual, divine and even religious order of nature and natural law system.[6] This concept owes its systematic philosophical discussion to Plato and Aristotle. Plato through Socrates strongly rejected the argument that all justice is merely conventional. However, neither Plato nor Aristotle actually formed, defined or explained the concept of natural law explicitly. Plato did not discuss the point that there is a formal natural law that is a pattern for good positive laws. Plato in *The Republic* demonstrated that there must exist an idea of justice, which allows men, in different political systems, to recognize some actions as just and others as unjust. Plato's idea of independent forms placed justice and other major ethical principles in a universal, permanent and unchangeable position. He was concerned to redefine the nature of ethical principles such as justice by relating them to something far more permanent and absolute than the norms of the city-state and thus he assigned 'reality' to unchanging archetypal forms. In the *Nicomachean* Aristotle defines justice as follows: 'Life has one difficult and thousands of easy paths. The difficult path is that of justice and thousands of easy paths are all branches from the path of justice in one way or another.'

It is thus tempting to suggest that the basic idea of natural law, though very vague and incongruous, came from Greece in the form of general philosophical speculations. Plato tried to establish more permanent, absolute norms above the city-state norms for law and morality by assigning reality to unchanging archetypal forms, i.e. ideas. He suggested that the knowledge of these ideas and forms, which is virtue, is only available to 'philosopher-kings' who are above the city-state. For Plato, as explained in *Politics*, law is the reflection of common human reason. There is however a contradiction in his opinion concerning human reason. Plato was aware of the contrast between the reason of ordinary man and the reason of the man of philosophy. Aristotle was more practical in method and aim. He suggested that man in his nature is moral, ratio-social and that these are innate. By doing this he prepared the ground for the doctrine of natural law. Aristotle was more interested in natural right than natural law but he provided a framework for the development of natural law theory. Aristotle held that there was a natural justice valid everywhere with the same force and that appeal could be made to it from the positive law. But he drew his instances from the Greek city-state with its obvious limitations and this is perhaps why he was not able to formulate the doctrine of natural law as a system and certainly not as a political system. The Greeks were generally interested in the philosophical aspects of nature, laws of nature and natural law. They were not juristically minded people. They did not produce jurisconsults and law specialists equivalent or near to the philosophers they produced. Greece with its city-state system did not really need an international inter-state universal legal system which could be based on natural law. The city-state polity was adequate except for a short period after Alexander's conquests. The Romans, on the contrary, had established themselves as an international state and thus needed a universal legal system for their vast empire. Rome produced lawyers of high calibre, such as Cicero. The efforts of these jurisconsults produced a proper legal and ethical system out of Stoicism and developed it as the natural law system with its international political implications. The crude tribal *jus civile* (civil law) of the Romans was thus transformed into a natural law system based on *jus gentium* (law applying to all people, Roman and non-Roman). This was done under the influence of Stoicism.

The origin of the ethical dimension of the concept of natural law goes back to the Greek Stoic school and to later development of Stoicism. The concept of natural law was developed and underwent refinement by the Stoic School of philosophy and ethics, which became active towards the end of the fourth century BC. The Stoics proposed the existence of a natural law, the *jus naturale*, which was an emanation of the *lex naturale*, the law of reason and cosmos. The existence of innately reasoning men linked everyone with the cosmic order and subjected all to a universally valid moral law. This concept thoroughly infused Roman thinking, largely as a result of the influence of Stoic philosophy on Rome. The early Stoicism of Greece concentrated mainly on the ethical dimension of the order of nature and left a great impact on the actual concept of the order of nature while the later Stoicism of Rome displayed much interest in the legal dimension of natural law. Legal specialists such as Cicero of Rome developed a legal and political system based on the conception of natural law under the influence of Stoicism. The political and legal history of natural law really starts in the Roman Imperial period, and goes back to Cicero and Latin thinkers. This is probably because the Romans needed a more international legal/political system to manage their multi-national empire. Cicero referred to natural law as 'right reason in agreement with nature' from which there can be no dispensation either by the senate or the people. To run counter to or try to restrict it is immoral.

Cicero, influenced by Zeno's Stoicism and the concept of man as world citizen, tried to base politics, law and ethics on a solid ground to answer the question of harmony of law and ethics and developed the doctrine of natural law. Stoicism itself as the forerunner of the natural law system was founded by Zeno (300 BC) and was influential during the Graeco–Roman period of mutual intellectual co-operation up to 200 Ad. Inspired by Socrates, Zeno's philosophy began and developed as a critical and radical school emphasizing the importance of duty, moral values, virtues and unity of man. The only criterion for happiness is virtue and nothing else. The ethical principles of Stoicism account for its appeal and influence. It transcends the conventional limits of race, status, sex, and worldly privileges, promoting virtues of wisdom, courage, justice, moderation, and unity of common humanity. It promotes the concept of world citizenship and natural law. Cicero handed down all these and the entire philosophy of Stoicism to Western civilization. In fact, we may call the natural law the Stoic/Roman Natural Law School.

The *jus civile* of the Romans needed to be transformed into a natural law system based on *jus gentium* to be able to meet the political and legal needs of Rome's vast empire, applicable to Romans and non-Romans. The Roman Stoics, including Cicero and Aurelius, established the teaching of classical natural law. For them natural law was the rational principle governing the universe. Because it is rational it can be known and obeyed by reasonable men. Properly understood it can guide man towards perfection and thus become the natural order of human behaviour. Such a law must apply universally. It is an objective standard for judging positive law and takes precedence over positive laws that conflict with one another. Thus the political and legal concept of natural law originated in ancient political philosophy based on the ethical philosophy of the Stoics.

As has been pointed out earlier, natural law is an inclusive concept covering, at the least, law, ethics and politics. A consideration of fundamental importance in the philosophy of law is the distinction between law and morality and the establishment of harmony between the two. Both law and morality aim at controlling human conduct: law from outside and ethics from inside. But both legal and moral norms change from time to time, place to place and people to people. This is why there has been a consistent and persistent attempt in the philosophy of law and ethics to find unchanging norms that are universally recognized by all and for all mankind. The most certain way of doing this is to base these non-facts associated with nature at large and with human nature in particular as a part of nature at large. This attempt for the written history of law in the past has been associated with the concept of natural law in its multi-dimensional versions. All theories of different versions of natural law have found it necessary, in one way or another, to rely on intuition, natural inclination, human instinct, and the innate insight of human beings, human primordial nature and human reason. Encyclopaedia Britannica has applied the term 'universal conscience of all mankind' in this context. A universal permanent natural law should thus be based on the principle of universal conscience and universal human conscience of all mankind. But here the dilemma from which philosophers of law were trying to escape returns because men's consciences do not coincide and do not fully correspond with each other. Individuals' consciences also contradict each other and are in conflict. This in turn means that human conscience may also err. It is thus necessary to find a more solid foundation than conscience for law. (We shall later explain that there is a difference between human primordial nature and conscience). Natural law, as has been noted, has many versions and interpretations and has gone through many phases and changes to the extent that some versions contradict others. But all theories of natural law share the principle of relying on man's universal true nature or some form of human primordial nature to avoid this conflict.

As has been pointed out before, the whole political aspect of natural law tradition as a system stems from Cicero, under the influence of Greek thought in general and Stoic philosophy in particular, as does the theory of the state as fundamentally a guardian of private property. Cicero left an impact not only on his contemporaries but also on the entire political thought up to modern times. Early philosophers, in their speculation about the regularity they had observed in the working of physical forces and the uniform growth they had perceived in living organisms, concluded that some force must be controlling the movement and processes of the material universe. Similarly, in their speculation upon man as a rational being, they had discovered general rules of his moral and physical constitution, and assumed that a force with an intelligent purpose directed these. This force they chose to call rational will. Having recognized reason as the harmonizing principle in man, they conceived of nature as an intelligent force moulding phenomena on regular lines towards definite ends. Consequently when the Greek philosophers began to speculate about human society and observed that certain rules and customs were to be found among all tribes and races, they concluded that these rules and customs must be natural, that they must be the results of reason, the intelligent principle. They shaped their speculation on human society in theories about law. Certain laws they found were common to all communities. And following the same line of reasoning as before, they concluded that the laws which were common to all communities must be natural, because they were apparently issued out of the mental and moral constitution of man, as man. These laws, which belonged to the human race as a whole, they conceived to be essentially anterior in thought and date to the laws that each particular community made for itself. They believed these laws to be imposed on the world by nature, the ruling force, and they called the laws that nature sets upon mankind, the law of nature or natural law and at the same time they are both legally and ethically discoverable and thus also in harmony.

Beside the universal human nature, there is also a universal human reason which can help the harmony of law and ethics. It has been pointed out already that human reason plays a major part in the discovery of the natural law, which is created by God. Human reason is not the whole natural law in the world of human beings but it is the harmonizing principle. In this case, those philosophers who accepted the authority of human reason, in one way or another, have surrendered to natural law. Plato, for example, believed that the essential requirement is that our souls and our actions be governed by reason, since reason alone is capable of determining what is truly good for us; if we are incapable of reasoning properly for ourselves, then others must do it for us. Hence the idea of philosophical rulers or kings. This is because only the philosopher-ruler is qualified to have access to proper reasoning. The forms and therefore the knowledge, which a grasp of them provides, are accessible only to a few, the philosopher-rulers. Plato also believed in the unity of virtue and knowledge and the natural conclusion for him was that only virtuous men could rule the community and only philosophers were the qualified knowledgeable people who knew what virtues were and were thus qualified to rule. Plato's ideas left an impact upon subsequent political theories and political theoreticians, especially through Aristotle, who came to Athens to work in the Academy, and later through Cicero. Both men based their own Utopian essays closely on the Platonic model. Cicero, the champion of the theory of the natural law, became the means through whom the Platonic and Stoic ideas spread.

As far as the position of Aristotle in the concept of natural law and his contribution to it is concerned, we must emphasize that it is more complicated than it seems. 'Man', said Aristotle, 'is by nature a political animal.' But he probably did not mean quite what a natural law reader expects. Human nature does not necessarily correspond to natural law fully. Aristotle suggests that the nature from which obligation (moral) must be derived is nature in its perfection. For man this is when his rational potential is actualized, developed and perfected and he becomes a different species of animal (man) distinguished from other creatures and animals. Natural law for him embodies these mature obligations. He also suggests that the 'union of man and woman is natural'. But at the same time he suggests that man should rule over woman because she has less reason than he does. He also suggests that some human beings (certain non-Greeks) are intended by nature to be slaves. In Aristotle's view human beings do not have a uniform nature. He divides them into groups, principally male and female, and free and slave, differing in capability. He thus rejects the basic principle of natural law. Although he believes that all living things, including human beings, are to be understood in terms of their nature, he means by nature of a thing, what it becomes when its growth is completed. This is not necessarily a natural law. He believes that human beings are innately different. So, when he said that 'man is by nature a political animal', he meant that man's potential is only fulfilled in a political environment by living in a political society. However, many supporters of natural law owe their appreciation of natural law to the approach adopted by Aristotle. Aristotle's influence has been considerable because his political thought has many sides to it. His ideas are an important component of the thoughts of Aquinas, who in turn used them to promote his concept of natural law. Machiavelli, for instance, appreciated his realism. Locke shared some of his views on the family. However, it is difficult to regard him as one of the proponents of the classical concept of natural law.

The Middle Ages

Natural law or the law of nature, preceded Christianity. Christian thinkers of the medieval period who found it initially difficult to embrace the theory of natural law were later persuaded to identify the law of nature with the law of God. The Church thus became the exponent of natural law. Nature was the product of the will of God and conformed to His prescriptions. Some medieval Scholastics, notably St Augustine and St Thomas Aquinas, altered the Stoic doctrine of natural law to make it compatible with revealed Christianity. For them, God replaces nature as the prime mover of the universe. Natural laws as products of God's reason are intelligible but God, unlike nature, has the power and the will to punish transgressors of the natural laws in this world and the next. This is in conflict with Aristotle's idea that natural law is the idea of universal order, conceived and shaped by human reason and the laws of nature. According to Aristotle, temporal felicity is man's end in this world, and it is also an end in itself. But according to Christians, in time, and in the end, which is subordinate to the ultimate end of man, eternal blessedness is only attainable in the next world. The temporal end is not only subordinate to the eternal end but itself must be directed towards that superior end. Politics determine the means by which man attains his temporal end, and they must always be directed towards man's ultimate end. The state has a position within the divine order. It must obey natural law if it is to be obeyed.

As the concept of natural law was developed in the light of human reason, it left an impact on both Christianity and the Western legal system. For Aquinas, natural law is the part of God's law which man by his reason can perceive. He distinguishes four types of law. First, eternal law, which is the one prior to all the others and is the divine wisdom known in its entirety only to God. Then comes natural law, which is that proportion of eternal law which human beings can perceive by their reason. The third is human law, which is deduced from natural law to be binding within the state. This positive law of the state is therefore in accord with natural law and ultimately with eternal law, and if it is not in accord with natural law then it is, for Aquinas, not law at all. And if it is not law at all, it need not be obeyed. It is not seditious, he says, to overthrow a tyranny. In fact he goes further than that. His fourth category of law is divine law, which God reveals to man to direct him to the ultimate end of eternal blessedness. This is the law which man is incapable of perceiving by reason alone. Not all that a man has, or is, is subject to political obligation, said Aquinas, but all that a man is, all he potentially can be, must bear a certain relationship to God. And that is revolutionary talk.[7] As we may notice, although Aquinas was influenced by Aristotle he developed his own version of natural law to make it compatible to Christianity. This is perhaps because the Muslim philosopher Averroes and his Islamic interpretation of Aristotelian philosophy also influenced him.

It must be pointed out that long before Aquinas, St Augustine (354–430 AD) moulded what later was recognized as Christian political thought. Although Augustine suggested that man and nature had been corrupted after the original sin, when Christianity became the state religion of the Roman Empire, accordingly political philosophy and law had to change profoundly. St Augustine undertook this task. Aquinas improved on the idea of harmony of political philosophy, law and nature of man but not exactly in the manner that

Augustine would have liked. Augustine no longer assumed as did Plato and Aristotle, that the state was either ideal or practical. He thus supported the natural law system politically. In this way a Hellenic–Roman–Christian political philosophy and law was formulated. By writing *The City of God* in 413 he in fact prepared the way for the '*civitas dei*' to be interpreted as the earthly Christian state. Augustine's influence in moulding the mind of the medieval West is immeasurable. Imperialist and church theories drew upon his writings to justify their social and political views. St Augustine admitted (in the *Confessions*) that he was moved by a personal quest for truth after reading a standard tract of the school curriculum, Cicero's *Hortensius*, and he also admitted that men like Cicero stood on a sound moral ground. He nevertheless believed that imperialist and papist theories made the Christian Roman Empire great and he thus showed his real commitment to Christian imperialism. His true state therefore is a true Church, nothing more. Augustine and other Scholastics, like John Duns, held that the fall of man had irreparably weakened human nature and that nature could not provide a pattern for human laws. Absolute submission to divine will was the only rule for human laws and human life. This form of Scholasticism paved the way for the modern doctrine of sovereignty and for natural law teachings in which civil authority replaced divine grace as the remedy for the evils of nature. For Augustine it was the divine will that ruled the universe and not the divine wisdom and reason. For Aquinas it was the other way round. There is still operating in the mind of the Western world an Augustinian notion that freedom – by which we mean the power to choose good and do it – is precisely what fallen man's nature is incapable of achieving. It was much later on, after Augustine, in the Middle Ages, in the thirteenth century, that Aquinas, with the help of Aristotle, would provide man's use of reason with the power to establish just politics rather than to accept injustice. Aquinas's major achievement as a political thinker was to gain acceptance in Europe for Aristotle's idea that man is by nature a political being, at a time when people thought about politics in religious and legal terms. It was probably thanks to Aquinas that European politics became less dominated by religious and legal traditionalism.[8]

In the twelfth and thirteenth centuries, numerous previously unknown works by Aristotle in various fields percolated into Europe via Muslim Spain and were translated into Latin. These contained clearly superior scientific knowledge and philosophical analysis but diverged from Christian belief in diverse fields. There was an intellectual crisis comparable to that produced by Darwin in the nineteenth century. Some wished to ban Aristotle. Others accepted his ideas wholesale. Aquinas sought to achieve a synthesis between Aristotle's ideas and Christianity and to establish that Aristotle's opinions did not conflict with those of Scripture. Aquinas suggested that divine grace does not take away nature but perfects it. Man's essential quality is reason, which differentiates him from other animals. Man is capable of knowing the truth and practising virtue. Aquinas extended Aristotle's vision by saying that all men, not just Greeks and Christians, possess reason. 'The light of natural reason is the impression of the Divine light upon humanity.' This was in direct conflict with what Augustine suggested. Aquinas said that whereas other animals are provided by nature with the equipment they need for survival, man has 'reason and hands' and man is 'by nature a social and political being'. Aquinas established that contrary to Augustine's view, political authority is not solely a corrective for sin or man's lust for power, but is natural to man, and thus non-Christians also can have legitimate states. Aquinas examined political justice and obligation in the context of a detailed analysis of law. God regulates the universe through the eternal law, which is impressed on all beings and inclines them to fulfil their destiny. A rational creature like man, however, is subject to divine providence in a more excellent way. Although man shares many natural and instinctive goals with other animals, yet there are goals that are properly only human, such as to know the truth by reasoning and participating in it in this way.

This 'participation in the eternal law by a rational creature', according to Aquinas, is natural law. Natural law tells man both what to do and how to attain happiness. Man's reason is able to distinguish good from bad and right from wrong. Aquinas developed the natural law theory, which dominated European philosophy and politics and jurisprudence until the eighteenth century and beyond. According to Aquinas, all men can know right and wrong through 'practical reason' and the basic principles of natural law are 'self-evident' (*per se nota* innate and, universal and in accordance with human primordial nature). Men are to avoid ignorance, not to offend those with whom they must associate and to harm no one. These principles are known to all men and are always to be followed. In a sense, Aquinas's position with respect to natural law in Christianity is similar to that of Cicero in the Roman Empire.

Aquinas's theory of natural law rests upon his notion of God's relationship with creation. The idea of a moral law implanted in man by nature would be difficult to justify otherwise. Wider knowledge of human societies and theories like Darwinism have done much to discredit it.

For Aquinas, natural law has the advantage of basing morality on humanity. It tells us how to behave towards all men, and thus makes one reject exclusive nationalism and cultural chauvinism. Similarly, the doctrine of natural or human rights explain how men in general, irrespective of their race and background, should be treated. At the same time, phenomena like Nazism have indeed led to a partial revival of natural law theory in our own times.

Natural law provides the standard by which all man-made laws are to be measured. Human law is a series of still more detailed specifications as to how the general tenets of natural morality are to be applied by particular people in particular territories. Murder must be punished, but what form this punishment takes is a matter for the legislator to decide. To qualify as law at all, human law must be just, that is in accordance with reason and natural law and aimed at the common good. Aquinas in many respects resembles Averroes. This is probably because of the impact of Muslim Spain on Western intellectualism and the translation of Arabic texts into European languages, which were of extreme benefit in the formation of Western intellectualism.

Although Aquinas tried to picture Christianity in the light of natural law, his theories of the state, politics and natural law put European political thought on a new plane. It legitimized the autonomy of secular rulers and a prudent rationality of decision-making. It influenced an increasing number of thinkers from the fourteenth century onwards. Thomism, the doctrines of Aquinas, also revived in nineteenth- and twentieth-century Europe and America. But the theory of natural law, of which Aquinas was one of the most influential exponents, helped lay a foundation for the theory of international law in Suarez and Grotius. John Locke also owed much to the Thomist theory of authority based upon and limited by natural law and the common good.

The concept of the natural law influenced the concepts and the development of law, ethics, politics and political thoughts and theories of the state and philosophers throughout the Middle Ages up to modern time. For example, being under the influence of natural law, Hegel suggested that the basis of the state is the power of reason actualizing itself as will. Men will co-operate the state in accordance with reason. The state is reason. It is mind on earth consciously realizing itself there. It is the actuality of the ethical idea. Actuality is the unity both of essence and of existence. Only when mind is present in consciousness, when it knows itself as a really existent object, is it the state

It must be explained here that different political thinkers have different interpretations of natural law. For example, Machiavelli tried to break the stranglehold of natural law, suggesting that there is no place for God in political power, and he believes that power belongs only to those who have the skill to seize it. But at the same time he even suggests that no government is safe without the goodwill of the governed. He also believes that it is better to rule by goodwill than force, not morally better, but better in the sense of being more likely to succeed. In fact, he proposes that the ruler must appeal to human nature of decency and morality, the natural law.[9] In fact modern interpretation of natural law theory, developed first by Machiavelli and Thomas Hobbes, transformed the ancient doctrine. They sought to construct an attainable rather than a utopian objective for political life. Modern theorists following Machiavelli suggested that natural law originated not in the heavens but in man himself. Nature supplies no pattern for the good state. In fact, in the state of nature there is no law at all, only individual desire and freedom. Everyone has an absolute right to preserve himself and his possessions. But because each looks to his own advantage, general conflict rages. Man then consults his reason for the means of self-protection, and reason points out specific legal principles that will establish peace. According to Hobbes and Locke, these peace terms are the laws of nature, which become the essence of any legitimate constitution. According to the 'social contract' interpretation of natural law, which gives effect to the natural laws, each person restricts his own rights to do anything he likes to protect himself as long as everyone else does the same. This agreement ends the conflict. Then the majority can set up a government strong enough to enforce the contract on everyone.

From the general right of self-preservation are derived specific natural rights. These include the inalienable right to life, liberty, and the pursuit of happiness appealed to in the Declaration of Independence of the USA. The spirit of natural law is the philosophical core of the governments of the USA, France and other democratic nations. The Romano–Germanic family of laws, with their interest in justice as the major objective of law, have benefited from the concept of natural law. For example, in France, following the Napoleonic codification, it was thought that the new compilations had expressed natural law in definitive terms having universal value.

The wide spread and influence of modern interpretations of natural law doctrine led to the formulation by Hugo Grotius (1583–1645) of a system of international law. It also resulted in the concept of natural economic order, as developed by Adam Smith and the laissez-faire school. It was also due to the influence of natural law, to some extent, that the modern concept of Human Rights was produced and promoted.

Political thinkers after Machiavelli went back to natural law. Calvin, Hobbes and others rejected Machiavelli's ideas and thoughts. But whereas medieval exponents of natural law began with God, law and obligation, Hobbes (1588–1679) began with man, freedom and right. Hobbes was not arguing from the state of innocence in which man had been in the biblical Eden but from a savage state of nature in which men free and equal in rights were each one at solitary war with every other. Hobbes defines a law of nature as a precept of general rules found out by reason, by which man is forbidden to do that which is destructive of his life. In the Medieval period the conflict between the Church fathers who believed in natural law and those who rejected it was mainly based on the conflict between those with the tendency to make divine reason prevail over divine will (as in Plato's call for philosophers to be kings or the Muslim scholar Averroes' calls for philosophers to interpret what is revealed) and those who thought the other way round. Machiavelli presented himself as seeking to escape from both transcendental will and reason at the same time into the empirical, into life as it is seen through the naked eyes of worldly men. He believed in describing rather than prescribing human nature. Before Hobbes, Grotius also tried to explain natural law in a non-theological way. He insisted on the validity of natural law even if we were to suppose that God does not exist or is not concerned with human affairs.

Grotius and Hobbes thus stand together at the head of that school of natural law which in accordance with the tendencies of the enlightenment, tried to construct a whole edifice of law by rational deduction from a fictitious state of nature followed by a social contract. Hobbes also starts introspectively with man's senses and emotions to find the source of will. This will is absolute because it is neither conditioned by rules nor directed towards some end. It is free both from law and from obligations. This freedom from obligation is man's natural right, his liberty to use his own power as he wills himself for the preservation of his own life. It derives directly from the character of individual will and not from some higher law or from higher reason or from reason at all. Neither law nor reason can create right. Man strives to attain what he has willed but the success of each individual is thwarted by the willed actions of every other individual. All men are competitors in their efforts to achieve what they have willed. Man's natural rights, however, include not only the liberty to act upon his will but also to formulate general truth by reasoning about the pursuit of what he wills. And reasoning leads man to formulate a general rule to forbid him doing that which is self-destructive. This rule is the fundamental law of nature, which is that man should seek inclusive peace (peace with himself, peace with his fellow human beings, peace with nature, peace with the entire creation and peace with the universe) as the only sure way of self-preservation. From this follows a second law, which is that to avoid war a man must lay down his natural rights and retain only the liberty against other men, which he would allow them against him. In other words man must will not to will and transfer his right to a beneficiary. This beneficiary must be the representative of each man possessing the authority to will in place of each separate man. He must be not a common will but a single representative will. This transfer of rights creates a civil society in which freedom is replaced by law and right replaced by obligation to do what is good. And it is artificial, not natural. It is the product of will. It is man-made, not the gift of God. And what man has put together, man can put asunder, if he wills to will again.[10]

Some of the major principles of natural law, according to certain proponents of natural law, are absolutism, universalism, and the authority of human reason and the unity of man. This is because the proponents and exponents of the natural law believed and suggested that man, regardless of race, culture, ethnicity, time and space, does believe in universal, absolute, rational rules which are applicable to entire humanity and have been applied throughout history. There have been some disagreements as to the exact number of these rules but not to the actual concept of natural law. We can thus understand that literalism, relativism, perspectivism, utilitarianism, historicism, positivism and similar schools do not believe in natural law and are in direct conflict with the natural law school. In fact any school that puts the truth at the disposal of circumstances is in conflict with the natural law school. We can see that the religions with a universal message and mission, the religions that support the unity of man, such as Islam and Christianity, are not in conflict with the concept of natural law. They may disagree on the method of applying them or on some principles and rules and their basis and philosophy, but they are in agreement on many points of principle. Both universal monotheistic religions and natural law reject moral relativism, scepticism and racism and claim universalism and absolutism as far as certain moral and ethical principles are concerned.

In the period between the sixteenth and eighteenth centuries, as a result of the conflict between Protestantism and Catholicism, and the conflict between the reformists and the anti-reformists, and also as a result of new scientific development by Copernicus, Galileo and others, relativism gained some ground, and thus both religion and natural law were threatened.

The conclusion so far is that the concept of natural law goes back to Greek philosophers, especially to the Stoics. As a system of law and ethics it has a long history that dates back to Roman times when Cicero referred to it as the 'right reason in agreement with nature' from which there can be no dispensation either by senate or the people. To run counter to or try to restrict it is immoral. Later on, for the advocates of natural law theory such as Grotius, Pufendorf and Locke, the idea of the most important issue, justice is closely linked with an assumed law of nature that is grounded in the physical and psychic constitution of man. Nature demands of man a certain amount of food and sleep and has endowed him with the faculty of reason, love for offspring, liberty and ownership, traits that no adequate theory of justice could afford to overlook. The classical theory of natural law, as Hart puts it is that 'there are certain principles of human conduct, awaiting discovery by human reason, with which man-made law must conform if it is to be valid. ' Any outrageous disregard of minimum human claims to freedom and equality would be offensive to natural reason. Christian thinkers of the medieval period who found it initially difficult to embrace this theory of natural law were later persuaded to identify the law of nature with the law of God. The Church thus became the exponent of natural law. Accordingly, natural and nature was the product of the will of God and conformed to His prescriptions. Christian thinkers and theologians like St Augustine and St Thomas Aquinas considered justice to be the overriding objective of the law and came to the conclusion that an unjust law lacked the attribute of a law. It should be pointed out here that Aquinas's synthesis of theology with Aristotle, and also to some extent his idea of rationality and natural law was deeply, extensively and importantly indebted to Muslim scholars such as Farabi, Avicenna and specially Averroes.[11]

Later History and Development of Natural Law

As a result of Martin Luther's Protestant movement and the Reformation, and Counter-reformation, many scholars were increasingly attracted to a kind of moral relativism. The revival of ancient scepticism, in the work of Montaigne and his follower Pierre Charron, was tremendously influential in this development. Its central message in ethical matters for the late sixteenth century was that 'there is no such moral law to be found which the fortune and temerity of chance has granted to be universally received and by the consent of unanimity of all nations to be admitted'.

As Charron said, 'Aristotle had uttered more gross absurdities than all other philosophers.' This message was delivered principally to the Aristotelians entrenched in all contemporary European educational institutions. The Aristotelians had believed in the possibility of genuinely objective moral standards, capable of being ascertained by men of practical wisdom thinking systematically about the nature of the virtues. Against this the sceptics pointed to the absurdly local character of the classic virtues: many societies had practised neither temperance, nor courage, nor prudence, and some had not exhibited any justice. The sceptical attack on Aristotelians was extended to physics, for the sceptics held that, whereas Aristotle had argued that observation of the world could tell us what it was really like, in fact illusion was commonplace and universal. There could be no confidence in our perception of size, shape, or colour, and hence no confidence in any physical theory.

It was at this juncture that Hobbes and his friends saw their task as transcending the scepticism of the late sixteenth and the early seventeenth centuries, and creating sciences. At the centre of this group was the intellectual entrepreneur Martin Mersenne, and around him gathered Pierre Gassendi (Hobbes's constant philosophical companion) and, most famously, René Descartes (1596–1650). Their sense that new sciences were possible in all branches of human enquiry, and particularly in ethics and politics, seems to have been engendered by various developments in the 1620s. The most spectacular was the work of Galileo, culminating in the publication of his *Dialogue on the Two Chief World Systems* in 1632. What Galileo showed was that while Aristotelian physics were indeed false, the sceptical objections to Aristotelianism equally missed the point. Observation alone could not determine the truth of a physical proposition, and therefore the fact of illusion did not directly overthrow the possibility of a true science. A genuine physics was possible which went beyond observation, and employed very general notions of simplicity and elegance to decide between competing theories. Galileo not only suggested what a new physics might look like; he in effect provided one. All the great physicists from then to Einstein worked within the framework which he had set up. With René Descartes one encounters that radical departure from the traditional perspective in the understanding of the order of nature that has influenced nearly all of later modern thought. For Descartes, extension is an essential attribute of matter, and all genuine properties of matter must derive from extension, which also includes duration. In his *Meditations*, Descartes considers even this conception to be innate to human intelligence like the concepts of God and mind. For him the basic quality of all things is related to extension and is mathematical.

Aristotle's belief that the mind at birth is a blank slate upon which experience writes (learning) was the basis for studying the effects of learning on behaviour (free-will learning). Descartes proposed the concept of mind–body dualism (innateness and learning, free will and determinism), which implies that human behaviour could be understood as resulting from both a free will, rational soul and from automatic non-rational processes of the body. This proposition led to the development of the concept of instinct (innateness) and its role in human behaviour and motivation as a counterpoint to education and learning as the most important factor, proposed by Aristotle.

Like most modern philosophers, Descartes mistook the mathematics of nature for the philosophy of nature and thus embarked upon the path that led to positivism. This positivism replaced the philosophy of nature with the ideas of Auguste Comte and Machiavelli in the last century and severed the link between the order of nature and all questions of ontology and causality. John Locke also followed the same path. It is mainly thanks to Berkeley that the ideas of Descartes and Locke were seriously challenged. Berkeley claimed that if there is one substance that is real, it is the mind (not matter) that first creates nature at its fullest and then abstracts from it the physical world of classic physics limited to pure quantity. This mind, however, is not the human mind but the divine mind that generates through His thought.[12]

Most subsequent historians have seen how spectacular this achievement was, but they have not seen how equally spectacular at the time was the achievement of another writer in ethics, Hugo Grotius. Until the late eighteenth century he was classed by historians along with Galileo and Bacon as someone who had founded a wholly new science, but for various reasons since then he has been relegated to the backwater of the history of international law. However, it is clear that for his readers in the 1620s his main work, *The Law of War and Peace* (1625), offered the same kind of possibility of an ethical science as Galileo offered of a physical science. For in that work Grotius explicitly attacked both the Aristotelians and the sceptics and proposed what amounted to a resolution of the relativists' dilemma. According to Grotius there are moral universals. But they are minimal by comparison with those of Aristotle, amounting in effect only to two: that all men have the right to defend themselves and to acquire possession of the necessities of life; and that no man has the right wantonly to injure another. If it is your life or mine, I am to prefer my own, but otherwise I am not to attack you. Grotius presented these principles as functionally necessary for any society, that is, no society could be imagined in which these principles were denied. However, everything else was up to the members of society to impose upon themselves, so to that extent the relativist was right, for, in Grotius's eyes, most strongly held and specific moral beliefs fell into the category of additions to the natural law represented by the minimalist principles. So did most religious beliefs, for Grotius argued that in nature man's only obligation was to believe in at least one God who had a care for humanity, and no other religious propositions were to be established by natural reason. With Grotius as with the Stoics, the normative or the moral power of natural law derives from the fact that man's innate nature (itself part of the nature of the cosmos) and his propensities are viewed as ideal or inherently good. Grotius used this theory in *The Law of War and Peace* primarily to expound the relationship between states (which by definition had to be conducted along the lines laid down by this universal core to all human institutions, rather than according to some locally agreed set of principles). But his readers immediately saw its general importance. And thus a great deal of seventeenth-century political thought is understood as an attempt to vindicate and systematize Grotius's ideas about minimal but universal moral science. Its attraction was that it appealed to both relativists and the exponents of natural law theory.

The group of writers associated with Mersenne seems to have seen that theories of the Galilean and Grotian kind could be made into new sciences, if they could be provided with the kind of general philosophical foundations which their original creators had neglected. Hobbes apparently developed his own account of these foundations in the late 1630s, partly after reading Descartes's attempt in the famous *Discourse on the Method* (1637). The core of Hobbes's thought is contained in his purely philosophical and metaphysical writings. He accepted the full force of the sceptical argument, but he, nevertheless, insisted that knowledge or science of a kind is possible. Unlike Descartes, he refused to use a proof of God's existence as an explanation.

Instead, his argument went as follows. If we reflect sufficiently, we can see that there must be moving material bodies in the universe. No body or thing can move itself, for if it could there would be no reason for it to begin moving at one time rather than another. So all motion is caused by the impact of other bodies. So we can have secure knowledge that a moral science of the Grotian kind is possible. He suggested that there is no secure knowledge of anything outside an individual's own skull, and his own thoughts and desires are all that can guide his actions. This was as far as a moral language could go. But even though this is true, there are some generalizations that can be made about all men's attitudes; in particular, whatever else they disagreed about, all men (according to Hobbes) would agree that death was the worst evil that could befall them. This general agreement that death is the greatest evil for anybody implied a number of other universal moral propositions – that is, propositions which would hold even in the absence of any superstructure of civility and custom. First, all men would agree that whatever a man did to preserve himself from death was right for him and that he had a right to do this. This corresponded to the first of Grotius's two principles, the right of self-defence. Second, no one could be said to have the right to do anything else, which is not intended to protect himself. This corresponded to Grotius's second principle, the prohibition of wanton injury to another. Third, and in some way more importantly, all men are by nature judges of what conduces to their own self-preservation. And he suggested that in the areas of uncertainty where men could not judge for themselves, they would hand over all calculation about what conduced to their self-preservation (in doubtful cases) to their representative body or institution. The representative body would be in breach of the law of nature if it went beyond its mandate.

As we noticed, Hobbes based his concept of natural law mainly on human rationale and humanity. God, for Hobbes, remained something to be apprehended by faith only and never by reason. With Hobbes, as with the Greek Sophists, the nature of man is not the ideal nature of Grotius and the Stoics. It is rather man's supposed actual nature and physical needs, before sociality and authority, that has tempered it. According to Hobbes, man naturally is motivated by desires and aversions and most of all by the desire to preserve his physical and biological existence. He suggests that the laws of nature, such as justice, equity, modesty, mercy and, in sum, 'doing to others as we would like to be done to us', in themselves, without the force of some power to cause them to be observed, are contrary to our natural passions that carry us to partiality, pride, revenge and the like. He suggests that covenants without the swords are but words, and of no strength to secure and satisfy man at all.

John Locke (1632–1704), on the other hand, based his concept of natural law on the existence of God. He said that the law of nature is God's rules for how his creation should operate. The rest of the world in which men live operates automatically in accordance with God's will. For men being all the workmanship of one omnipotent, and infinitely wise maker, all the servants of one sovereign master, sent into the world by his order and about his business, they are his property, whose workmanship they are, made to last during his, not one another's pleasure. Locke calls the source of men's duty to respect claims of right justifiably advanced by other men the law of nature. Locke departed from Hobbesian pessimism to the extent of describing the state of nature as the state of society, with free and equal men already observing natural law. However, human beings can and do choose whether or not to follow God's rules, the law of nature. In his book *The Letter on Toleration* Locke even confines his concept of religious toleration only to those who believe in God and refuses to extend it to the atheists. He strongly rejects any kind of intolerance in religious matters for the followers of religions and strongly supports religious freedom. But he denies this freedom to the atheists. For Locke, the right to toleration was a religious right based upon the immediacy of an individual's responsibility towards and relationship with the Deity. Atheists, to the best of their ability, enjoy no relationship to the Deity and hence can hardly claim the privileges. He believed that within the natural order all men are created equal. He suggested that government power is a trust to serve those it represents. Any misuse or abuse of power by government is wholly out of place within God's workmanship, a direct violation of natural law. The essential task of governmental power is to secure a far higher level of observance of the law of nature. He distinguishes between legitimate and illegitimate governments. This distinction rests mainly upon their differences in their origins or in the basis on which they claim authority. Illegitimate governments do not have any political authority over people. In so far as legitimate government fulfils its mandate, it is entitled to the obedience and support of its subjects. The clearest institutional distinction, which Locke draws, between legitimate and illegitimate governments and forms of rules rest on the role of an elected legislative body.

Locke accepted Grotius's natural law concept of property but with his own justification. Grotius assumed that God had originally given the world to mankind in common. But how could any particular human being come to have a right to any bit of it against all other human beings? Grotius's own answer was that they could do so by coming to an agreement with one another. In the fifth chapter of his *Second Treatise*, Locke attempted to provide a different answer and justification. He argues that God indeed gave the world to men in common, but for use and enjoyment. That to use and enjoy it they needed no consent from one another and that the basis of their individual title to use or appropriate was the labour, which certainly by nature belonged to each of them, at least against any other human beings. Those who work hard and observe the law of nature deserve and are entitled to enjoy God's world. This is the divine order of nature. Locke's concept of divine natural law has retained its value for the proponents of the natural law who believe in God. But it seems very unlikely that in a world in which nature is dealt with only scientifically and is no longer conceived by scientists as God's work it will be able to keep its attraction.[13] However, both Hobbes and Locke reduced the natural law rules to two or three. But because of other reservations, we may regard them as half-hearted natural law thinkers.

Hobbes/Locke/Bentham supporters of individual rights based on their version of natural law and the nature of man, formulated in the shape of liberalism, did not meet either the challenge of true supporters of natural law or the challenge of supporters of democracy. It was because of these challenges that another concept of man's essence was proposed which introduced its own nature of man. This school was the political school of liberal democracy. The liberal democratic thinkers who took this position – most notably Mill and Green – were of course going back to much older traditional version of natural law and theory of man than those of Locke/Bentham ones. They were, in a sense, supporting traditions that went back to Greeks, Romans and medieval natural law. They were exposing Locke/Bentham as a deviation from the humanist, Christian and classical supporters of natural law. There seems to be a conflict between justice and freedom in Western political thought. But how could freedom exist without justice or vice versa. There has been an attempt to reconcile these two concepts. While the supporters of liberalism introduced man as individual consumer and user, who follows his individual natural desires, the liberal democrats tried to inject an element of social equality and justice into it. The pre-democratic liberal theory was based on a concept of man as essentially a consumer of utilities, an infinite individual desire. This concept, clearly dominant in Benthamism, where it is displayed to perfection in James Mill's *Essay on Government*, goes back through the classic economists, at least as far as Locke. Liberal democracy injected a mild element of justice and equality to the nature of man. Social democracy injected an even milder version. Going back to our main theme, we would like to point out that Aristotle also injected a mild form of social element into the nature of man by introducing man as a political animal, rather than as only an individual being.

In France where Montesquieu (1689–1755) had argued that natural laws were pre-social and were superior to religion and the state, Jean-Jacques Rousseau (1712–1778) postulated a savage who was virtuous in isolation and actuated by two principles prior to reason: self-preservation and compassion (innate repugnance towards the suffering of others). Rousseau presented another interpretation of natural law. He accepts neither Hobbes's transference of will

– 'willing not to will' – nor Locke's giving of it on trust. He wishes to compromise neither the freedom of the individual nor the authority of the state. He postulates instead the 'general will' starting with the assumption that all nature is a harmony. He argues that because of this harmony all men have a real will which is identical in all men. In their heart of hearts, if they are really true to themselves, they all want the same. This will, which is common to all men, is the general will. It is by definition good, and men are free only in conforming to it. Men should obey the state, in Rousseau's ideal state, because the sovereign is a moral person expressing the general will. The people are both the subject and the sovereign, and therefore in obeying the sovereign the individual is obeying his real self. The only just social contract is the agreement of people to obey the general will, the agreement of people to obey their real selves, not to obey someone they appoint. But in practice people are not always aware of their real will and must commission a wise legislator to interpret the general will for them. The wise legislator is the declarer of the law, not a maker of the law, and therefore cannot be above the law. He cannot be an instrument for anything but the good because he alone knows what men really want. He forces them to be free. He forces them to live in a rational manner, to discard their chains.

Rousseau came face to face with the paradox of two absolutes that he had constructed: liberty and authority. Liberty he saw as a religious concept, identical with human personality. A man is free. If he is not free he is not a man. Freedom cannot be bartered for security. There cannot be compromise between freedom and authority. But men live in society and society must have rules, and these rules are engraved on the heart of nature. They are inherent laws, laws seen not as conventions but as sacred absolute truths. How then can these absolutes and authority be reconciled? Rousseau suddenly saw the light, the one and only answer, which he alone had discovered. It was possible to obtain personal freedom, which was the state's complete authority. Each man giving himself to all gives himself to nobody. Only those who know what they want are free. And as nature is harmony (Rousseau's basic dubious premise), all rational men will want the same. Corrupt and irrational men seek ends which conflict with nature. Natural, good, rational men seek the same ends that nature demands. These ends are equally good for all other natural men. Men who know what they truly want, want the same. These are the real men. Rousseau invented the real self.

Jean-Jacques Rousseau turned the concept of natural law around and suggested that human nature should be in its place. He insisted that people are what the political systems and governments make of them, and therefore their vices and virtues stem not from human nature but rather from the ways in which they have been governed. He attributed both vices and virtues to political sources and regarded them as political values. But he regarded political systems as artificial and the life of man within them as a transformation of human nature. Even his most famous theory of the social contract is based on his concept of human nature. That is to say, because man is born free naturally he must remain free. 'Man is born free, and he is everywhere in chains.' (*Emile* was written by Rousseau to explain the natural man). No political system can deprive him of this freedom. Only the social contract can safeguard his freedom, as will be explained later. He studied human history in detail and formed his own concept of human nature. Rousseau believed that while our creator had made everything good and natural, all that had been forged by man was corrupt, depraved and unnatural. Rousseau's picture of human nature, stripped away from society, drew savage man closer to other animals than to civilized man. Much of the *Discourse on Inequality* is concerned with zoology and it is noteworthy that the savage, Rousseau believed, was the characteristic outcome of human enterprise, if not always the object of human design, providing us a drastic picture of human beings. The savage creature he fabricated and sometimes termed an orang-utan – solitary, nomadic, indolent and amoral – bears an uncanny resemblance to the real orang-utan of South-East Asia. However, Rousseau's portrait of animal instincts in the *Second Discourse* is almost as striking as his description of the nature of man. It led him to suppose that we differed innately from animals. First, by virtue less of our behaviour than our capacities, in particular, our freedom from domination even by harmless instincts. Second, by our perfectibility, a word he coined to explain how we alone in the natural world had the potential for moral improvement/perfection or corruption. Mankind, he thought, was for better or worse the only creature that could make its own history

Through his hypothetical reconstruction of the past, Rousseau was drawn to several notable observations in political and social theories, of which perhaps some three themes should be emphasized. The first is that the conception of our moral decline around the institution of private property, directly challenged a number of mainly seventeenth-century philosophers of natural law, and was also designed, in particular, to refute the doctrines of Hobbes and Locke. Most natural law thinkers, Rousseau claimed, ascribe to man's essential nature complex traits or institutions – such as reason, language or sense of justice – which could not be acquired except in society. Rousseau therefore charged that such theorists had premised their unacceptable prescriptions for government upon unfounded accounts of human nature. Hobbes and Locke above all incurred his wrath in this matter, since the one supposed that war was natural to man, the other that this was so of private property. Neither of these institutions, he retorted, could in fact have figured in our original state of nature; both were social institutions that had developed in the course of human history, with the condition of war such as Hobbes had described indeed arising both after and from Locke's state of property.

As we see, the doctrine of social contract is socio-political. The relationship between natural law and socio-political issues is very close, clear though sometimes tense and complicated. This point has engaged the mind of other philosophers, especially political philosophers. This is because the doctrine of natural law is a multi-dimensional doctrine. It has its political dimension as well as its legal dimension. The normative political theories (*de jure*) are naturally more agreeable with the doctrine than the descriptive ones (*de facto*). A distinction is, and should be, made between normative political theory or political philosophy on one hand, and descriptive/explanatory theories of the social sciences on the other. The former refers to theories about the proper form of political organization and includes accounts of such notion as liberty and equality. The latter refers to attempts to characterize actual phenomena and events and is marked by a strong empirical element. The distinction, thus, is between theories which focus on what is desirable, what should or ought to be the case, and those that focus on what is the case. The political writings of people like Hobbes, Locke and Mill are generally placed in the first camp, while those of, for instance, Weber are put in the second.

As far as the first camp is concerned, in *Leviathan* Hobbes tries to explain that the state is necessary because of human nature. It is through the theory of human nature that he sought to prove that the state must be regarded as ultimately both absolute and legitimate, in order that the worst evil – civil war – might be permanently averted. He started his theory of Leviathan from a set of postulates and observations of human nature. As for Locke, the state's *raison d'être* is the protection of individuals' rights as laid down by God's will and as enshrined in law. It is interesting that the doctrine of natural law and state of nature can yield a variety of political positions. Locke, like Hobbes, saw the establishment of a, or the, political world as preceded by the existence of individuals endowed with natural rights. For Locke the state of nature is the state of liberty not the state of licence. Individuals are bound by duty to God and governed only by the law of nature. The law of nature, according to Locke, specifies basic principles of morality. This law can be grasped by human reason but it is the creation of God, the infinitely Wise law maker.[14] Humans are free and equal because reason makes them capable of rationality, of following the law of nature. They enjoy natural rights. The rights of governing one's affairs and enforcing the law of nature against transgressors is presupposed, as is the obligation to respect the rights of others.

But it should be pointed out that the line between the two types of theories of the two camps, and their relationship with natural law is not as clear as it sounds. There are some political theories, which have accommodated both tendencies at the same time. Many political philosophers see what they think the state ought to be like in the state as it is. Social scientists, on the other hand, cannot escape the problem that facts do not simply 'speak for themselves'; they are, and they have to be, interpreted. Having explained this point briefly, we would like to go back to where we left.

Second, Rousseau's abstraction of natural man from social man was drawn around a fundamental dichotomy between our physical and moral attributes. Morality, he insisted, did not stem from human nature but rather from denaturation of man in society, with the striking inequalities that shaped our lives utterly different in kind from the insignificant natural variations between us. Private property, especially, was not an expression but a deformation of human nature, artificially established, and contrary to Locke's view, requiring the consent even of those who have none. Third, was Rousseau's concept of human nature, as explained before.

Rousseau's *The Social Contract* of 1762 was to develop some of these theories pertaining to man's denaturation in society, but almost in reverse, that is, along an uplifting path of virtue rather than the descending slope of vice. Confronted by the famous remark in the first chapter that 'man was born free and everywhere he is in chains', readers of *The Social Contract* might have expected it to be a further elaboration of the *Discourse on Inequality*. In fact, however, it provides an alternative and corrective picture of society, a prescription of how the political systems described in the *Discourse* might be changed. In *The Social Contract* he addressed himself to a reform of our political will and intended to inspire moral uprightness. Promoting that end required as profound a transformation of our nature as we had already undergone in the opposite direction. Rousseau believed that the true social contract must realize our liberty and equality together, and not one at the expense of the other. These were the two principles that ought to be the main object of every system of legislation. Having already differentiated the moral and political from the natural and physical spheres of our lives, Rousseau now contended that distinct forms of liberty or freedom were appropriate to each. Without government, he argued, men can be naturally free, in the sense of not being subject to the will of others, but their freedom is attached merely to the satisfaction of their organic impulses. Only in political society, whose establishment requires that our natural liberty be laid down, can we realize either civil or moral liberty, of which the first makes us dependent upon the whole community and the second obedient to laws we prescribe to ourselves. He attempted to show how political systems might actually enhance our freedom.

According to earlier social contract theorists, the liberty or rights that men naturally enjoyed must be largely forfeited when they enter into society and accept the protection of law. For Rousseau, by contrast, liberty would not be lost so much as gained when in giving up our right to do as we please, we bind ourselves collectively to act as we choose. It is his unswerving commitment to political liberty, which marks him off most sharply from all other social contract theorists. He maintained that the state could serve as the instrument of freedom only when all its subjects were at the same time sovereign. Rousseau stressed the significance of a religious as well as a political foundation for our civil responsibilities, according to which citizens performed and loved their duty as a matter of patriotic faith, joining them together in common devotion to the Almighty, beneficent and tolerant Divinity. Nevertheless he condemned Christianity as favourable to tyranny because its believers were made to be slaves. Rousseau's belief in divinity was that of informal and natural divinity. His profession of faith of the Savoyard vicar in *Emile*, published in the same year as *The Social Contract*, set forth the fullest and most eloquent statement of his philosophy of natural as opposed to official religions. In *Emile* he sets a natural framework for a natural educational system. He regarded formal morality, private property, and virtue and vice, war and reason as artificially developed by social and political circumstances and factors. Rousseau can therefore be regarded as a naturist rather than a natural law thinker though the actual concept of the Social Contract is really based on the concept of natural law.[15]

The majority of thinkers and intellectuals of the last two centuries have placed the concept of natural law on the back burner and concentrated mainly on social, economic and other newly publicized socio-economic sciences. But Baron d'Holbach (1723–1789) in *Système de la Nature* and Thomas Paine in *Common Sense* and *Rights of Man* stand out in this period as the two thinkers who supported natural law.

The Later Modern Period

During most of the twentieth century natural law ethics has lost its appeal. But as a result of many events, such as the two world wars, the use of atomic weapons and the threat to the environment, there has been a revival of interest in nature and natural law. Shammer in his *Leben von dem Recht* (1902) sought the a priori social principles of just law concerning respect by all. His call for 'natural law with a changing content' based on these a priori principles quickly became a twentieth-century slogan.[16] There have been some attempts by writers such as the German, Stammler, and the French jurist, Francors, to revive natural law in spite of some resistance they faced from the proponents of positive law. The German legal philosopher Gustav Radbruch converted to natural law from a lifelong commitment to democratic legal relativism and positivism. His conversion was a reaction against the Nazi legal positivism of 'law is law'. The French legal philosopher Maurice Hauriou and writer and historian Georges Renard also helped the revival of natural law. Some have even attempted to seek kinship between existentialism and natural law, e.g. the German legal philosopher, Werner Maihofer. At the same time the twentieth century has been a century of doubts about human reason. The rise of analytical and metaphysical philosophy gave intellectuals rather strong grounds for doubting whether there was such a thing as rational or natural commitment. Books such as A. J. Ayer's *Language, Truth and Logic* (1936) popularized the notion that moral expressions were a sort of emotional bludgeon rather than candidates for truth or falsehood. This was often called the 'boo–hooray' theory of ethics because of the way it analysed statements such as 'democracy is better than fascism' as hooray for democracy, boo for fascism. Even before these philosophical movements got underway, turn-of-the-century sociologists and psychologists had already made the move, which Stuart Hughes chronicled in his *Consciousness and Society;* towards exploring the irrational, an unconscious spring of our behaviour. Freud of course stands out among these explorers of the unconscious, but among sociologists, too, writers like George Sorel wrote of the role of irrational myths in rousing men to action, and dourly reasonable thinkers like Max Weber struggled to explain the paradoxical ways in which reason and unreason interacted.

In the *Principles of Social Reconstruction* Bertrand Russell addressed himself to the problem of why people did not behave in what he and they would usually have called a reasonable fashion: why did men fight one another on the Somme when they had no real quarrel with one another? The answer seemed to Russell to lie in two directions. First, men are moved by passion rather than by calculation, propelled by instincts which demand satisfaction at all costs, not guided by a calculation of what would do themselves good or make them happy. Certainly men get some pleasure out of satisfying their impulses – when men fight they do not enjoy it but they hurl themselves into it willingly. Russell always feared that industrial civilization was chronically vulnerable to warfare because it stifled so many impulses, thwarted the instinct to grapple with and master the world. The second part of Russell's case is that men are motivated by two sorts of instincts: possessive instincts and creative instincts. Possessiveness drives men in pursuit of things that simply cannot be shared, whose possession therefore sets us at odds with other men. The creative instincts on the other hand lead us to seek what can be shared, such as painting and other arts. We must realize that although instincts in animals and in the animal dimension of man is part of the law of nature, they are not what we may call parts of the natural law in human society. This is because men naturally have reason to control and direct their instincts and thus through the process of reasoning and common sense have come to realize that there are universal principles of right and wrong, good and bad, which must be respected.

The issue of a universal human intelligence is closely related with one of the most profound questions of modern times, which Bertrand Russell posed in the following words: 'How come that human beings, whose contacts with the world are brief and personal and limited, are able to know as much as they do know?' What Russell meant was that the amount of knowledge which each one of us possesses is staggeringly large in spite of the fact that we rarely live beyond 60 or 70 years of age. Anybody who has tried to programme a computer to perform the simplest recognition of patterns, or to make it understand elementary concepts, will understand the full depth of Russell's question.

The modern theory of linguistics suggests that Russell's question may be answerable on the basis of scientific research. This research has underscored the importance of the language faculty as a superb mirror of the mind and our ability to comprehend. Noam Chomsky, the well-known philosopher of linguistics, argues that we know as much as we do essentially because we were born to know. He says that humans are born with the faculty of language essentially in place. Rational man has emerged from the realm of biological evolution endowed with innate mental structures capable of abstract thought. In essence he is an intricate 'pre-programmed' computer needing only external stimuli to set cognitive and creative processes in operation. The discovery of a universal human grammar brings to us the clear implication that, at the most fundamental level, many human thoughts and behaviour are entirely universal. It demolishes many theories especially racist theories of development and establishes the oneness of humanity and its universal principles. (*Britannica*, 'Existentialism') John Rawls in his book *A Theory of Justice* (1971) puts forward an idea about the justification of moral judgements. First, was the method of 'reflective equilibrium'. Moral theory, he suggested, is the attempt to describe our moral capacity, just as a linguistic theory is an attempt to describe our capacity of language. Native speakers are able to distinguish well-formed from ill-formed sentences, even without a theory of guidance. Similarly we are able to judge intuitively that some actions are right, and others are wrong.[17]

The main features of the system of natural law are as follows:

1. Nature follows a certain basic pattern and order.
2. Man as a part of nature also conforms to a certain basic pattern.
3. This pattern for man has taken the shape of certain general rules or principles, which are absolute and above the will and the authority of people, governments and legislative authorities.

4. These principles are permanent and are not subject to change, alteration or modification.
5. These rules and principles are universal and universally accepted by all humanity without being limited by time, space, or other relativistic circumstances.
6. These principles are self-explanatory and self-evident, though some natural law proponents have rejected this characteristic and feature of natural law.
7. These principles are rational, discoverable and understandable by human reason, though some have rejected this characteristic and feature of natural law
8. The system of natural law to a large extent supports liberty and the right of individuals and thus liberalism. This feature of natural law is rejected by many of its supporters.
9. These principles established by natural law enjoy a kind of sacredness and divinity, though some have denied this and have excised the spiritual dimension from the order of nature and the natural principles of man and natural law.
10. The system of natural law is indeed a school of philosophy of law rather than an inclusive legal system, a code of law or a collection of legal rules. The number of its basic and fundamental principles varies according to the views of its supporters, which is probably its major shortcoming.
11. It supports and promotes abstract general principles such as justice, equality, freedom, rights of possession, rights to life etc, which can be interpreted in conflicting ways. This is why natural law has been used or even misused by fascists, Nazis, racists etc. Individualism, liberalism, socialism and communism have been explained and justified by their supporters in terms of natural law too.
12. Natural law is very flexible. Its basic principles are subject to conflicting explanations. The Greek supporters of natural law, such as Aristotle even justified slavery on the basis of natural law. In modern times racists, fascists and Nazis justified racism on the basis of natural law.
13. It is at the same time a school of philosophy, ethics, politics, law, philosophy of law and thought.

Challenges to Natural Law Theories

Natural law has faced challenges throughout its history and development and has been the subject of more serious challenges recently. The disappearance of all traces of solid moral, ethical, spiritual and metaphysical schools, thoughts and aspirations and certainty, and also the reduction of philosophy into practically no more than the discussion of trivial and superficial issues, all led and contributed to the appearance and establishment of certain so-called schools of thought under these titles and names, which led to challenges to natural law. The development of the schools of empiricism, utilitarianism, secularism, materialism, social Darwinism, scientism, historicism, atheism, ethical relativism, individualism, humanism, logical positivism, self-centrism, nationalism and other recent 'isms' put natural law into serious question. These schools declared war on nature, natural law, ethical values, spiritual norms, social maxims, rational mores, order of nature and all other traditional and cultural standards and absolute values.

The recent assault on natural law and natural rights began during the late eighteenth century and it intensified during the nineteenth and early twentieth centuries. Here we shall briefly deal with some of these schools and their challenges to natural law.

Utilitarianism

Utilitarianism was the doctrine which adopted as the test of all moral rules and social arrangements, their contribution to the general welfare, or, as it is often summarized, the greatest happiness of the greatest number. The English utilitarian movement was founded by Jeremy Bentham (1748–1832), liberal and non-believer. The utilitarians sought to base the art of legislation on a science of human nature, but both Bentham and his follower James Mill believed in a clear but limited view of man. Men were conceived as particularly natural objects, as passive creatures whose mental life is governed by the law of the association of ideas and whose actions are aimed at the achievement of pleasure. According to Mill, part of human fault lies in man's conception of human nature. In spite of his efforts to free his view of man from the crude errors of classical utilitarianism, his account still seems to us at once narrowly rationalistic and optimistic. The steady trajectory of progress, which he expected, depended in the end on the realism of his account of human nature. Jeremy Bentham wrote: 'Right is the child of law'. From real law comes rights, but from imaginary law comes imaginary rights. David Hume (1711–76) agreed with Bentham. He insisted that natural law and natural rights are unreal metaphysical phenomena. Utilitarianism spread to other parts of the world.

There appears to be a dilemma for these utilitarians. It seems as if they are torn apart between different sets of ideas. They do not seem to be able to discredit human nature and natural law easily. Hume also faced this dilemma. Hume also believed in a continuous universal human nature with unified human natural feelings, inclinations and innate human moral principles and in this respect he was influenced by Latin thinkers, like Cicero, rather than by

Greek thinkers. Utilitarianism itself faced quite a few difficulties and was challenged on many grounds. During the middle decades of the twentieth century, utilitarianism's chief rival was the intuitionism of W.D. Ross. As early as 1930, in his book *The Right and the Good*, Ross had pointed out that utilitarianism leads to conclusions that seem plainly wrong. Ross argued that people's relationships with each other are that of the prima-facie duties which are more or less incumbent on them. Ross argued that we have an indefinite number of these prima-facie duties including at least the following:

1. resting on some previous act of our own, such as the duty to keep our promises and the duty to make restitution for wrong we have done;
2. the duty of gratitude, to return favours others have done for us;
3. the duty of justice, to distribute goods fairly;
4. the duty of self-improvement, to develop our own talents and abilities;
5. the duty of beneficence, to act in a way to benefit others;
6. the duty of non-malfeasance, not to injure others.

These duties are, according to Ross, independent of one another, they are not reducible to one another, nor are they reducible to any other or more general principle such as the principle of utility. They are not hierarchical either.[18]

Contrary to what Ross suggested, the liberals, it may be said, reduced the natural law rules to only one. According to liberals all values are personal except one: the value of respecting personal values, which is universal. The close connection, or even identity, between liberalism and utilitarianism explains the position of both of them towards the concept of natural law. John Stuart Mill believed in human nature and he tried hard to free his view of man from the crude errors of utilitarianism. But his theory of human nature was very narrow.[19]

Although Utilitarianism in modern contemporary civilization is prevalent, the main justification and explanation for the United Nations UDHR is natural law, though this has been denied. The Declaration of Independence of the USA also refers, though only briefly, to the laws of nature before citing equality and other inalienable rights as self-evident. The French Declaration of the Rights of Man and of the Citizen asserts liberty, property, security and resistance to oppression as imprescribable natural rights. On the level of international politics, the recognition of the international laws, norms, conventions, commercial treaties, the concept of the United Nations and the UDHR represent the recognition of natural law rather than an empirical and utilitarian search for common values, which in turn also is based, somehow, on the recognition, somewhat, of human universals.

Empiricism

Empiricism was not confined to the realm of natural sciences. Social scientists, like everyone else, are philosophers of knowledge. They also have their theories of knowledge – epistemologies. Empirical methodology was thus applied to social sciences and humanitarian studies too. Empiricism is the doctrine that proclaims that all knowledge, ultimately, originates in experience and not in universal human reason, primordial nature or intuition. Although empiricism deals mainly with the question of the means of acquiring knowledge, it indirectly challenges natural law by denying the authority of the means of natural law. However, empiricism has been recently the subject of strong criticism even in the field of science. The critics of empiricism claim that it never was and it never could be the method of science and that conscious or even unconscious adherence to its principles can retard progressive scientific discovery. There are four major problems with empiricism: selectivity, certainty, error and interpretation. Empirical method has to use a deductive approach along with an inductive approach to be able to generalize and come to conclusion. It cannot be a sound method of acquiring knowledge on its own even in the field of natural sciences let alone in the fields of social and humanitarian studies.[20]

Karl Popper has criticized crude empiricism in his essays and autobiography. But Kuhn explains and shows that Popper himself is really an empiricist. 'For all the advances his theory has made over the earlier forms of empiricism, Popper remains an empiricist at heart.'[21] 'Popper's position amounts to empiricism of a non-inductive variety, if he is unambiguously to be able to claim that scientific progress is always the result of bold theoretical conjecture and rigorous empirical refutation. This is the central doctrine of his critical rationalism and he himself is the target of the same criticism,' states Len Doyal.[22] The most influential and overtly non-empiricist writer to explore the problems and implications attending this view is Thomas Kuhn. The gist of Kuhn's argument is that dogma plays just as important a role as criticism and experience in the growth of scientific knowledge. Kuhn suggests that experience alone can never force you to change your mind, for with imagination you can always find an interpretation which is consistent with your beliefs. Kuhn argues that it is precisely this imperviousness of paradigms to empirical refutation that makes successful science possible at all. How can one justify such a paradoxical claim?

The conclusion is that empirical method, experience and induction on its own cannot produce a sound conclusion. It needs to employ explanation and deductive rational means to be able to do this. Deduction and deductive methods have to rely on universal law in order to produce true conclusions.

Generally speaking, explanations in modern physical science are deductive in that their premises logically entail their conclusion, and they are nomological in that at least one of their premises is a law. If an explanation employs universal law, the *explanadom* follows from the *explanas* with the same sort of logical necessity as the conclusion follows from the premises in this famous argument: All men are mortal = major premise. Socrates is a man = minor premise.Therefore, Socrates is mortal = conclusion.

As we see, the major premise is a universal law. It is important to distinguish between the logical necessity which deduction derives from their validity, and the necessity with which events occur that fall under the law of nature. For the logical necessity clearly remains even when the explanation is false and yields a false conclusion – it is from these false conclusions that we deduce the falsity of explanatory premises. Results that inductively confirm a theory, do not allow the deductively valid inference that it must be true, no matter how many times it happens. Only true premises produce true conclusion and falsehood of conclusion implies the falsehood of at least one of the premises.

Atheism

It is interesting to note that throughout the history of ethics and humanity ethical absolutism has been associated with theism, religion and the spiritual tendencies of man. Plato, in his *Laws*, prescribed the death penalty for certain kinds of atheists on the ground that their views undermined both morality and law (Book X, 908–10). Even John Locke, the great European advocate of religious tolerance, exempted atheists from the application of the principles he was advocating on the ground that, as he put it, 'Promises, covenants and oaths, which are the bonds of human society can have no hold upon an atheist' (*Letter Concerning Toleration*). Atheism, he argued, in that it is not only not a religion but also a philosophy that undermines all religions, could not come under the privilege of toleration that was rightly claimed by all bona fide religions. In England, until the Evidence Amendment Act of 1869, atheists could not be trusted and could not give evidence in English courts of law, because they were unable, as atheists, to take an oath which was couched in theistic language. Atheism has also been associated with ethical relativism. Within the Western tradition, absolute atheism has, overall, been linked to the rejection of religion, which is regarded as another source of ethical absolutism. Such rejection has usually been based on philosophical naturalism and materialism, which denies the existence of any reality other than that which is accessible through sensory experience.

Atheism was not the only means that led to ethical relativism. Deism has also contributed to it. The seventeenth-century thinker Thomas Hobbes, who is often regarded as an atheist, and was regarded as such by many of his contemporaries, was, on his own admission, not an atheist but a deist. He held that God was necessary to account for there being a world, but that, having created the world, He took no further part in its affairs. The first avowed atheist of modern times was the French materialist philosopher Baron d'Holbach, the second volume of whose book *Système de la Nature*, published in 1754, contained a vigorous defence of atheism. From the eighteenth century onward an increasing number of thinkers, the best known of whom were Karl Marx, Friedrich Nietzsche, Sigmund Freud and Jean-Paul Sartre, advocated atheism and the rejection of all religions. This they did by drawing on Ludwig Feuerbach's suggestion that God was a 'projection' of certain aspects of human nature. The main features of atheism are materialistic ontology, an empirical epistemology and hedonistic ethics.[23] Contrary to the approach adopted by atheists to link atheism with naturalism, a group of scientists, represented in modern time by Ian Graeme Barbour, introduced theology of nature and natural theology.[24]

Ethical Relativism

Ethical relativism (versus ethical absolutism) is the view that what is right or wrong is not absolute but relative, depending on the person and external factors and circumstances. The view is as ancient as Protagoras, a leading Greek sceptic of the fifth century BC. Ethical relativism is the view that what is really right depends solely upon what the individual or the society think is right. This is because what one thinks will vary according to time, place and circumstances. What one thinks is right will also vary accordingly. Ethical relativism is a view about the truth and status of moral principles, according to which, changing and even conflicting moral principles are equally true, so that there is no objective way of justifying any principle as valid for all people and all societies.[25] Thus there is no innate and intuitive right and wrong, truth and falsehood, duties and responsibility, good and evil, ethical universals and principles. A second argument for relativism is that of the sceptics, who hold that moral utterances are not cognitive statements, verifiable as true or false, but are instead emotional expressions of approval or disapproval, or are merely prescriptions for action. In this view, variation and conflict between moral utterances are relative to the varying conditions that occasion such feelings, attitude or prescriptions, and there is nothing more to be said. Critics of the sceptical view may observe that moral utterances as emotive expressions do not in themselves disqualify them from functioning simultaneously as beliefs with cognitive contents. Or again, one may observe that. even if moral utterances are not cognitive, it does not follow that they are related in a special way to needs and wants that are common and essential to human nature and society everywhere and in every age. If so, the criticism continues, these needs can provide good reason for justification of some moral utterances over others. The relativists will then have to reply either that human nature has no such common enduring needs, or that, if it does, they cannot be discovered and employed to ground man's moral discourse.[26]

The question of relativism can be discussed, at least, at three distinct levels: ethical relativism, cognitive relativism and cultural relativism. They have all been both justified and refuted by different people. Postmodernism would seem to be rather clearly in favour of relativism. Postmodernist relativism is hostile to the idea of unique, exclusive, objective, external or transcendent truth. According to relativism truth is elusive, polymorphous, inward, subjective, and perhaps a few other things as well. Postmodernist relativism may be regarded as an ephemeral philosophical/cultural fashion, but it has left some impact on modern thought.

The doctrine of primordial nature (*fitrah*) rejects moral and ethical relativism at all its levels. According to this doctrine morality is beyond culture and even beyond knowledge. Cultural morality is not exactly ethical morality. Everything about the history of mankind makes it fairly plain that ethical relativism is false and that man has always believed, in one way or another, in primordial, innate and universal values and principles. Absolute relativism denies the possibility of morality and knowledge beyond culture. It supports moral relativism, according to which we cannot establish values or that there are moral values. It supports the idea that the values that guide our life and inspire human beings are contingent and have no foundation other than those circular self-confirming systems of thought and sentiment we call cultures. At the same time we must understand that the denial of the possibility that morality could be beyond culture, and knowledge beyond both, is in fact an extremely acceptable definition of relativism.[27] What we desperately need is precisely a morality beyond culture and even beyond empirical knowledge. The real and greatest objection to relativism is not that it proposes a false solution (though it does), but that it prevents us from even seeing, formulating and solving our problem. Relativism is objectionable because it entails moral nihilism as well as cognitive nihilism. It thus challenges natural law, universal values and religions in two fronts: ethics and knowledge. It has been suggested that cultural relativism has a deeply inherent bias towards idealism or a permanent and original ethical value system.

It is important to appreciate that ethical anti-relativism does not necessarily lead to cultural absolutism. Ethical principles derive their value mainly from the primordial nature of man while cultural values are based on culture, which is subject to time, space and circumstances etc. One culture cannot sit in judgement on another culture. But this is not the case with ethical principles and values. We cannot agree with the subjectivist–relativist theory of ethics, which states that the notions of values are self-invented; that is the value of truth, beauty and goodness is a projection of man outside himself. The recognition and pursuit of virtue is an innate property of man, born out of his natural state of *fitrah*. Virtue has an absolute value of its own which must be discovered. One of the major problems with relativism is that it carries an inner contradiction, mainly that of contradicting itself. The relativist contradicts himself if he would proclaim the absolute truth of the proposition that there is no truth.[28]

Social Darwinism

The theory of evolution has been largely discredited by scientific advances in the fields of physics, chemistry and genetics, among others. However, the Darwinism of the middle of the nineteenth century with its contradictory dimensions tried to put an end to the old idea of man as a human being and introduced him as an animal only. It thus put an end to the natural order and to the idea of human nature and natural law and to the classical idea of a permanent universal order of nature. It also led to the idea of designed natural selection, which in turn led to the eugenics movement and also to the racism and the racial selection of Nazism. The concept of the survival of the fittest also contributed to the concept of the 'white man's burden' promoted by the West to justify colonialism, imperialism, exploitation and genocide. In fact, and to some extent, the theory of Darwinism and evolution and natural selection was based on environmentalism (environmental factors). Nature in natural selection meant environmental circumstances. Geneticism in its Darwinian version was another contributing factor in the war against natural law. Darwinism was in fact the philosophy of 'becoming', as against the philosophy of 'being' on which natural law was based. The theory of evolution does not limit itself to the field of biology; rather, it has socio-political, economic, religious, scientific and ethical repercussions and affects all spheres of life. The objective, or at least the end result, of evolution is to destroy the concept of man as an ethical and spiritual entity with its own properties and dignity and to destroy belief in God. Natural selection replaced both God and natural law and order. Racism, the eugenics of selective breeding, the social Darwinism of introducing the upper and middle class as the fittest who are naturally selected to survive, and other products of Darwinism caused it to retreat to academic circles for a while. However, the discovery of very old fossils, which proved that many species have remained the same for tens of thousands of years, have led scientists to suggest that there are more additional laws than the evolutionary theory ruling nature. Also, the results of the recent research of new disciplines like social and evolutionary psychology, group psychology and even genetics have produced results suggesting that there are universal, inherent innate tendencies, such as altruism and co-operation.[29]

Individualism

Another dimension of postmodernism and relativism is the individualism on which Western democracy and liberalism are really based. The justifying theory of Western liberalism and democracy rests on two maximizing claims: a claim to maximize individual freedom to use all resources and a claim to maximize individual power and pleasure. Neither of these claims can be made good, partly because of inherent defects and partly because of changing circumstances. The changing circumstances both permit and require a change in some of the theory's assumptions. Changed circumstances have created new difficulties for democratic theory because of the very breadth of its claims. One of the central values of Western democracy has been the surpassing importance of freedom of choice of individuals. This unlimited freedom of choice is self-refuting and challenges the concept of universal standards and principles of morality and thus the concept of natural law. The claim to maximize freedom to use all resources means that man is viewed as essentially a consumer and the seeker of pleasure. This claim implies a particular concept of man's essence and nature which does not really fulfil man's ethical, moral and spiritual responsibilities. This concept of man denies man's absolute, primordial and comprehensive identity. Besides the claim to maximize individual use of resources contradicts the second claim, the claim to maximize individual power. While the first claim introduces man as a consumer utilitarian animal the second claim presents almost the opposite view of the essence of man from that of the utilitarians. It is thus self-refuting.[30]

Individualism and its by-product, liberalism, put ethical, spiritual and absolute values at the mercy of individuals and deny human primordial nature, the universal and social dimension of man. Virtue is an inborn quality and the learning of it is a rediscovery of what is already known. According to Islamic sources man's soul has already acknowledged his true primordial nature and its voluntary commitment to fulfil its requirements.[31]

Secular Fundamentalism of Enlightenment

There is another position, which shares something with relativism but at the same time challenges it. It is a position, which, like that of fundamental religion, is firmly committed to the denial of relativism. It is committed to the view that there is external, objective, culture-transcending knowledge, i.e. there is indeed knowledge beyond culture. But this position, on the other hand, also does have something in common with relativism. It does not believe in the availability of a substantive, final, world-transcending revelation. It does believe in the existence of knowledge which transcends culture, and it is also committed to the mundane origin of knowledge and its fallible status; but it firmly repudiates the very possibility of revelation. This position is located mid-way between religious fundamentalism and relativism. Unlike the relativism of postmodernism, the secular fundamentalism of the enlightenment is certainly more than a passing academic fad and fashion. Sketched out at first in the course of scientific revolution in the seventeenth century, worked out in details in the eighteenth, the position which might be called the secular fundamentalism of enlightenment, has become the unwritten, but widely recognized, code of cognitive conduct of many thinkers. Nevertheless, not all scholars of scientific and industrial civilization accepted it. Recently it has been out of fashion with many intellectuals. How can this position both deny the possibility of revelation from outside and yet affirm extraneous, culture-transcending knowledge? This is indeed the crucial question. Alasdair MacIntyre has produced a critical analysis of the Enlightenment. His book *After Virtue* begins with the 'disquieting suggestion' that moral discourse in the West has lost its meaning, that it serves as a disguise for the expression of preference, attempts to gain power, emotions and attitudes, but that it has ceased to have any relation to what is truly good or right. He pins responsibility for the collapse of Western ethics on the Enlightenment. Much of the book goes on criticizing various aspects of enlightenment thought in Hume, Kant, the utilitarians, the emotivists, and in contemporary liberal political philosophy, especially as elaborated by John Rawls. However, MacIntyre accepts in *After Virtue* that there is no absolute moral truth. He suggests that each of us must view the world from his own position in history and society. It is this admission that led many of critics of his book to accuse him of relativism or historicism. It is largely in response to this criticism that *Whose Justice? Which Rationality*? was written. In this book he rejects relativism and come to the conclusion that it is possible to have access to absolute truth. He argues that both relativists and perspectivists are wrong because they fail to admit the absolute timeless character of the truth and would replace truth by what is often called warranted assertibility.[32]

Existentialism

The question whether there is or is not something called human nature and human primordial nature has been asked often, especially recently. The question of human nature has been dealt with in quite a few disciplines: psychology, philosophy, sociology, epistemology, psychotherapy and even in genealogy just to mention a few. There has been an explosion of animal behaviour studies. Comparison between animals and man has become immensely popular in dealing with human nature and instincts. Freudian psychology suggested dependence on instinct. On the other hand, many sociologists and psychologists support the theory of what may be called the 'blank paper' view, which suggests that man is a creature entirely without instinct, nature and certainly primordial nature and a sense of ethical value judgement. So do existentialist philosophers.

According to the blank paper view, man is entirely the product of his culture. He is formed completely by the society in which he grows up. Man's behaviour is just the result of his conditioning. Man is what he is becoming and not what he is being. Existentialism at first appears a very different standpoint, because the existentialist asserts man's freedom and will not let him call himself a product of anything. But existentialism also denies that man has a nature; if he had, his freedom would not be complete. Thus Sartre insisted that

> there is no human nature ... Man first of all exists, encounters himself, surges up in the world, and defines himself afterwards. If man, as the Existentialist sees him, is not definable, it is because to begin with he is nothing. He will not be anything until later, and he will be what he makes himself to be. For Existentialism there is only the human condition, which is what happens to man and not what he is born like. He is what he chooses to be. Existentialists must never talk about human nature or instincts.'[33]

This type of modern existentialism is different from the traditional philosophical existentialism which is termed in Islamic philosophy as *isalato al-wujud.* In fact Sartre's existentialism corresponds with the opposite school which is essentialism or whatism, which is termed in Islamic philosophy as *isalato al-mahiyyah.* This is because Sartre suggested that man is nothing until later and becomes what he will be as the result of what happens to him.

The so-called modern 'existentialism' is a different form of the subjectivism publicized by Jean-Paul Sartre. As a philosophical movement it claimed that our existence precedes our essence (hence existentialism). Because there is no human nature for Jean-Paul Sartre, human beings have not been created for any particular purpose. Because we have not been designed for any specific end, we are free to choose our own essence, which means to choose how we will live and how we exist. To say that we are compelled by our situation, our nature, or our role in life to act in a certain way is to exhibit ' bad faith'. This seems to be the only term of disapproval (moral judgement) the existentialists are prepared to use. As long as we choose 'automatically' there are no moral standards by which our conduct can be criticized. This is the official view held by the majority of those who claim to be existentialists. But in a pamphlet entitled *L'existentialisme est un humanisme* (Existentialism is humanism, 1946), Sartre backs away from so radical a subjectivism by suggesting a version of Kant's idea that we must be prepared to apply our judgement universally. He does not reconcile this view with conflicting statements elsewhere in his writings.[34] He re-evaluated his ideas after two world wars and the atrocities committed in those wars.

Rationalist Fundamentalism, Fundamental Rationalism or Enlightenment Rationalism

Rational fundamentalism repudiates any substantive revelations and belief in the absolute and in this sense it resembles relativism. But at the same time it treats as absolutes some formal principles of knowledge, at least procedural, and perhaps also of formal valuation. Absolutist and non-relativist in procedure rather than relativist in its substance is the basic stance of enlightenment rationalist fundamentalism and fundamental rationalism. This movement suggests that there are no privileged or a priori substantive truths. It thus eliminates the sacred form of the world. All facts and all observers are equal. There are no privileged sources or affirmations. All of them can be queried. Nothing can escape scrutiny. According to this movement, the laws to which this world is subject are symmetrical. This levels out the world, and thereby 'disenchants' it, in the famous Weberian expression. It desacredizes, disestablishes and disenchants everything substantive: there are no privileged facts, occasions, individuals, institutions or associations. Nothing is sacred and everything is subject to inquiry and scrutiny. The only thing that is absolute and sacred is this method itself, which leaves its shadow and impact on the world and establishes its own order. This makes the proper sense, which is to be attributed to the Kantian doctrine that we 'make' our world and that an orderly, systematic, law-bound nature is really the shadow of our cognitive procedure. This method is beyond and outside culture and beyond this world. The Enlightenment was eager to deny religious transcendence but at the same time affirmed the transcendence of this method, and affirmed that everything was to be found within a single, orderly system of nature.

The mainstream of the Enlightenment did not properly come to terms with the tension between its naturalistic, relativist view of everything within the world, and its privileged perception of itself. Kant faced and challenged this contradiction. As the deepest thinker of the Enlightenment, Kant suggested that everything inside nature was indeed subject to its laws, but knowledge itself

– and morality – were outside it (*a fortiori*, they were outside and above culture). Kant saw with great lucidity that inside nature, conceived as an orderly system subject to laws, there was no room for a universal and unique reason: there was only room for causation. Applied to the higher form of life, this in effect meant the cognitive adaptation of each organism or each culture. But nature, as a unique orderly system, was the construction, precisely, of a reason determined to treat all like cases alike. The result of these considerations was the stressful Kantian dualism, which consigns everything within nature, including man, to causality. Hence, by implication, when this is applied to culture it consigns it to relativism. But it exempts us, as moral and cognitive agents, from being members of nature, and allows us to have access to uniquely valid knowledge and morality. In a sense we created the world, which is but the shadow of our rationality, and for this very reason we neither can nor need be part of it.[35]

The Social Contract Theory of Ethics

'In its pure form, the social contract view is that morality is a set of rules that rational people will agree to adopt to further their own interests. It is obvious, for example, that each of us will be better off if we are able to live in a society in which murder, assault and theft are prohibited. Therefore we have good reason to accept such rules, and others like them, provided that other people will accept them as well.'.[36] According to this theory, moral rules are justified by showing that they are necessary if we are to co-operate for our mutual benefit. It is reasonable to follow them because it is to our own advantage to follow these rules and to live in a society in which moral rules are accepted. It is reasonable for us to follow them because we agree to follow moral rules. The utilitarians and others like them find it difficult to establish morality on an objective basis. But for the partisans of social contract theory morality is a rational enterprise. It is easy to explain the role and objectivity of these moral rules. However the theory of social contract also has its shortcomings and faults. It fails to account for absolute character of moral obligation. Is it wrong for me to murder you *only* because we have made a deal that forbids it?[37]

Positivism

Positivism would appear to mean a belief in the existence and availability of objective facts, and above all belief in the possibility of the said facts by means of an objective testable theory, not itself essentially linked to any one culture, observer or mood. According to positivism, a theory could be articulated, understood and assessed without any reference to its author and his social identity. Accordingly, objectivity is the main characteristic of positivism. Positivism has been challenged along various lines. One may not be satisfied with relativism but one can find the challenges launched against positivism by the relativists quite interesting. The relativists challenge the positivists by suggesting that the world is not the totality of things, but of meanings. Everything is meaning and meaning is everything and hermeneutics is its prophet. The meaning conferred on it makes it whatever is. It is the meaning with which it is endowed which has singled it out from the primal flow of uncategorized existence and thereby turned it into an identifiable object. Facts are inseparable from the observer, who claims to discern them, and the culture, which applied the categories in terms of which they are described.[38] Although both contemporary positivism and relativism borrowed their legitimacy mainly from postmodernism they produced two distinct opposite movements, challenging each other. But they both challenged the authority of primordial nature, intuition and ethical absolutism of monotheistic religions.

The methodology of the argument between the positivists and the relativists/hermeneutists resembles that of the discussion which was going on for a long time amongst the Muslim philosophers, between those who supported the authority and priority of existence (*wujud*) over essence (*mahiyyat*) and those who did the opposite. The supporters of each theory based their argument on whether the opposite group was subjective or objective in their cognitive approach. From the cognitive point of view, it sounds like the argument put forward by the architect of the last great philosophical system in Islam, Sadra al-Din of Shiraz (d. 1059/1640) in his monumental work entitled *The Four Journeys* (*al-Asfar al-Arba'ah*). Having accepted from al-Suhrawardi (founder of the school of philosophy of Illumination, *Maktab al-Ishraque*, executed in 587/1191) the monistic doctrine of the 'grades of being' in terms of 'more or less', he developed his own doctrine of cognition and the nature of the human soul. Sadra al-Din suggested that the human soul is not a single-level entity having different faculties of cognition, but is of different levels (*nash'at*) corresponding to those of the ontological reality. The powers of the mind are not mere power but are literally constituents of reality. The soul, therefore, not merely 'knows' reality but participates in it and is identified with it; it is not merely receptive but creative. It follows that at a higher level of experience the mind experiences and becomes whatever it wills and thus attains absolute freedom from the finite existence of the material world. [39]

Logical Positivism

Along with modern ethical relativism, logical positivism challenged intuitionism. During the 1930s, logical positivism, brought from Vienna by

Ludwig Wittgenstein, and popularized by A. J. Ayer in his manifesto, *Language, Truth and Logic* (1936), became influential in British philosophy. According to logical positivism, all true statements fall into two categories: logical truths and statements of fact. Moral judgements cannot fit comfortably into either category. They cannot be logical truths, for they are near tautology that cannot tell us more than is already contained in the definition of the terms. Nor can they be statements of fact, because they must, according to logical positivism, be at least in principle verifiable. There is no way of verifying the truth that the intuitionists claimed to apprehend. The truth of mathematics, on which intuitionists had continued to rely as the one clear parallel case of truth known by its self-evidence, was explained now as logical truth. In this view, mathematics tells us nothing about the world, it is simply a logical system, true by the definition of the terms involved, which may be useful in our dealings with the world. Thus the Intuitionists lost the one useful analogy to which they could appeal to in support of the body of self-evident truths, known by reason alone.[40]

Contemporary scientific development has led to the idea of cognitive absolutism. It is claimed that an enormous mass of facts establishes it. The new learning and sciences respect neither culture, religion nor morality. It is not only beyond culture and morality, but also against it. Cognitive absolutism has challenged ethical absolutism.

Ethical Scepticism

Ethical theorists are generally divided into two groups. For the group which suggests that there are objective moral truths moral objectivity may be explained in two major theories:

1. Ethics could be objective in the sense that moral problems can be solved by rational methods. These methods would show that some moral views are acceptable while others are not.
2. Ethics could be objective in the sense that moral predicates – good, right, and so on – refer to real properties of things. Moral facts are part of the fabric of the world.

The group which, on the contrary, suggests that ethics is based upon nothing more than our feelings and social conventions challenges these ideas (moral subjectivism). The question of ethical objectivity and subjectivity is as old as philosophy itself. In Plato's *Republic* Socrates encountered Thrasmachus, who believed that right and wrong are the inventions of the strong that help them dominate the weak. The partisans of this view assume that there are no such things as moral facts.

Emotivism

Modern sceptics, who also believe that there are no moral facts, suggest that morality originates in the desires and emotions of individuals and societies. Thomas Hobbes supported this view. But it is David Hume, more than any other figure in modern thought, who is associated with this idea. The approved version of subjectivism is emotivism which became the most influential theory of ethics in the mid-twentieth century and was developed by logical positivism and its partisans, most notably Moritz Schlick and A.J. Ayer and the American philosopher Charles L. Stevenson. In the mid-twentieth century many philosophers believed that emotivism had solved all the problems of ethics. There are quite a few interpretations and versions of moral objectivity, moral subjectivity and emotivism. One version of moral subjectivism, emotivism and relativism is utilitarianism, which for a long time held the centre stage. In the year of the French Revolution Bentham declared that all moral duties are derived from one ultimate principle, the principle of utility. In the nineteenth century John Stuart Mill and Henry Sidgwick developed and extended this idea and utilitarianism became the leading idea in moral philosophy. The central principle of this school was to promote 'the greatest happiness of the greatest number'. The twentieth century witnessed a great reaction to utilitarianism in one way or another. Some supporting it and some challenging it.[41]

The emotivists who base moral judgement on purely emotional ground (hence the terminoligy) held that moral judgements do not make statements of fact at all. The emotivists were branded as subjectivists. But unlike other subjectivists in the past, modern emotivists claimed that those who say, for example, 'stealing is wrong' are not making a statement of fact about their own feelings or attitude towards stealing. This view is more properly known as subjective naturalism, because it makes the truth about moral judgements depend on natural facts about the world, albeit subjective.[42]

Racism

Although racism (which in its present form is a product of Western culture) has no scientific and philosophical basis, its proponents have tried to justify it by one means or another. The human genome project recently found that all human beings share 99.9 per cent of their genes with other human beings, which makes racism a scientifically meaningless concept. Science simply confirms what has been revealed to us, in the Qur'an, of the unity and singleness of our shared Adamic nature as human beings.[43] Racism in all its different shapes, forms, degrees and interpretations denies the universal characters, properties and potentialities of mankind. It is anti-natural law, (though its supporters explain it in terms of nature) anti-universal human rights and anti-universal human nature. Theorists like Max Weber, for example, would like us to believe the following theory. If science (civilization and intellection included) is the result of intelligence, the birth of modern science in Europe was on account of genetic superiority of the European people! By propagating this theory Weber denies the universal intellectual potential of the large portion of humanity. The discovery of a universal human grammar brings to us the clear implication that, at the most fundamental level, many human thoughts and behaviour are entirely universal. It demolishes many theories, especially racist theories of development, and establishes the oneness of humanity and its universal principles. We know that modern psychology has found no scientific ground for this in spite of countless tests.[44]

One of the problems with natural law in its Western version is that it is very flexible. Both the racists and the anti-racists appeal to it to justify their views. To justify, that is to find a moral basis for, their views, many schools of thought and behaviour found it necessary to derive the rights from and base their views on the very nature or essence of man. In this way they try to show that man being so was in accordance with natural law or morality. The explanation, which was needed, was one that would serve as a basis of moral justification. It had to be one on which an acceptable moral theory could be built. It would have been too outrageous to postulate that hatred for and inferiority of a section of human society, or racial discrimination, for example, without having natural justification is morally right. This is why even the Nazis, Fascists and racists try to justify their views in terms of natural law and their version of human nature. The Zionists justify the doctrine of 'chosen people' in even religious terms. It had to be justified in an acceptable way. In the following chapters we shall explain that this is not the case with the Islamic version of natural law in the context of *fitrah.* The world and human community envisioned by Islam is that of an inclusive view of mankind, a vision of unity in diversity, inclusivity and universality.

Materialism

'While individual philosophers continue to produce and defend as wide a range of metaphysical views as they ever have, today two outlooks have become dominant (in Western) American and French philosophy', states H. Putnam. He continues,

> These are respectively the outlooks of materialism and relativism. Although few American philosophers actually call themselves materialists, and I do not know of any French philosophers who actually call themselves relativists, the terms 'physicalism' and 'naturalism' have become virtually synonymous with materialism in analytic philosophy, while the thrust of deconstructionists' views is often clearly relativist, if not down-right nihilist. There are happily many philosophers who have rejected both materialism and relativism. The only thing we can learn from them is the failure of their points of view.[45]

Other Challenges

There are other schools of thought, which in one way or another, do not support, and even reject, the natural law system. They include sociologists, anthropologists, ethnologists, historicists, Communists and many others. What they all have in common, with regard to natural law, is that they all put the truth, ethical values and their recognition at the disposal and mercy of various different unfounded conjectural secular, materialistic, relativistic, social and even economic explanations. They suggest that the notions of truth and moral values are self-invented, that the values of truth, beauty, law and goodness are projections of man outside himself and that they are the fabrication, results and creation of factors outside natural law and beyond divine will and thus really not universal.

The result of these speculations has been the idea that ethics is not needed at all, that there is something to be said for going beyond ethics, or even a suggestion of taking a stand against ethics. It was Heidegger who first openly suggested these thoughts in the recent history of ethics. He even suggested that to be against ethics is just as much to be for something more primordial, a more original ethics, so that one can show one is not being immoral or illogical. This is because he believed that the question of ethics appeared for the first time in the school of Plato and it was Plato's invention.[46] This led to an open campaign against ethics and even books under the title of 'against ethics' have been produced.[47]

After at least a century of relative neglect among legal scholars and after various challenges to the theory of natural law, the last quarter of the twentieth century has seen a strong support for and revival of natural law. Contemporary thinkers have been developing the idea of the basic good in human nature, and showing both how this can lead to the elaboration of moral principles, and then how positively enacted laws can be understood as the concretization of fundamental principles.[48]

Two

The Position of Natural Law in Islam

In this chapter we try to explain the concept of natural law according to Islam and (briefly) the major issues in Islam that correspond with the basic principles of classic natural law. In this context, we may have to make comparison between the position of Islam towards nature, natural law and the nature of man and that of some other religions. This comparison is made only to clarify the points we intend to make. No offence is intended whatsoever.

The first subject, the position of Islam concerning natural law, should be treated at five distinct levels, namely:

1. The nature of man, as part of the entire creation.
2. God as the Creator of the universe, man, nature, and the order of nature.
3. Nature, the universe, natural law or the laws ruling nature and creation.
4. Natural law as a system, and whether Islam recognizes or rejects it.
5. Human primordial nature and human reason, common sense and human intellect as the sources of law both in the natural law system and Islamic legal and jurisprudential system.

In this chapter we shall discuss these issues, though not in the same order. There may also be some overlapping of the issues, because they are very interrelated. The last issue, human primordial nature and human reason, is dealt with in the later chapters on *fitrah* and Islamic rationality.

The concept of laws and the order of creation, nature and universe (natural law) in Islam has a long rich history. Its history goes back to the time of the prophet and the revelation of the Qur'an. The Qur'an in many verses explains certain orders in the universe. A verse, for example, reads as follows: 'And the Sun runs along a set course, for her: that is the decree of (Him), The exalted in Might, The All-knowing. And the Moon – We have measured for him stations till he returns like the old lower part of a date-stalk. The Sun is not permitted to catch up with the Moon, nor can the night outstrip the day: Each (just) swims along in its orbit (according to law and order set for each) (Qur'an,

36:38–40). Another verse reads: 'The sun and the moon follow courses (exactly) computed' (Qur'an, 55:5). 'And He raised the sky (heaven) and set the balance' (scale and measure with which the universe is run) (Qur'an, 55:7–10). A tradition, reported authentically, reads 'By justice (balance, law and order) the heavens and earth are raised'.[1] Hast thou not seen how to God prostrate themselves all who are in the heavens and in the earth, the sun and the moon, the stars and the mountains, the trees and the beasts, and many of mankinds' (Qur'an, 22:18). Muslim scholars exploited these verses and developed their own concept of the divine order of the universe, creation, natural law and natural law ethics. The Mu'tazili movement and school, before Muslims became familiar with Greek and other philosophies, suggested that Allah is just, all knowing and all wise. On this basis they believed that the order of nature and creation, which is the manifestation of His will and action, is the most just (balanced), harmonious and thus in excellent order. Justice of Allah means *inter alia* that He is far from committing evil, wrong and disorder. This justice is of genetic and structural nature. That is in the order that prevails and rules over the entire sphere of creation and creatures. Everything is thus created good, balanced and is in its proper place. This just and balanced order covers man and his nature as well. This idea of inclusive justice, balance, harmony and order of nature has been one of the main subjects of emphasis and discussion amongst the Muslim scholars since the Mu'tazilah time and has been going on up to present time. Murtada Mutahhari, wrote a book on the topic under the title of *'Adl-e-Ilahy* in 1970 in which he explained the balance and harmony of creation and nature in the light of the justice of Allah. In fact the order, balance and harmony of creation and universe has been regarded as one of the major ways of knowing the Creator (Allah) of the universe. Muslim theologians have termed this concept as 'the best (possible) order of creation and universe' (*al-nizam al-ahsan*). Some Muslim scholars suggests that the justice (*'adl*) of Allah is based on His attribute as all knowing (*'ilm*) for injustice is based on ignorance (*jahl*) (Demeshqi, S.M. Afnan, *Wajeh nameh-e Falasafi*, '*'adl*'). There is order, balance and harmony in the universe because Allah is just and all knowing, for disorder is caused by ignorance and not knowing. The doctrine of the inclusive unity of Allah (absolute monotheism) also contributed to the concept. This is because the unity of the Creator establishes the balance and harmony of the creation, for if there were more than one God there would be chaos in the creation and universe. 'If there were in the heavens and earth, other gods besides Allah, there would have been ruin (chaos) in both' (Qur'an, 21:22).

Having pointed out briefly that the entire creation is created with order and harmony mainly because of the unity of the Creator and His justice (we shall deal with this issue again) we try to explain the Islamic position concerning the nature of man. Islam introduces man as a part of the creation with natural properties. It thus suggests that belief in a divine being (God) is very natural for man. This is termed in Islamic sources as natural religion or *din al-fitrah.* The Qur'an (30:30) states, 'turn towards the religion in earnest (*haneef*). That is the natural religion with which mankind has been created. No exception or change befalls Allah's (swt) creation'. Islam also suggests that Muslims and the entire human race possess a universal primordial human nature, *fitrah* or Ur-religion or *religio naturalis*. This consists of the unerring discoveries of *sensus numinis* by which man recognizes God as transcendent and holy and hence worthy of adoration. The late Prof. Ismail al-Faruqi explained this point as follows.[2] 'This is not a repetition of man's natural capacity to know through science. It is a new knowledge, a knowledge of the Holy, of the numinousness of God. ' This natural vision of God or *din al-fitrah* stands to be enriched by man's other natural knowledge, that is the discovery of his theoretical and axiological consciousness. Man's reason and sense of value stands at the ready to enlighten his service to God. Both faculties, the numinous and the theoretical–axiological, belong to man by virtue of his humanity. As he grows older, the cumulative products of science and morals are his as shortcuts to truth, just as previous revelations are equally his as shortcuts to certainty of what the divine imperative is.[3] Islam recognizes two distinct religions, *din al-fitrah* or *religio naturalis,* which any human being possesses by birth, and the religious traditions of history. What God has implanted in human nature – the recognition of His transcendence, unity, holiness and ultimate goodness – is prior to any tradition. Hence *din al-fitrah* properly speaking is Ur-religion, or original religion. Its possession by man, regardless of the religious tradition or culture in which he was born or nursed, defines his humanity and casts upon him a very special dignity. It entitles him to full membership in the religious community of man, the universal brotherhood of man under God. Islam calls this *din al-fitrah* or Ur-religion, 'Islam'.

Islam supports the view that the historical religions are the outgrowths of *din al-fitrah*, containing within them different amounts or degrees of it.[4] It explains their differences from *Din al-fitrah* as the accumulations, figurations, interpretations or transformations of history, that is of time, place, culture, leadership and other particular conditions.[5] Islam thus suggests that all humanity enjoys the same natural religion or *Din al-fitrah* or Ur-religion.

From the Islamic point of view, the first law of human nature is man's natural desire to know his own creator and the belief and faith in God. According to Islamic sources, especially the Qur'an, Allah has granted man with what has been described in the Qur'an as 'vicegerency of Allah' and it is his natural/moral duty to be appreciative of this, his high calling, and to strive to attain to those qualities of character that are recognized in the attributes of

Allah himself. Man was made vicegerent (*khalifah*) on earth (Qur'an, 2:30–3), and this trust (*amanah.*) of vicegerency, refused by the heavens and the earth and the mountains, 'man alone undertook to bear' (Qur'an, 33:72). Such is man's natural place in creation, and on this premise, in so far as Islam makes duties and privileges explicit, it may be regarded as a religion of nature. Islam is also and at the same time a religion of revelation. In this respect, Islam promotes the harmony of natural theology and revelation. 'Allah is he who has revealed the word with the truth and the balance' (Qur'an, 42:17). Allah has set the balance.' 'That in the balance you should not transgress.' (Qur'an, 55:1–9).

The second law in human nature, in this respect, is the inclusive liberation and freedom of man from all forms of servitude, submission, obedience, surrender, and acceptance of the authority of anything and everything but that of God alone. Man is a natural worshipper. The alternatives are either to worship and accept the authority of God alone or other forms of false objects of worship. By accepting the authority of the true God, the whole truth, man liberates himself from all other forms of worship of all other forms of feigned gods. In secular societies the concept of human dignity and freedom does not really have a metaphysical or for that matter a sound philosophical foundation. In Islam the dignity and freedom of man is based on the dignity and freedom of humanity as divinely ordained.

The third law in human nature in Islam is the equality and unity of man on a theological basis. The unity of God leads to the unity of the entire creation, which in turn leads to the unity and equality of human beings as inseparable parts of humanity as a whole. The Qur'an states 'Whosoever gives life to a soul, shall be as if he had given life to mankind altogether' (Qur'an, 5:32). Mankind may be looked at from the point of view of either its differentiation or its equality and unity. The hierarchical differentiation of mankind finds expression in Hinduism (with its caste system and its four main castes: brahmins, kshatriyas, vaishyas and shudras); in Christianity (with its four estates: Lords spiritual, Lords temporal, craftsmen and merchants, serfs) and in Judaism (with its division of mankind into the chosen people and non-chosen people, Jews and Philistine, Semites and non-Semites, and then the double racism of dividing Semites into Jews and non-Jews). From this point of view, men are manifestly unequal, and hierarchy goes hand in hand with heredity. The purpose of heredity is precisely the unnatural preservation, or perpetuation, of quality, challenging the unity and dignity of man. Not only the colour of one's eyes but also intelligence and character depends on birth. With the privileges of birth, be it noted in passing, go obligations, *noblesse oblige.* Islam, on the other hand, is based on human unity and equality. This shows itself both positively and negatively: first, man's 'theomorphic' nature is common to all, and second, all human beings are inescapably faced with the same natural disasters and suffering.[6] At the same time that Islam recognizes the natural facial and physical differences of different groups of human beings and the biological differences of the sexes, for the purpose of natural identification, and the cultural variations, it strongly rejects the inequality of human beings and supports the unity and equality of mankind. The Qur'an explains these points as follows. 'O mankind! We created you from a single (pair) of male and a female, and made you into nations and tribes, so that you may know each other (not that you may despise each other and discriminate against each other). Verily the most honoured of you in the sight of Allah is (he who is) the most righteous and the most pious of you' (Qur'an, 49:13).

One of the main causes of conflicts, discrimination in human society and aggressive behaviour against each other, against nature and its order is power in its various forms and shapes. In Islam power is exclusively the property of God and man has nothing but responsibility; the responsibility to respect the power of God and His laws for nature, for creation and for man as an inseparable part of nature and creation. In Islam man's rights are based on his responsibility. The entire Islamic religious and political system is based on this concept. We must understand that the power of God is not transferable to anyone or anything, thus rejecting theocracy as the power and government of religious and spiritual leaders. The Qur'an (23:21) states this point emphatically where it says 'God is the only authority with no responsibility and everybody else is only responsible'. In a sense, there is no ruler within the conceptual framework of the Muslim state except God. The Qur'an on many occasions has categorically asserted that all powers belong exclusively to God, thus leaving man with the responsibility to fulfil only God's will and thus liberating man from all forms of servitude. Man is only a trustee of God's will. Sovereignty belongs to God and not to people or religious authorities or leaders. The doctrine of the exclusive authority of Allah gives man complete and absolute freedom from everything and everybody but Allah. It has become fairly clear that the Islamic concept of human freedom and liberty provides man with a sound and metaphysical liberation; liberation from everything and everyone. The whole approach of Islam towards the question of man's freedom is radically different from the one in which human rights and man's freedom are viewed in the framework of secular philosophies of *Weltanschauung*. There is hardly anything in common between the two.[7]

The fourth law in human nature, according to Islam, is man's freedom from the burden of original sin. His duty in life is not thus a negative one. He is here for a positive purpose and objective, that of earning his own salvation through his own efforts by perfecting his existence and life and improving his noble position. This may be achieved by actualizing his potential and becoming the perfect man, *l'homme parfait*, *al-insan al-kamel* by means of simply being man, (existence, *wujud*) and continuously improving this existence (*tashakukiyat al-wujud*). According to Islam man is not just an animal. He is a human being with special potential, characteristics and consciousness and a sense of moral and ethical values, duties and responsibilities. In the contemporary secularized world this dimension of man has been trivialized. Those who believe in the moral and ethical values of man place it on a materialistic or unsound intellectual basis. The Islamic concept of morality is founded on a sound theological basis with deep roots in human nature. The cornerstone of all moral values is the concept of justice. The single principle and value, the lack of which leads to natural and social disorder, chaos and disharmony and the presence of which leads to peace, order and harmony, is justice. In Islam injustice begins with man being unjust to himself by denying his own basic fundamental natural human right to believe in and worship the true God, by denying his dignity, his primordial nature, and his spiritual needs and potentials. The Qur'an suggests that the most unjust act is the injustice that a man inflicts upon himself by denying his own right to believe in God.[8] Injustice thus begins with injustice to oneself. If man cannot be just to himself and does not do justice to himself how can he be just to others? Justice in Islam is not a concept referring to a state of affairs only, which can operate only within a dual relation situation. Other religions or philosophies have not given a consistent clear-cut answer to the question 'Can one be unjust to oneself?' Islam provides a clear concept and a clear answer to this question. Many Muslim scholars have dealt with this point.

S. Muhammad al-Naquib al-Attas has explained this point as follows.[9] It is true, in Western society, for example, that a man who commits suicide may be considered as committing an unjust act. But this is considered as such only insofar as his suicide deprives the state of the service of a useful citizen, and that his injustice is not to himself but to the state and society. We have pointed out earlier that the concept of justice means a harmonious condition or state of affairs whereby everything is in its right and proper place, such as the cosmos, or similarly, a state of equilibrium, where it refers to things or living beings. With respect to man, we say that justice means basically a condition and situation whereby he is in his right and proper place. 'Place' here refers not only to his total situation in relation to others, but also to his condition in relation to his self. Justice in creation, nature and universe means that everything is in its proper place and functions according to the order set for it. 'Justice in human society means that everyone enjoys and benefits according and in proportion to his ability, potential and aptitude. When this is the case the society will be well ordered, peaceful and harmonious.'[10] So the concept of justice in Islam does not only refer to the rational situation of harmony and equilibrium existing between one person and another, or between the society and the state, or between the ruler and the ruled, but covers far more, fundamentally and profoundly. So it refines in a primary way to the harmonious and rightly balanced relationship between the man and his self, and in a secondary way only to such as exists between him and others, between him and his fellow men and state and society. Thus to the question 'Can one be unjust to oneself?' Islam answers in the affirmative. This answer not only has metaphysical implications but also moral and ethical implications too. The justice of man to himself and his peace with himself is a natural principle.

In Islam justice and injustice begins and ends with the self ethically too. The Qur'an repeatedly stresses the point that when man does wrong, he is being unjust to himself and that injustice is a condition wrought by man upon his self. Even disbelief or the rejection of the unity of God is regarded as the greatest injustice of man to himself. The Qur'an states 'the denial of the unity of God (*shirk*) is the highest form of injustice' (Qur'an, 31:13). When a man commits a crime and wrong against others, against nature and creation and against the order of nature, he in fact and deed is committing a crime and wrong against his own self, and when he does justice to others he does it to himself first. Though in Islam justice ostensibly applies between man and God, and between man and man, and between man and himself, in reality, however, injustice is ultimately applicable – even in the two former cases – to man's self, alone. In the Islamic world-view and spiritual vision, whether a man disbelieves or disobeys, or whether he does wrong to another man, it is really to his own self that he does wrong and he alone is answerable to God on the Day of Judgement. Besides, injustice, being the opposite of justice, is putting a thing in a place not its own (creating disorder). It is to misplace and abuse a thing, to misuse it or to do wrong. It is deviation from the right course; it is disbelief of what is true, or lying about what is true, knowing it to be true; and it is thus disturbing balance and order and interfering with harmony. Thus when a man does an act of injustice, it means that he has wronged his own soul for he has misused it; he has made it deviate from its real nature and natural course and order and he has interfered with harmony in his own nature, nature at large, the order of nature and creation and the harmony and order of the human society.

Having discussed the issue of the nature of man, we now move to the issue of order of nature. Islam is a monotheistic religion, and calls itself *din al-tawhid wa al-fitrah,* in the strictest sense of the term. The entire edifice of Islam is placed on the doctrine of unity of God (*tawhid*). This doctrine is the core of Islam. In fact Islam is a mono-doctrinal religious system. All other Islamic principles emanate from the doctrine of *tawhid.* They all revolve around this doctrine and are based on it. The unity of God means the unity of His being, His action and His attributes. The unity of His action means the unity of His creation. The unity of creation means the unity of the entire creation, the entire universe, the unity of humanity, the unity of man as a whole. The unity of the entire creation means the harmony of the entire creation. The entire ideology of Islam is based on the doctrine of unity and harmony. Islamic monotheism, unlike that of Judaism and Christianity, has not been and cannot be diluted. Christian and Jewish monotheism represents a kind of contradictory doctrine. In Judaism the doctrine of a universal God is challenged and contradicted by the doctrine of a tribal god of Jews, exclusive membership of the tribe of Israel, racial Zionism. Jews are the children of a greater god and non-Jews are the children of a lesser god. Both in practice and according to Talmudic teachings, Jehovah is merely a tribal god or a community god. The Christian concept of monotheism is riddled with the Trinity and the family of God. Hence the development and even justification of racial tendencies and movements within both Judaism and Christianity on religious grounds. Islamic monotheism supports not only the unity of God but also the unity of creation and thus the unity of man.

There is no room for multiplicity and conflict in Islamic ideology. The doctrine of *tawhid* or unity is not just a belief that God exists or that He is just one. It is also a system of understanding the creation, humanity, and man's relationship with the universe and humanity. It is a harmonious system of understanding, belief, behaving and worshipping. It is a complete system of absolute harmony. The doctrine of *tawhid* leads to the belief that the entire creation should be regarded and understood in the light and the framework of the doctrine of unity, balance, order and harmony. That is, balance and harmony within the entire universe; harmony between man and the universe; harmony of man with himself; harmony of the individual and the human community; harmony of different dimensions of man and his activities; harmony with nature; the harmony of different needs of man; the physical, spiritual, social, political, psychological needs of man so that he is in harmony with himself, with his human nature, with the universe, with creation, with nature and, in a word, with everything which concerns him.

In Islam the order of the cosmos and nature and that of human behaviour is clear. Here three issues are involved:

1. The order of the cosmos and nature.
2. The order of human society and human behaviour (human nature).
3. The inseparability of these two sets of orders (inclusive harmony, natural law).

As far as the order of the cosmos and nature is concerned, the whole ideology and theology of Islam and many Qur'anic and innumerable Islamic traditions clearly suggest and support it. Allah (swt) has many attributes, qualities and names that are ultimately one, but are means to represent His reflections and manifestation and theophany (*tajalli*) in the process of creation and governing of all universes and the whole of our universe. His quality as the Creator (*khaliq*) is in total unity with His quality as the All-powerful (*qadir*) and His quality as the creator of order, balance and harmony (*muqaddir, 'ādil*) is also in total unity with His quality as All-wise (*al-hakim*). Allah (*swt*) by His power (*qudrah*) created (*khalaqa*) everything, the entire cosmos, universe and man according to his wisdom (*hikmah*) in special order, balance and harmony and measure (*miqdar, ta'ādul*) and governs and rules the entire creation according to His divine order. Everything is thus created according to divine wisdom in accordance with order, harmony and balance (*ta'ādul*) and man as an integral part of nature and cosmos is also the subject of the order and is requested to respect the order and behave orderly, justly (*'adl*) and in harmony with universe. The term *'adl* (justice) and the term *ta'ādul* (balance, harmony) share the same root ('a/d/l). They both have quite a few meanings interrelated with each other. The word *'adl* means justice, fairness, equity, impartiality in judgement, freedom from corruption, perfection of personality, giving things the correct ratio or proportion they deserve, to place things in their proper/appropriate place, to do what is good (*ihsan*), to act in accordance with our original nature (*fitrah*), which like the whole of creation, is created, as the Qur'an puts it, 'in due measure and proportion' as a 'fitting' reflection of divine harmony, balance and order (*ta'ādul*).

Justice thus is an inclusive concept covering the fields of creation and man's understanding and behaviour. So a just society is the society which is just to itself and to the entire creation at the same time. In Islam the laws governing nature are not separable from those governing man and human society. The divine order/harmony/balance is applied to man as well as to the entire creation. The Qur'an and the major schools of Islamic thought speak distinctly of an order to be observed and also contemplated in nature and of a harmony to be respected. In fact, the term *sunnat Allah (swt)* (divine pattern and order) which is described as being unchangeable and unchanging is interpreted by many Muslim scholars as applying to the cosmos as well as to the world of man. The Qur'an (25:2) declares 'And He created everything and calibrated it with precision'. There is thus a harmony between laws governing human society and possessing moral character and those governing nature. Both issue from the divine reality whose wisdom and power are reflected in the order of nature and also in the human order as long as man abides by divine law, which, in contrast to nature, he has freedom to obey or disobey.[11]

Al-Shahristani (d. 1153 AD) has summarized the teaching of the Muslim philosophers of his time on this issue as follows:

> The world order moves towards good, because it proceeds from the origin of good, and good is what everything desires ... When the First being knew the perfect good *in potentia* ... it emanated from Him ... and that is the eternal providence and will. Thus good came within the divine decree essentially, not accidentally, while evil came accidentally ... Evil may be said to be deficiency. In fine, evil *per se* is privation, i.e. the loss of a thing's true and perfect nature. (Existence is equivalent to goodness) Evil absolutely does not exist. Whenever we find nature and the divine determination over human choice and acquisition prevails, evil prevails, so that we return to the position that there is no evil in God's work; and if evil is to be found therein it is relative to one thing and not to another. Evil only enters into man's voluntary acts.[12]
>
> 'Professor Guillaume remarks that this would seem to mean that man's will, if surrendered to God, will produce good; but if his free-will is exercised apart from God's will evil must result.' [13]

Islam regards the universe and nature in a manner that is related to God, its creator. God did not create the universe just by accident. Nothing occurs accidentally with any relation to other parts of creation. Everything is created orderly and for purpose and in harmony with everything else. However, this concept of the universe at the same time negates the divine character attributed by some to the universe. Thus the universe and nature are not divine but divinely created by the will of God. The natural laws that govern the universe are not an arbitrary authority inherent in or emanating from nature. God designs them as the orders of nature. Nature and matter are not gods. God makes natural laws and orders. Although they don't change, they can be changed by God if He wills to do so. Universal divine phenomena and laws do not necessarily have to conform and follow laws familiar to man. This applies to human nature too. God is constantly in charge of everything; the universe, nature, matters, the natural laws, human nature and so on (Qur'an, 55:29). We are not in a position to explain in detail here the theosophical bases for these beliefs. This must be dealt with separately. We simply intend here to explain the beliefs briefly, so that we can follow the consequences of these beliefs.

The doctrine of the unity of God or *tawhid* is an inclusive doctrine covering all areas of human thoughts and actions individually and collectively. Neither nature nor man nor, for that matter, anything else, is God. The humanists regard man as God.[14] Darwinism suggests that man is only an animal and nothing more. In Islam man is neither God nor merely an animal. Man is a whole with physical, psychological, spiritual and other characteristics and needs unique to him alone. Human nature is decent and not evil as Hobbes suggests. Human nature is fashioned on the divine pattern (*Fitrat Allah alti fatara al-nas 'alaiha*).[15] Islam treats nature itself as God's revelation with divine purpose. Human nature is also made in divine mould with divine objectives.[16] The purpose of man's life which is fashioned on the divine pattern, is none other than the securing of his awareness of his true nature and nature at large. God has pre-emptively implanted in man the love of the good values which are the constituents of the divine will. Man is thus predisposed by nature towards such fulfilment and responsibility. Man's essence is not evil and is potentially innocent. He is neither good nor evil until he earns his own salvation or wickedness. Man shares many instincts with other animals but is provided with reason, which makes him unique. Man with the help of his primordial nature and reason is capable of moral and ethical judgement and can control himself with moral values. He is free to choose to be only an animal or to use his moral potential and be a man. He is not born evil. He earns his own happiness and eternal salvation. In Islam man is born innocent and his destiny depends on what he does after birth and not before it. Islam repudiates original or hereditary guilt or evil. Man is not a fallen creature or inherently evil. God has created him in an order that makes him capable of fulfilling the responsibility of being man. It is reported that Mohammad (puh) in an often quoted tradition said: 'Every infant is born according to the *Fitrah* then his parents make him a Jew or a Christian or a Zoroastrian'. (*'ala'l-fitrah*, i.e. Allah's kind or way of creating 'on God's plan'.[17] This is one of several traditions on human primordial nature and the salvability of the infants of unbelievers. This text evidently means that every child is born naturally a believer, a Muslim; but is perverted after birth by his environment. This issue will be explained in the chapter on *fitrah*.)

A brief comparative study of different concepts of nature and nature of man would further clarify the position of Islam. The late Professor Ismail al-Faruqi has made this comparison as follows.[18]

'Hindu cosmology regards nature as an unfortunate event that happened to Brahman, the Absolute. Creation is an objectification of it (the absolute) that should not have taken place because it is a degradation of its perfection as absolute. Everything in nature is hence regarded as an aberration, as something encased in its creaturely form, hoping for release and return to its origin and as Brahman. While it continues as a creature in the world, it is subject to the law of karma through which it is upgraded, or further degraded, according to whether it acknowledges and complies with this first cosmological principle, namely, that it is merely an ontological mishap of the Absolute.

Christian cosmology regards nature as the creation of God which was once perfect, but which was corrupted in the 'fall of man' and hence became evil. The evil of creation, ontological, essential and pervasive, is the reason for God's drama of salvation, of His own self-incarnation in Jesus, of His crucifixion and death. Theoretically and practically, the Christian mind continued to hold creation as fallen, and nature as evil and man as corrupt and sinner. The great enmity to matter which characterized gnosticism passed on to Christianity and reinforced its contempt and antagonism for nature and 'the world' so avidly pursued on every level by Christianity's first enemies, the Romans. Nature, with its material potentialities and propensities, was the realm of Satan. On the material level, its momentum is the pull away from 'the other world' to 'the flesh', to 'sin.' On the social level, it is the temptation to politics, to will-power and self-assertion, to 'Caesar'. Pragmatism – the will to order the movement of history towards transformation of nature – is by Christian definition vain. For a millennium or more, 'nature' contrasted with 'grace' as its opposite. Both were treated as mutually exclusive; pursuit of the one was necessarily violation of the other. Western Christian critiques of nature, natural man, natural religion and natural theology have an entirely different approach and flavour from those of Muslims.'

Islamic culture refuses to produce a concept of *iman* (faith) like that of Christian faith, as the latter is taken to stand independent of and beyond reason, balance and knowledge. This is probably because Christian theology, as has been presented, is not able to correspond with reason, knowledge and a natural balanced judgement. It has been generally conceded by Christian theologians, since the Middle Ages, that the doctrine of Trinity, for example, is a doctrine of faith and must be accepted as a matter of faith, (because it cannot be rationally explained and justified) where faith is understood as a way of accepting that which cannot be accepted according to the standard of reason. They thus announced the divorce between reason, religion and faith. This caused problems and dissatisfaction for and with the church, because a large group of intellectuals drifted away from the church and leaned toward atheism. In the West the problems with Christianity have been typically generalized and considered as problems with religion *per se.* Few have considered the possibility that Islam may be immune from the failings which led to their dissatisfaction with Christianity. Islamic culture has not produced any sort of theological antirealism of the sort debated in Western circles. Islamic thought has not given rise to the atheism and agnosticism that have emerged from Christian culture.[19] In Islam theological discussions are demonstrated through reason and knowledge and once satisfied *iman* is left at the disposal of *qalb* (heart), where the true *iman* resides and *'aql* (reason) and *qalb* interact. According to Islamic tradition, it is not the soul that contains the heart and intellect, but rather the soul and reason in proper harmony give rise to the heart. Hhihab al-Din Suhrawardi suggests that the marriage between soul and intellect give birth to heart and that the product of the union of soul and intellect or spirit is heart.[20]

Christianity as developed by the Holy Roman Church caused an unnatural split between matter and spirit, denigrating matter in favour of spirit. When St Augustine invented Trinity, and after St Paul invented grace, the Roman Church created a dead power known as 'spirit'. This alienated humans from their bodies and men from nature and their natural needs cutting them off from the path of salvation advocated by all divine religions, self-cultivation and self development, and replacing it with vicarious atonement in the blood of a celibate Christ. Church innovation led to the renunciation and denigration of human flesh and thus of nature, all in the name of deliverance to the supposed Saviour. It became necessary to kill the body in order to save the soul and to declare a war on nature. This war on body and nature led to the extreme, as has been pointed out already, introducing man and nature as gods. However although Western civilization went through a period of secularization, diffusing much of the economic and political power of the Church, many of the Church's innovations continued into the age of supposed enlightenment. Descartes demanded a dichotomous mind–body split as the basis for his ontology. Bentham advocated a strict surveillance of the body to cultivate the mind, while Comte invoked an elite rule of the technological scientists. The subject of Islamic theology is obviously God. God in Islam is not material. He is transcendental. Even the world's most transcendental religions, Judaism and Christianity, have somehow managed to reduce God to matter. The consciousness of transcendence was confused and misunderstood by the anthropomorphic understanding of the concept of deity in Judaism and the doctrine of incarnation in Christianity. Islam takes its distinguishing characteristic among the world religions precisely by insisting on an absolute metaphysical separation of transcendent from temporal. Only God is transcendent and the rest is only temporal. As we see, the subject of Islamic theology is a natural, rational one.

Going back to the main issue in this chapter, the position of natural law in Islam, we need to discuss, briefly, the comparative theological impact of major religions on the doctrine of natural law. The ideological and theological principles of different religions leave a great direct/indirect and positive/negative impact on the concepts of nature and human rights accordingly. In the case of Judaism, God has been racialized and even tribalized, thus creating a two-tier humanity: the 'chosen people', the Jews and the gentiles, or the descendants of Jacob and the rest of humanity. Judaism has thus produced not only a two-tier humanity, but it has also introduced two different types of rights, two different kingdoms. The tribe of Israel, the children of Jacob are the first-class citizens of the kingdom of David, the Kingdom of Jehovah with special privileges and rights; and the rest of humanity are second-class citizens with the responsibility of respecting the rights of the first-class citizens. This challenges both the natural unity of humanity, natural law and the universalism of human rights. In the case of Christianity, it has Christified and Aryanized God. It has further corrupted the whole of nature. Frithjof Schuon has explained this point as follows.[21]

'In terms of the ordinary Christian perspective, the whole of nature has been corrupted and more or less cursed as a result of the fall of man and his consequent corruption. It follows from this that the pleasures of the senses are justified only in so far as they are necessary for the conservation of the bodily individual, that is the earthly species. Under the impact of Islamic thought first, and later of the Renaissance, Scholasticism and enlightenment, Christians opened themselves to life and world affirmation. World denial and condemnation, however, was never eradicated but only muted. In more recent times, with the triumph of romanticism and secularism following the French Revolution, 'naturalism' came to occupy and sometimes dominate the Christian's attitude to nature and the world and finally nature was declared virtually as God.'

In Islam, if pleasure remains within the limits set by nature and within the frame of religion, it includes in addition a contemplative quality, *al-barakah*, or a blessing which is related to celestial archetypes and is therefore of profit to both virtue and contemplation. Islam thus finds its support in incorruptible nature in general and in the innocent and divine nature of man by virtue of which he cannot cease to be what he is, not by conferring a new nature upon him, but by restoring to him his primal perfection through the medium of the normal elements of his immutable nature. In Islam the unity of the Truth (God) has led to the unity of the entire creation, to the unity of humanity and to the unity of man as a whole and thus to the universality of his message and to the universality of human rights. This is not the case with the religions which are based on the principle of multiplicity of deity and polytheism. In the same way that anti-religious, secular Western rationalism developed as a revolt against Christian emotionalism and ended up introducing human reason as the only source of knowledge (thus replacing God with man), so did anti-nature Christian theology produced anti-Christian naturalism (thus introducing nature as God with the power of making laws of its own and non-religious rights). In Islam the doctrine of the unity of creation, the harmony and the unity of the entire creation have produced harmony between man and nature and harmony between reason and revelation and consequently the unity–universality of man and his rights.[22]

There remains a point of importance, which must be explained here. Islamic theology, throughout its history but mainly fundamentally, is different from other theologies. The question of divinity, the divine being, the absolute truth, the necessary essence, or God has been discussed at three different levels:

1. the nature and essence of God (if the term nature and essence can be used for God) *(al-dhat)*;
2. the attributes of God (*al-sefāt*); and
3. the acts of God *(al-af'al)*.

The doctrine of unity is taken into consideration at each level and between the three levels. The Islamic doctrine of inclusive monotheism, at all these three levels, has left its impact on the concepts of natural law, nature, nature of man and other related issues in Islam

As we have already pointed out, the concept of human nature *(fitrah)* in Islam and its position in leading to the recognition of the actual existence of God is a major issue in Islamic theology. This is mainly because God being God and man being man, man cannot really understand the nature of God. The responsibility for appreciating the actual existence of God has been left to human nature. It is in the fields of God's attributes and actions that Islamic theology has been involved and active. This is not to say that human reasoning has no role in the area of appreciating the actual existence and the attributes of God. In this field human reason (*al-'aql al-salim*) and human nature are introduced as the same.

In Islam, nature is a creation and gift of God. As creation it is teleological and orderly; as a gift it is an innocent good, placed at the disposal of man. Its purpose is to enable man to do good and achieve felicity. This treble judgement of orderliness, purposefulness and goodness sums up the Islamic view of nature. The principle of *tawhid*, or the unity of God, the recognition of Him as one, absolute and transcendent, is also at the centre of the Muslim's curiosity regarding nature from another viewpoint. Islam taught its adherents that God created nature and implanted therein its laws, order and ends.[23] It commanded man to discover these in order to enable him to enjoy nature as God has entitled him to do. Islam suggests that God has created everything in nature perfect. He has fashioned each creature and given it an essence, a structure that determines its life and from which it never deviates. He has placed every creature and all parts of nature within the general nexus of nature so that its birth, its whole life and its death all happen according to patterns which are themselves constituents of the divine will. To every creature He has ordained a career and objective to which its existence is forever subject. There is no gap or conflict in nature. No object or event in nature is an accident. Everything that is or happens does so because of predictable causes and with predictable consequences. That is why nature is a real cosmos, not a chaos where events never take place with cause, or sometimes with and sometimes without cause. The Qur'an (67:4) says, 'Look and look into nature, will you see any discrepancy?'

It seems necessary to say a few words about the pioneers of classic Islamic theology; the Ash'arites and the Mu'tazelites. This is because the Ash'arites have been accused of denying both the secondary causes (the law of causality at the level of nature) and denying the natural laws. The Ash'ari school of theology founded by Abu al-Hasan al-Ash'ari reduces the function of the intellect to a purely human level. For this school, truth is what God has willed and the intellect has no function outside the external tenets of the religion. For this school, good is what God has declared to be good and not what man regards as good. Only God has the right to decide what is good and what is bad. This school believed in an absolute moralistic approach to all human behaviour. Schuon puts this point as follows. 'Ash'ari conceives only the opposition between the created and the creator, and not the participation of the first in the second; hence the negation of the secondary causes and natural laws.' The Ash'arites and the Hanbalites refused to reconcile relative or cosmic causality with absolute or divine causality. They insisted in their violent and stubborn option for the second at the expense of the first by claiming that it is hypocrisy (*al-nifaque*) to admit ordinary causality – the laws of nature, for example – because this would be to associate (*al-shirk*) an 'aid' (*al-sharik*) with God. Schuon suggests that there are two types of cause and causality; physical causality which is 'horizontal' and metaphysical causality which is 'vertical'. Schuon believes that the Ash'arites could not reconcile these two and thus denied the horizontal causality completely. If we look for a prime mover in Ash'arism, it is the wish to relate everything, absolutely everything, to the divine cause alone. This means denying all cosmic or horizontal relationships in favour of 'vertical' or ontological relationships alone, as if the first were incompatible with the second and as if the 'horizontal' relationship were not, on the contrary, the necessary images of the 'vertical'. As we see it Ash'arism is engaged mainly with the understanding of the will of God and not with reaching the universal dimensions of the intellect and discovering the God-gifted human rational potential. They may not be regarded as rationalists in the wider sense of the term. They denied the authority of human reason to understand what is good and what is bad. For them good was what was declared by God to be good and they did not see any place for secondary or horizontal causes in the universe (orders and laws). This is why some scholars, as pointed out before, have been tempted to regard the Ash'arites as anti-rationalist and opponents of natural law. But a careful study of the Ash'ari movement does not seem to support these claims. The Ash'arites put the concept of natural law on the foundation of Islamic and Qur'anic texts, instead of on their abstract speculations.

The Mu'tazili school of theology represented all the principles that were rejected by the Ash'arites. The Mu'tazilites are recognized as the pioneers of Islamic rationality. But we must emphasize again that Islamic rationality is not the same as anti-religious Western rationalism. There is common ground in the field of Islamic rationality on which both the Ash'arites and the Mu'tazilites stand.

Almost all Islamic schools of thought, law and theology have appreciated the divine dimension of nature and also the order of nature. For example, the Mu'tazilah appreciated it on the basis of their general systematic approach and the Asha'irah on the basis of Qur'an and Islamic tradition. A Qur'anic verse states 'And the sun runs unto a resting place for him. That is the decree of (Him), the exalted in Might, the All-knowing. And the moon we have measured for her stations (to traverse), till she returns, like the old (and withered). It is not permitted to the sun to catch up the moon, nor can the night outstrip the day: Each (just) swims along in its own orbit' (according to law).[24] The Qur'an not only refers to the harmony in the universe and to the order and balance in the entire creation, but it asks people to regard them with respect as the signs (*ayat*) or manifestations of Allah and also ask people to ponder the relation between the outward manifestations and the essence.

Islamic thinkers have always pondered the relation between the outward manifestations of the order of nature and the essence, based on the Qur'anic words: 'We put Our signs into the horizons and into themselves' (Qur'an,41: 53). For the Muslim, everything in creation and universe could serve as a sign (*ayah, Ġiå*), a sign from God. The Qur'an repeats this again and again. These signs are not only in the 'horizons', that is the created universe, but also in human souls, that is, in the human capacity to understand and admire; in love, human inquisitiveness, in human primordial nature or *fitrah*, and in human intellectual potentials. The significance of the concept of a sign is so great that the verses of the Qur'an are called *ayah* (plural, a*yat)*. This concept explains the divine dimension of nature and its order. The importance of the concept of *ayah* in the Qur'an and Islam has been fully appreciated and explained by Prof. Anne-Marie Schimmel and has even introduced this as the phenomenological approach to Islam.[25]

As has been pointed out, the entire edifice of Islam rests on the doctrine and principle of *tawhid* (the unity of God, Allah, and the Creator). The unity of God as the only creator leads to the unity of creation, the unicity of existence and the unicity of all that exists, which in turn means the harmony of creation. Islamic hikmah (philosophy) developed these principles as the doctrine of unity of the cause of existence, the doctrine of the unity of entire existence (*serf al-wujud la yatathana wa la yatakarar*), the doctrine of divinity of entire existence with regard to whatever enjoys existence (*basit al-haqiqah kul al-ashya' wa laisa be sha' in menha*), and the doctrine of goodness of actual existence and evil as non-existence or *'adam, al-wujud khairon mah*d. Nature and man as parts of the creation and existence are good and thus in the state of harmony and balance and this means that there is an order in nature. What is interesting in this connection is that this harmony and order of nature is divine. There is thus a spiritual and divine dimension in nature, its harmony and its order. And thus there is also harmony between the world of creation–universe and the world of spirit–heaven.

The doctrine of the oneness of being or *wahdat al-wujud* has led some to believe that it is a form of pantheism. This is entirely misleading. The term pantheism is normally used to designate certain European philosophic concepts of recent centuries that have nothing to do with any traditional doctrines, whether scholastic or mystical. Pantheism (the belief, for example, that God is the sum total of all things) implies a 'substantial' identity between the principle and the manifestations, or between the Creator and the created. This is foreign to all traditional doctrines, which insists on the gulf between the absolute and the relative, or the Infinite and the finite, going so far as to call the first element in each case 'real' and the second (relatively) 'unreal', because ephemeral. The Islamic doctrine of monotheism in the form of *shahadah* insists that 'there is no reality except "Reality". The doctrine of *wahdat al-wujud* or the oneness of being has been called "monism", but which is perhaps more accurately translated as "no-duality". There is, however, an "essential" (not substantial) identity between the Creator and the created, specially man, whence the relative reality of the world in which we live and hence the respect for the world of creation and nature.'[26]

The doctrines of *tawhid*, the unity of the source and cause of existence (*wahdat wajib al-wujud*) and the unity of existence (*wahdat al-wujud*) have all contributed to the doctrine of natural law in Islam. Repudiating and rejecting belief in the multiplicity of independent gods with arbitrary wills, creating chaos and interfering with the phenomena of nature, Islamic monotheism provided a natural, even scientific, approach and mode of explaining nature and its order. The Qur'an states that 'If there had been more than one God there would have been total disorder and chaos' ' If there were in the heavens and the earth other gods besides Allah, there would have been ruin and chaos in both' (Qur'an, 21, 22). The unity of God means the unity of creation and the unity of the order in creation. The unity of God means that the entire creation and universe is wisely governed by divine laws and order which are of His making.

As far as the relation between nature and morality is concerned, Islam teaches that nature is indeed orderly, but that its orderliness is God-given and God-sustained. There is good reason why God made nature orderly. Since God has put on us the obligation to act morally, and as moral action implies intervention into the causal processes of nature and the deflection of its flow to pre-conceived ends, it would be impossible on the part of man to fulfil the moral purpose of God without the provision of effects and their assumption as targets of action, which only an orderly cosmos can make possible. Both an orderly nature and the scientific knowledge of it are necessary for morality. Had nature not been orderly, that is, were it a realm where causes do not produce effects and effects do not follow upon their causes, this would be a 'ship of fools' where morality is not possible. Such creation would be a cruel and senseless act on the part of a malevolent deity. God, however, is most beneficent, just and merciful. He created us and charged us with a mission – fulfilment of His commandments – that we may succeed. Our success in our mission is our actions based on moral value, which is nothing but the will of God Himself. That is why God placed us in a theatre of malleable nature, where moral action is possible, i.e. where provision of causes and production of their effects are possible. For this not to be the case is to put the divine will in contradiction with itself, or to charge it with malevolence and cynicism. However, there is another side to the question of causality, which is spiritually as valid. (This part of the question has been explained by the Islamic scholar Ghazzali).

How then did the illusion arise that the world is causal, but necessarily so; orderly, but blind? Causal regularity does indeed seem to be the inexorable law of nature. Islam suggests that even the law of causality is a divinely ordained law and does not apply to its Maker. It is true that the research scientist in his laboratory assumes causality to be necessary in all cases. But his assumption is regulative rather than constitutive. He has no categorical proof that effects do in fact come from their causes. Modern science has repudiated the dogmatism of the nineteenth-century scientists. Theoreticians believed in causality, which is as ontological as it is absolute. In this century science has come of age, and is far more sober and modest in its claims. The same immodesty has characterized a few Muslim philosopher-scientists; but they were put in their place by Ghazzali as early as the eleventh century. This argument anticipated David Hume's by seven centuries. Ghazzali argued that nearly all the causal sequences of nature do not prove one necessary cause. All they prove is that in the normal course of events, E, the 'effect', does follow after C, the 'cause'. As Ghazzali puts it, 'following after' proves neither 'following from', nor 'following by'. It only proves itself; namely 'following after'. But this following after, which is termed as habit of nature is indeed causality but does not apply to the maker of the habit of nature. Accordingly God Himself, who is the maker of the law of causality, is not bound by it. He can, if He desires, alter, suspend or annul it altogether, as is the case in miracles, which are exceptions. If God were not omnipotent, and if He did not stand outside of space, time and causality and was not their creator, He would not be God. This idea of Ghazzali, however, does not contradict and challenge the principle of the divine harmony and order of universe, existence and creation. He simply excludes God Himself from the law of causality, which He designed for the universe. The exclusion of God from the law of causality, as may be understood, does not necessarily mean that there is no order, harmony and laws running the universe.

Ghazzali had to, and I believe he did, appreciate the divine dimension and order of nature, because this is recognized by the Qur'an. He rejected only the system of causality of nature and replaced it with his atomistic approach, which relates every natural phenomenon and events directly to the Divinity without the need and intercession of the chain of causes. This group of Muslim intellectuals also replaces the term 'order of nature' with the term 'habit/norm' of nature *'adah.* (Conceptual atomism breaks the apparent continuity of the world and of its matrices, time and space and makes God the direct agent in all events.) It should, however, be pointed out that, as far as the question of freedom of will of man and its relation to infinite and final cause (Allah) is concerned, the majority of Muslim scholars suggested that there was no conflict between the two opinions. They believed that Allah created and caused human beings fully capable of causing all their actions and effects in accordance with their nature and will. Otherwise there would not be any sense in revealing religions. This was in fact one of the major issues supported by the Mu'tazilah and their followers.

This atomism, which has its roots in the specific character of Islam, and which asserts the absolute transcendence of the divine principles, flourished in Islam after the fourth /tenth century. Although atomism might be supposed in the Western perspective to be scientific, in Islam it is regarded as belonging to theology. The Ash'arites who represented this school were theologians. Al-Baqilani, one of its outstanding representatives, promoted the 'philosophy of nature' of this school. According to this atomism the continuity of external forms is broken by an atomistic doctrine of time and space and by the denial of the Aristotelian notion of causality. For the Muslim atomists, the Ash'arites, the world is annihilated and recreated at every moment; the cause of all events is the Creator and not a finite created agent. But this does not necessarily mean that this annihilation and recreation does not follow a pattern. On the contrary it has a pattern and order of its own which has been continuing ever since the creation.

The Qur'an suggests that God is constantly in charge of the creation. It suggests that there are two aspects to reality: the world of nature-creation and God, a being other than nature who is the creator of nature and all its laws including the law of causality. God is the ultimate Cause. Universal as these categories of time, space and causality may be in nature, they are inapplicable to Him, for He is their creator. God's will is embedded in the structure and essence of all creatures, in which it is fulfilled by the necessity of pattern and order, which is natural law.[27] The same is true of man's physical and psychic nature, except that man is free to choose to obey or disobey, to follow his divinely gifted nature or not to do so and this by itself is an order. We can thus conclude that even the Ash'arites supported the order, balance and harmony of nature and nature of man though in a different manner and through a different approach from that of the Mu'tazilites.

The order of nature, therefore, is not merely the material order of causes and effects, the order which space, time and other such theoretical categories make evident to our understanding. Nature is equally a realm of ends where everything is for a purpose and thereby contributes to harmony and balance both in the field of morality and ontology and in the universe. The Qur'an (65:3) states that 'To everything We have given a balance and a measure proper to it'. Nature, therefore, in Islam has many dimensions; metaphysical, ontological, teleological, rational, cognitive and ethical amongst other dimensions. Because of the divine dimension of nature, according to all schools of thought in Islam, it must be thus treated with respect. The balance and harmony of nature must not be interfered with. nature is not man's property. The order of nature is subject to man who is allowed to enjoy it, exploit it and benefit from it but ethically, responsibly and justly. Islam also demands of man to study, search and understand the pattern, order and sign of God in nature. The fact that nature is God's handiwork, His planned design and the actualization of His will casts upon it a halo of dignity. Man himself is part of nature and is designed by God to recognize his natural potentials, and follow his natural order.

There is also the Sufi concept of nature and order of nature. In this respect the doctrine of unity of being, or *wahdat al-wujud*, or unity of existence, itself plays an important role. The school of unity of being, founded by Muhy al-Din ibn al-'Arabi, sees the entire creation in the light of unity and regards creation as theophany, *tajalli.* Ibn al-'Arabi expressed the Sufi and 'Irfani conception of nature in formulations based not only upon Qur'anic terminology but also upon the spirit of Islam and the Qur'an (*'irfan*). It was he who expressed for the first time in Arabic the conception of nature as the 'breath of the Compassionate' (*nafas al-Rahman*).[28] According to this school, what appears as the laws of nature, i.e. the uniformity of sequence of cause and effect, is a matter of 'habit' too (*'adat*), determined by the will of God and given the status of law by Him. Miracles, which seem to break the apparent uniformity of natural phenomena, are simply exceptions from the habit of nature. As we notice, the term 'habit' is replacing the term 'order', but the actual concept of the order of nature is left intact. It just proposes a different terminology as far as the balance, harmony and the actual order of nature is concerned.

What is intended here is to point out that despite their differences, almost all Islamic schools of thought, theology, philosophy, and even law may be said to supported a certain 'philosophy of nature' and, in conformity with it, cultivated the sciences dealing with the universe, its laws and orders. Some of their writings, primarily those of the Peripatetics, were to be translated into Latin to help form Western Scholasticism, which was later to give way to seventeenth-century 'natural philosophy'. The Western world has since concentrated its intellectual energies on the study of the quantitative aspect of things, thus developing a science of nature. Islamic rationality and science, by contrast, seek ultimately to attain such knowledge and the dimension of the science that will contribute towards spiritual perfection, towards the divine dimension of nature. Its fruits thus are also inward, hidden, spiritual and ethical as well and more difficult to discern.[29]

This leads us to another approach to the question of natural law, harmony, order, balance and laws of nature. Man has been given by God means and potential of understanding, appreciating and reasoning through which he can discover and grasp the secrets, laws and orders of nature (*nawamis*) and draw ethical and moral principles and strength from them. This brings us to the question of the position of human reason, intellect, common sense, intuition and human primordial nature as the means to discover, understand and appreciate nature, laws of nature and the system of natural law in Islam. The question of Islamic rationality and the position of human reason, primordial nature and intuition have been explained in chapters dealing with these issues. Here we just would like to explain briefly the position of reason and primordial nature as a means of appreciating nature, natural law, order of nature and their ethical implications.

Rationalism has been vigorously appreciated in modern Western ethics, from British moralists of the eighteenth century to Kant and his disciples, then to more recent intuitionists such as Moore and Ross. The common elements have been the beliefs that the values of acts and intentions, to which we refer by words such as good and obligation, are objective and factual. The common elements have also been the belief that they are recognizable by intellectual acts which are different in kind from those by which we recognize characters of sense data or our own mental states. There are other issues which have influenced the concept of Western rationalism.[30] One cannot appreciate the development of rationalism without appreciating the factors that led to it.[31]

Modern rationalism has followed roughly the tradition of Aristotelian thought and ethics. No doubt one can trace its lineage through medieval Christian theories of natural law. In medieval Islam also the existence of rationalist ethics has been a familiar issue. Mu'tazilite theology, with its insistence on the objective nature of good and evil, justice and injustice explains this. But Mu'tazilism did not oppose naturalistic ethics, as in the modern West, but challenged the voluntaristic theory of the Ash'arites out of Shafi'ite jurisprudence.[32] In a Mu'tazilite theory the concepts of value are predicable of God's acts in the same sense as of man's. But the ethical thought of the majority of Mu'tazilite theologians moved constantly between two levels, human and divine. The most noticeable feature of both divine and human good and evil is praiseworthiness and blameworthiness, thus making it comparable with that of a modern intentional ethical system. For the majority of the Mu'tazilites, general truths are recognizable. Evil means it is deserving of blame and good is whatever deserves praise. There are absolute general truths, such as evilness of wrongdoing, lying, useless acts, tyranny etc., which are always evil. Such truths have the status of axioms of reason, which every sane man can recognize immediately. The Mu'tazilah also claimed that God would never permit *istifsad al-adillah*, 'corruption of evidentiary proofs', that is, contravention of the customary pattern of the way things happen in the physical universe (nature). Thus for the Mu'tazilah confidence in the rational and knowable nature of physical reality is based on theodicy: God would not deceive His creatures by creating an irrational universe and not appreciable by man.[33] As with Montesquieu many centuries later, early Mu'tazilah also held that God operated according to rational laws. The Mu'tazilah held that the constantly created reality behaves according to known patterns of events or 'nature' on which human reasoning about the world is based. In only one case – the sending of prophets with miracles – does God permit the contravention of this pattern, but even here there is an order.[34]

These are primarily what give the Mu'tazilah ethics the rational–intuitional character and feature, which in turn establishes a kind of harmony between rationalism and intuitionism and between reason and primordial nature of man. The means to recognize the general truth is both human reason and human intuition in their decent, original, natural forms.

A careful and comprehensive study of the term *al-fitrah* covering, thus, intuition, innate, primordial nature and its frequent uses in the Qur'an reveals that it applies both to human knowledge and to innate moral and ethical properties and potentials of man. In Islam there is no schism between these two areas. The Qur'an suggests that certain knowledge is innate in the same way that certain moral values are, e.g. there is the innate knowledge, *fitri*, that the world has a Creator and the soul a Maker. In the same way this creates a faith in man which enters the inner hearts of men and that is the innate faith. Without this innate knowledge man would not be able to acquire any knowledge and appreciate the divine order of nature. The acquired and secondary knowledge would be impossible without the innate primary knowledge. The Qur'an suggests that even the heathens and the idolaters had an innate faith in God, but took the idols for God by mistake. This is called in the Qur'an as a natural religion (Ur-religion or *din al-fitrah*). It is God that trusted man (*amanah*) and had sown in all men's hearts the innate general truths and moral and ethical principles which are intuitional and innate. There is therefore a natural marriage between innate knowledge and natural reason and between innate faith and moral universal truths. They both draw their authority from the same source.

As far as the question of the role of learning and education in the process of understanding and appreciating nature, natural law and natural innate ethics is concerned, Islam seems to support the middle theory between absolute innateness of knowledge and that of absolute learning (innateness versus learning). This middle course theory suggests that human beings have some knowledge that is innate. But there are other forms of knowledge which are acquired by reasoning and learning. The first type of knowledge includes man's awareness and consciousness of God; the principle of moral perfection, rightness and wrongness; certain mathematical, logical and general theorems, such as the rejection of contradiction; vicious circles; out of nothing nothing comes; cross-cultural and inter-cultural moral beliefs and practices, such as prohibition against murder, incest, untruth, deception, hypocrisy, injustice etc.

Another closely related issue to the issue of innateness versus learning or complementing it is the question whether human beings are genetically programmed (innately programmed) and motivated or not. Islam here too has taken the middle course. Some motives are genetic, innate, and instinctive (pushing), such as the human motive to understand, love and worship his Creator, while other motives are external (pulling), such as achievement, happiness, success, salvation, etc.

Another way of explaining the issue of innateness versus learning or complementing it is to explain motivational processes as either mechanistic (automatic, genetically programmed) or cognitive (the active processing of information influences motivation; learning). Here again, given the complexity of the motivational process, it is safer to choose the middle course; that is, both horizontally and vertically motivational processes involve mechanistic and cognitive influences. Islam thus suggests that there is a combination of both internal and external motives, both pushing and pulling.

Closely related to the issue of innateness versus learning or complementing it is the question of the main source of knowledge; and whether it is reason, or experience. The rationalists who support innateness of knowledge regard reason as its main source and the empiricists regard only experience as the source of knowledge. Islam does not reject the role of experience in the process of learning. We can thus understand the relation between rationalism, innateness and experience in Islam.[35]

All these arguments have their origins in the theological and philosophical issues of free will versus determinism. Even John Locke, the champion of empiricism, accepted that there is a kind of knowledge, which the mind recognizes without the intervention of any other means and is immediately present: 'The knowledge of our own being we have by intuition.' Locke says of this kind of knowledge that 'the mind is presently filled with the clear light of it', even using a religious and spiritual metaphor. 'It is on this intuition that depends all the certainty and evidence of all our knowledge.'[36] It seems as if he has turned Descartes's idea of 'I think, therefore I exist' (for what does not exist, *nothing*, cannot think) upside down. Whereas Descartes suggests that 'thinking' is innate and the proof for 'I think' is intuition, and whereas he deduces from 'I think', 'therefore I exist', Locke regards his existence as intuitional and innate, and the rest is deduced from existence. (It is interesting to note that, like Ghazzali, Descartes came to his conclusions by a study of his own self. Al-Ghazzali's starting formula was 'I will, therefore, I am', and Descartes's being 'I think, therefore, I am'. Descartes also followed al-Ghazzali's derivation of the negative and positive attributes of God from the concept of necessary existence.)

Some intuitionists such as G.E. Moore attempted to define good only in terms of natural quality, as a simple and an analytical quality which cannot and does not need to be defined in terms of something else, including something metaphysical, ethical or supernatural, such as 'good is what God wills'. Moore believed that universal ethical terms are self-explanatory and that all attempts to derive ethical conclusions from something not itself ethical in nature are bound to fail.[37] Moore considered Hume's own account of morality to be naturalistic, because of its definition of virtue in terms of the statements of the spectator. Richard Price and many other intuitionists claimed that ethical knowledge is gained through an apprehension of its truth. In other words, a true ethical judgement is self-evident as long as we are reflecting clearly and calmly and as long as our judgement is not distorted by self-interest or moral upbringing. Alfred Ewing proposed a theory of intuitive knowledge of good and duty (deontology), which dispensed with the necessity for an essential concept or definition of the good. He advocated the theory of normative ethics (as against the purely descriptive). He emphasizes these points in his books,

Reason and Intuition, and *Ethics*. The intuitionists differed on many points, but they all shared the idea that innateness and intuition are the source of moral judgements and values.

The concept of human reason and the concept of Islamic rationality are therefore completely different from the modern Western concept of rationalism. While Western rationalism developed outside Christianity and mainly against Christianity, Islamic rationality grew out of Islam itself. Thomas Paine represents Western rationalism and Averroes represents Islamic rationality. While Paine in *The Age of Reason* shows beyond doubt the conflict between reason and Christianity, Averroes (also known as Ibn Rushd) in his discourse *Fasl al-Maqal fi ma Bayn al-Shari'at wa al-hikmat min al-Ittisal* (*On the Harmony of Islam and Reason*) explains how these two are in harmony. Western rationalism and political freedom and the doctrine of popular sovereignty were gained as the result of a long campaign against the Church authorities. Western rationalism owes its success to its challenge to church doctrines. This resulted in the divorce between reason and religion, matter and spirit and man and nature and so on. Western rationalism adopted profane characteristics and hence the divorce of knowledge from the sacred. Western rationalism recognizes human reason as the only source of knowledge and relies on human reason as the supreme instrument for the attainment of knowledge, and in its emphasis on the human senses as the final criterion for the distinction between truth and error. As the entire teaching of Christianity and Christian ideology is emotional and as it relies on a sense of 'numinous awe', Western rationalism had to grow outside the realm of Christianity, and almost against it. This is not the case with Islam. In Islam, rationalism and the harmony between reason and revelation has been maintained under the umbrella of the doctrine of *tawhid*. Western rationalism is based on total reliance on human reason as the sole source of knowledge. Islamic rationality is profoundly non-anthropomorphic. A truly Islamic rationality cannot but derive its ultimate legitimacy from the intellect, which is divine because human reason is regarded as the divine gift of God. This is why even all the Islamic mystical and gnostic terms in no way stand opposed to reason (*al-'aql*); rather, they serve as its complement. Islam has never recognized a dichotomy between intellect and intuition and between human reason and revelation. In fact human reason has been introduced as an inner prophet and source of revelation and the Prophet (puh) as the outer intellect. It is thus reasonable to suggest that Islamic appreciation of the laws of nature and natural law has a spiritual and divine dimension, but Western rationalism led either to the denial of natural law or based it on non-divine foundation.

While in Western culture and civilization the distinction between intellect and reason is usually forgotten, in Islamic literature there is a clear distinction between the two. The term used for reason is *al-'aql* which generally applies to reason, intelligence, keenness of perception, foresight, common sense and many other related concepts. The term used for intellection is *hikmah.* It is interesting to know that the term *al-'aql* and the term *al- hikmah* literally mean the same thing. They both mean to bind and to restrain, because they both bind man to God and restrain him from doing that which is not good.

It should also be pointed out that the Islamic intellectual and rational movement (*al-harakat al-fikriyyah wa al-'aqlaniyyah fi al-Islam*) is founded entirely on purely Islamic ideology, principles and Islamic sources. It was initiated and launched long before the establishment of Islamic theosophy and philosophy and quite some time before the translation of Greek literature into Muslim languages. Even Islamic mysticism (Sufism) and Islamic gnosis ('irfan*)*, in one way or another have some kind of relationship with Islamic intellectualism and they do not stand opposed to *al-'aql*: rather, they serve as its complement in its profoundest sense.[38]

The position and authority of *al-'aql*, human reason and human intellect has been discussed from different points of view by the scholars of Islam in, at least, four different fields: Islamic theology (*kalam*), Islamic law and jurisprudence *(fiqh)*, Islamic theosophy (*hikmah*) or philosophy, and Islamic ethics (*akhlaq*). As far as Islamic concepts in these fields are concerned, they are rational both in their contents and their methodology and approach. Islamic theology is rational–intuitional. This point will be explained in the course of discussion.

The position of Islamic law is very important in appreciating the position of natural law in Islam. We must therefore point out here that there has been a difference of opinions as to whether the source of law is reason (direct divine reason, indirect divine reason or independent human reason) or will and power (direct divine will, indirect divine will, or independent human will) and also as to whether human reason is capable of discovering or appreciating divine wisdom and will or not. There are also a variety of theories with regard to the question as to whether the divine wisdom and will are reflected and implemented in the form of order of nature and principles inherent in humans and are by their nature normative or not. As far as the first group of theories are concerned, exploration of the nature of humans as rational beings and as creatures endowed with divine rationality may help humans to underpin and discover the idea of that which is right by nature though it has to be implemented by external power and authority, in the form of law-stating, law-applying and law-enforcement. The underpinning of these natural principles is done by divine inherent 'written reason' but their implementation is done by practical reason. Rationalism, which treats law and its fundamental principles as emanating from and produced by reason (divine and non-divine) and as discoverable by reason, however, in some way contrasts with voluntarism. If we believe that the foundation of law is reason and that the fundamental principles of law are discoverable by reason we have the concept of some higher law. And if this belief depends in some way on a teleological understanding of human nature and its relation to the Creator and the rest of the created universe, then we may reasonably enough call this law of nature or natural law. Of course there is another concept of higher law; the law laid down by God for His creation, the foundation of which is divine will, and thus the law is whatever God, the Creator, wills it to be, and not related to the nature and nature of things. Indeed the nature of things is what the Creator of things wills it to be. This is another interpretation of natural law. In this case natural law as a kind of higher law does not presuppose rationalism. There can, therefore, be a voluntaristic species of natural law, though the voluntaristic tradition will more likely speak of divine law or God's law than of natural law.[39] From this point of view we may regard the Ash'arites too as the supporters of natural law.

As far as the position of Muslims towards natural law, in this respect, is concerned, the Mu'tazilah, their sympathizers and the jurists who followed their school of thought supported the first theory of natural law (that is, that the foundation of law is divine reason and that divinely gifted human reason is capable of appreciating it, teleological). The Asha'irah, their sympathizers and followers, on the other side, supported the second interpretation of natural law (voluntaristic natural law, the foundation of law is divine will, non-teleological). This point will be developed further in the following chapters. It is interesting to notice that both schools and, also other schools, base their arguments about law and natural law on theological ground.

Going back to the question of the rationality of Islamic theology, we must also emphasize that the methodology of Islamic theology thus has to be rational as well as intuitional. This is why Islam requires that every individual has to conduct his own theological thinking and search. Before practising Islam one has to sort out one's own belief and faith (*al-iman*) in the God who has commanded one to follow His way (*shari'ah*). All Islamic theological schools are united on this point. Islam is grounded on the transcendent, the truth, the absolute truth, the whole truth and the source of the truth. It starts with the actual truth and not with the manifestation, the incarnation and the presence of the truth, though manifestation of the truth has a special position in this process. The truth exists outside man without man and is not dependent on man. The truth, therefore, has to be discovered, recognized and known. In Islam one must start by knowing God and God's love. In Islam knowing is virtue. Man has been provided with the means to do this: the reason, intuition, primordial nature and intellect. Virtue follows knowing and does not precede it. But man being what he is; a combination of reason and emotion, the emotional needs of man have to be taken into consideration also. Emotional needs are fulfilled after rational needs are fulfilled. Of course God was merciful to man by providing him with reason but He blesses man with more mercy after man has used his intellectual potential to know Him and the order He has set. The presence of God in the heart of man and manifestation of truth in man comes as the result of knowing God and serving Him and surrendering and fully submitting to Him. Man in this way become *khalifato Allah*, (swt) and in this way both his rational and emotional needs are met.

The responsibility of saving and salvation is placed upon man himself, for he is provided with reason and freedom by God (strength from outside which leads to the strength from inside and finally he is blessed by the further mercy of God's presence in his heart). Islam thus strikes a balance between the rational and the emotional needs and potentials of man. While the bounty and mercy of God provide humanity generally with reason and intellect, the actual salvation of every individual is earned by the individuals themselves and after earning their own salvation they are further blessed with faith and *iman.* This is also the case with nature, and laws and orders of nature. They are absolute, discoverable by human reason and human primordial nature and respecting them are fulfilling rationally and emotionally.

In Islamic philosophy and theosophy we can distinguish at least three schools which have dealt with the methodology of knowledge and the full amplitude of the meaning of the intellect and its relation to reason, intuition, primordial nature and natural law. The Mashsha'i school (Peripatetic) doctrine concerning the intellect can be summarized by saying that there are degrees of intellect which are attained as man advances in knowledge with the aid of the active intellect which is divine. The Ishraqi school (Illuminative philosophy) emphasizes the intuitive aspect of the intellect. The third school, the Transcendental, Falasafat al-Muta'aliyyah, incorporated the views of the other two schools. These schools are engaged mainly in discussing Allah's (swt) attributes and their implications in the world of creation, laws of nature and natural law in the light of their philosophies.

Finally it is in the fields of Islamic jurisprudence and law and consequently in Islamic ethics (Islamic ethics is interrelated closely with Islamic law, i.e. Islamic codes of practice, which is regarded as practical philosophy by Muslims) that we must seek the role of human reason and intellect and their implication on natural law. This subject needs to be dealt with in detail, with an independent discussion, and we have done this in the section dealing with Islamic rationality. But dealing with it briefly here we would like to point out that the harmony of *shari'ah* or Islamic law/jurisprudence and reason has been reflected in the well established doctrine of *Usul al-fiqh,* namely the doctrine of 'close correlation and inseparability of the *shari'ah* rules of law and those of reason'(*quaèdato mulazamate hukm al-'aql wa al-shar'*). This doctrine was established as the result of another more comprehensive principle, namely that of the full harmony of religion (Islam) and Islamic philosophy (*hikmah*). These two doctrines have been properly dealt with by Averroes in his famous treatise, *Fasl al-Maqal fi ma bayn al-shari'at wa al-hikmah min al-Ittisal* (The final and decisive word on the harmony of philosophy and religion).[40] It was in the science of *Usul al-fiqh* that Muslim jurisconsults came closest to the doctrine of the harmony and the concept of natural law. According to traditionalists, the sources of law were *Kitab* and *Sunnah,* the word of God and the exemplary life of His messenger (puh). According to traditionalists, the legal system of Islam is one of divine voluntarism. In such a system there was no room for the authority of human reason, the harmony of reason and revelation and for the classical concept of natural law. According to traditionalists obligations and the rules of law do not inhere in the nature of things. Muslim jurisconsults found the answers to these problems and questions through the science of *Usul al-fiqh.* And because this science was essentially based on Islamic foundation and theology, it cut across the lines of schools of law. It should, however, be pointed out that the first recognized writer on *Usul al-fiqh,* namely al-Shafi'i, has also been introduced as a traditionalist and that there is a direct connection between Ibn Taymiyyah and Shafi'i.[41]

Major features of Islam and natural law:

1. In Islam, Allah is the only legislator, and the means to the will of Allah in matters of law are textual sources such as the Qur'an and Islamic tradition, or basic secondary sources, such as consensus, *(ijmu')* and sound human intellect (*al-'aql al-salim*), or supplementary secondary sources, such as public interest, analogy, established legal precedent (*ittifaq*). Human nature as such is not officially recommended as a source of law unless it is founded on natural sound human reasoning, which corresponds with *'aql.*
2. Islam recognizes both the natural order, the order of nature (*takwin*), and the divine order of law, the order of divine law (*tashri'*), and suggests that not only do they not contradict each other but they complement each other (*takmil*). It also recognizes the primordial nature of man (*fitrah*).
3. The divine law and the divine order of nature have roots, basis and genesis in human nature, and thus human nature and divine law are in absolute harmony.
4. The Islamic legal maxim of 'whatever is recommended by human intellect is also recommended by *shari'ah* and vice-versa' is a conditional and limited

maxim. Its authority is conditional on the certainty of both aspects of the maxim.

5. Islamic law in general, except the Ash'ari lawyers, accepts that things can be good or bad in themselves and outside the sphere of legal considerations and *shari'ah.* But even the Ash'arites support their own version of laws of nature and natural law though through different sources.
6. Man is capable of discovering and understanding values but not able to create all and every good and bad. The vacuum has to be filled by divine law. Khajah Nasir al-din Tusi in *Akhlaq-e-Naseri* suggests that the foundation of human behaviour is either nature (*tab'*) or decision (*wad'*). The first is what people of wisdom and experience find acceptable and recommended. The second type is either the decision of people in general, which is common sense and custom, or the resolution of certain individuals, such as the Prophets. This last one is regarded as divine law.[42]
7. Natural law suggests that there is an order in nature, that there are universal moral and ethical principles, that ethical principles are inherent in the nature of things and are apprehensible through human reason or human primordial nature. Some Muslim jurists may not recognize the package as a whole. The Islamic schools of law that follow the Ash'arite school of theology, especially the Hanbalite, have reservation about many parts of the process. But the majority of Muslim jurists and Islamic schools of law have recognized most of it in one way or another. There are some Muslim jurisprudents, specially the Shi'ites, who accept the whole system. The Islamic legal system, however, does not recognize nature as the source of law, but accepts it as a means to understand and even to formulate some basic principles of law in the absence of definite textual sources.
8. All Muslims unanimously accept that the most fundamental principle of Islam is the doctrine of the unity of Allah (absolute monotheism). *Tawhid* is the fundamental statement of oneness of the creator. The unity of Allah as the only creator means the unity of the entire creation. This is the primordial testimony to the balance, harmony and order in the entire creation and the existence of primordial nature and the laws governing the entire creation including nature. (Allah is *'adil* and created everything in balance, *'adl.*) This is because the whole of creation, being the work of one creator-originator, has to work within one stable pattern and in balance and complete harmony. The Qur'an points out that 'if there were more than one God there would have been chaos in the creation and universe'.[43]
9. Islam suggests that creation was designed to function as a whole and in full harmony. It states, 'So set thy face to the religion of the primordial nature, (*hanif*), God's original pattern, order and nature (*fitrah*) in which and upon which He made and originated mankind. There is no changing in God's

creation. That is the true/right religion, but most among mankind know not.'[44]

10. God has also originated and created man within the pattern of His entire creation. Humanity is thus subject to God's immutable, general laws, order and balance, with its own primordial nature, as is the rest of creation. This balance in humanity is created through and based upon man's primordial nature (*fitrah*) the part of which is his reason (*'aql*). All creation has an order, balance and primordial nature and so does humanity with man's own human primordial nature. The entire creation including humankind has to obey and conform to this balance and to natural laws.
11. Man has to recognize, respect and obey these laws, balance and order as responsibilities. In Islam man has been entrusted with and made the guardian and trustee (*khalifah*) to fulfil this responsibility. Man is capable and is provided with the means and sources of appreciating both divine revealed law and laws of nature and appreciating that they are responsibilities.
12. Islam suggests that from the principle of the unity of Allah man can deduce the principles of balance and order of nature, that there is primordial nature in general and human primordial nature in particular, including his reason, and that man has the responsibility of obeying and respecting the laws and balance of nature. According to the system of natural law, nature is: deterministic, with secrets (laws and rules), predictable and rational. These rules also apply to man. Man is also deterministic, with his own laws of *fitrah* and *gharizah* (instinct), predictable and rational.
13. Islam favours and supports the idea that although both nature and man are created by Allah and follow fixed rules and laws, Allah Himself is always in charge and may change the rules. There is thus a macro natural law but not a micro one, at the level of creation. Macro in the sense that the final arbiter, decider and mover is Allah who has decided to create and rule the universe according to rules and law. Allah is the maker of the laws and orders of nature and the law of causality. He himself cannot be the subject of these rules otherwise he would not be God. This is probably what al-Ghazzali meant by denying the law of causality. This point will be explained later.
14. The main and major means of approaching, dealing, explaining and appreciating universal and natural law and laws and orders of nature are human primordial nature, and universal human intellect which are divine gifts. Revelation has been added to these two sources but works as the only code of spiritual behaviour and code of practice. Islam is a religion and not a system of sciences. The Qur'an is a book of faith and not an encyclopaedia of sciences, as some zealots try to make it, and nor is it in

conflict with science, as some accuse it of being. (In certain areas where the Qur'an deals with issues of sciences it is for spiritual and religious purposes.) Both these approaches bespeak an ignorance of what the Qur'an is meant to be. The Qur'an is concerned with human essence and it is located in human condition. It intends to foster a broad concept of existence, the necessary existence, the contingent existence, the source of existence and the way humans relate to the source of existence, Allah, the Creator. It defines where man is located in the arrangement of all things, universal, natural, social etc. The Qur'an is addressed to man: his perceptions, conceptions, doctrines, belief-system, his manner and behaviour, his interaction, amongst many, with nature and other forms of life on earth. As for physical sciences and technological advance and scientific and technological approaches, these are the outgrowth of the disciplined mind and cultivated character that the Qur'an prepares for the mind to do its work with. The Qur'an maintains and sustains man's state of nature (*fitrah*).

The epistemological and cognitive sources, means and approaches, in Islam, are the cognitive trinity of revelation (*wahy*), reason (*'aql*) and human primordial nature (*fitrah*), we shall be dealing with these issues in the next chapters. However, the responsibilities of man in treating the laws and order of nature have been set by revelation.

THREE

Fitrah, Human Primordial Nature

In the course of our discussion in the last sections we explained that natural law is both the general order of nature and the natural order of human behaviour. Natural law ethics, as the major part of the overall natural law, is not, as is sometimes imagined, based on favouring what is 'natural' as opposed to what is 'artificial'. The main idea behind natural law ethics, as part of the natural system, is that we have, within our own nature (reason and human primordial nature), a guiding mechanism which leads us to what is good and what is evil. The guiding properties of human beings are human reason/intellect and human primordial nature, which are called in Islam *al-'aql* and *fitrah*. In this chapter we shall deal with *fitrah*.

The question of the position of natural law in Islam cannot be answered without dealing with the position of human reason and human primordial nature in Islam. This issue enjoys a very important position in the Islamic eschatology, thought and belief system and works both as a normative and as a cognitive agent. Since Islam introduces itself as Ur-religion or *religion naturale* it has to be based on, and has to explain itself, in terms of man's primordial nature (*fitrah*).

It is very difficult to give a proper definition of *fitrah* and it has been dealt with by explaining its attributes, properties and functions. *Fitrah* is a 'noun kind' to the infinitive *fatr.* It literally means 'a kind or way of creating or of being created'. It occurs in the Qur'an: 'So set thy face truly to the religion being upright. The primordial nature [*fitrah*] in which Allah has made mankind. No change [there is] in the work [wrought] by Allah.' (Qur'an, 30:29) Other forms of its verb occur fourteen times in the Qur'an. It is an Islamic term for primordial nature and human primordial nature. Ibn Abbas, a companion of the Prophet, did not understand it until he heard a Bedouin using the verb *fatara* for digging and creating a well.

The term *fitrah* is used to denote both what is termed in Islam as common sense (*'urf*), undiluted sound rational judgement (*al-'aql al-salim*), primordial nature and human primordial nature. *Fitrah* thus covers a large area of intellection, intuition and reasoning. As far as human beings are concerned, the distinction is between *fitrah* (primordial nature) and *gharizah* (instinct), and not between human intellection and ethical nature. It must be noted, however, that the term *fitrah* has been used in Islamic literature to denote animal instincts and indeed all-natural dimensions of even the world of the inanimate. This seems to imply that the entire creation, including man, has been endowed with primordial nature. The terms used in Islamic literature to denote man's primordial nature, intuition, etc. do not by any means oppose intellect and ratiocination. In no way do these terms, as used in traditional Islamic literature, stand opposed to each other. Rather they serve as complementary to each other.

> Islam has never seen a dichotomy between intellect, reason, intuition and human primordial nature. It has created a hierarchy of knowledge and methods of attaining knowledge according to which degrees of both intellect and intuition and primordial nature become harmonized in an order encompassing all the means available to man to know.[1]

Islam suggests that discovering the truth, learning the truth and believing in the truth are possible. This is because, deep down by *fitrah*, we are all seeking the truth and are learners of it. No one has to teach infants. They are intrinsically inquisitive and later on in life they are equally interested in finding the truth because it is in our human primordial nature to seek the truth, discover the truth and love the truth. Humanity collectively has been after the truth and humans helped and complemented each other, in the course of their history, to discover the truth and respect it in one form or another because they all share the same primordial nature.

In Islam *fitrah* has a divine dimension. But conscience, in its modern and secular meaning, seems to be not necessarily so. Conscience is the mundane personal sense of the moral contents of one's own conduct, intention or character with regard to a feeling of obligation to do right and be good, without divine dimension and almost replacing *fitrah*. It is thus a personal sense of moral judgement. It varies from one person to another and does not necessarily correspond with human primordial nature. But, historically almost every culture has recognized the existence of such a faculty and thus arises the concept of universal ethical culture. The view that holds human primordial nature to be an innate, intuitive faculty, determining the perception of right and wrong is also called intuitionism. There are of course other views concerning conscience.[2] However, if we hold that conscience is a universal divine property of man and capable of intuition then the tension between conscience and *fitrah* can be resolved and they may be used interchangeably.

There are some major issues concerning *fitrah,* which must be dealt with briefly in the course of our discussion. These include the definitions, interpretations, and implications of *fitrah.* The etymology of the term, its roots, its origins, its literal and practical applications, though essential and interesting, are beyond the scope of the present discourse. However, it is of importance to know that the term is uniquely Islamic and an accurate synonym is almost impossible to find in English literature. Ibn Athir in *al-Nihayah,* and Raghib in *al-Mufradat* have fully dealt with the term and have shown that the term is Islamic and that it was not in current use by Arabs before Islam.[3]

The terms *al-hanif* and *al-sibghah* have also been used as synonyms of *fitrah* in the Qur'an.[4] The Qur'an fully sanctions the position and the authority of *fitrah* or primordial nature of man. Islamic traditions also confirm this.[5] Man's primordial nature has been dealt with by Muslim scholars from different points of view: philosophical, educational, ethical, theological, spiritual and religious. Contemporary Muslim scholars discuss nature and terms and concepts associated and dealing with it at three distinct levels: Nature in general (*al- tabi'ah*), instinct (*al-gharizah*), and man's primordial nature (*al-fitrah*). They apply nature to inanimates (vegetation, solid and inorganic), instinct to animates and to the animal dimension of man and apply primordial nature only to man. The three of them share being general, absolute (not relative), inherent, necessary, primary, of existential genesis, deterministic and beyond the control of time, space, and free from environmental and circumstantial conditions. Instinct is different from primordial nature, being known by animals but without their being aware of knowing it. Primordial nature provides man with double knowledge, i.e.,knowing and knowing that one knows what one wants. Instinct is also purely corporal, animal and physical but primordial nature is incorporeal, human, ethical and spiritual.[6]

The word *fitrah* comes from the Arabic roots *fatara* The root action means to split, to slit, and to crack. *Fatara* also means to create and to cause to exist. The root action of *tabi'ah* also means to create with a disposition to the affair, state or condition. *Tabi'ah* is synonymous with *jibillah, fitrah, sajjiyyah, khaliqah* and *mizaj* which are also names for innate natural disposition which cannot change and which exist at birth in all human beings. Thus *fitrah,* having the same meaning as *tabi'ah,* linguistically means an inborn natural disposition. It literally means the natural constitution with which a child is created before he or she was born. It is said that this is the meaning of *fitrah* in the Qur'anic verse, (Qur'an, 30: 29) and in the well-known *Hadith* (tradition) which reads as follows. 'Every child is born in a state of *fitrah*'.[7]

The linguistic and positive religious explanations of *fitrah* define it as an inborn natural disposition which cannot change, and which exists at birth in all human beings.

Human nature has been discussed in different disciplines from different viewpoints. Psychologists, philosophers, theologians, educationists, lawyers, criminologists, and others have shown special interest in the subject. Psychologists have generally confined the question of human nature to the area of personality (individual and group). Psychologists in the West do not even agree upon any single theory of personality.[8] Dozens of books are available on the subject of 'human nature' especially in English language, but most of them begin with a philosophical, moral or religious perspective, or even a mixture of these views. It is evident that studies that have a psychological approach to the subject are rare, even in the West. Western psychologists, in general, have not been concerned with the so-called 'universality of social behaviour' until recently.[9] There are some reasons for this lack of interest. The main reason is that modern psychology is a behavioural discipline and suggests that it is futile to explain human behaviour in terms of human nature and primordial nature.

Scholars, whether philosophers, sociologists, or psychologists have become more and more interested in the subject of human nature. This has been felt by many Western scholars such as Stevenson,[10] Chaney, Wrightsman, Schultz[11]and Kant. These authors have studied the subject of human nature from various viewpoints. The nearest idea in Western thought to the concept of *fitrah* is that of Immanuel Kant in *The Metaphysics of Morals.* First, he places ethics and morals on metaphysical ground and then he suggests the following concept:

> There are certain moral endowments such that anyone lacking them could have no duty to acquire them. They are moral feelings, conscience, and love of human beings and respect for oneself (self-esteem). There is no obligation to have these because they lie at the basis of morality. All of them are natural predispositions of the mind (*praedispositio*) being affected by concepts of duty, antecedent predispositions on the side of *feeling.* To have these predispositions cannot be considered a duty; rather, every human being has them, and it is by virtue of them that he can be under obligation. Consciousness of them is not of empirical origin; it can, instead, only follow from consciousness of a moral law, as the effect this has on the mind.[12]

There are certain questions concerning human nature that are of common interest to all disciplines. But they have been dealt with and answered from different angles and points of view; i.e. the questions of human nature, human primordial nature, human emotions and feelings, freedom of man, even freedom from moral obligations, whether man is a single-dimensional (material) or a multi-dimensional being, (material, spiritual and ethical), whether man is basically good and innocent or not, what is the role of education, religion and reason in the development of man, and finally the question of the relationship between man and his primordial nature. Muslim scholars have discussed these questions and have their own answers, which may or may not correspond with answers by others. In a way some of the famous scholars of Islam such as Ghazzali and Avicenna (Ibn Sina) can be regarded as Muslim scholars who dealt with these questions from the viewpoint of Islam and Islamic psychology. For example, *'aql* was discussed in terms of the difference between inborn or innate intelligence (*gharizi-fitri*), versus acquired or learnt intelligence (*muktasab*, *mustafad*), employing the imagery of innate *'aql* as eyesight and acquired *'aql* as light, for operation of insight. There were, of course, differing views over the degree to which *'aql* is inborn, innate, instinctive, and natural (*jibelli, tabi'i, malikah, gharizi, fitanat*).

However, having said this, we would like to point out that although on the surface some of the answers to these questions, by modern psychologists, for example, may agree with the views expressed by Muslim scholars the approach and the foundation of their conclusions are different. One or two examples may shed some light on this point. Freudian theory suggests that man has no free will, for he is controlled by unconscious forces like the instincts, aggression and sex, which he can never conquer. In this sense Freud gives the role of primordial nature to instinct.[13] This Freudian theory has been rejected by the neo-Freudians like Fromm. Fromm has a positive attitude towards the free will of man. While Muslim scholars view the good and positive nature of man in the light of man's divine primordial nature, Freud and Freudians see it within the framework of instinct. This is also the case with the actual question of man's free will. Another example is the attitude towards the relation of good and evil to man. Maslow, as a modern philosopher, in his *Humanistic Theory* affirms that the innate human nature is basically good. This corresponds with the Islamic view on *fitrah*. But this innate good human nature of man is for Maslow material whereas in Islam it is divine and spiritual. We shall deal with the issue of conscience at the end of this chapter.

Having said this, I would like to point out that the term *fitrah* cannot be clearly and concisely translated into a single English word. However, there are four classical views of *fitrah* as follows:

1. The predestinarians' view which was originally held by scholars during a period before the middle of the eighth century Ad. This view is based on the doctrine of predestination as understood by Jahm ibn Safwan, a member of the Jabriyyah deterministic school. The Jabarite school supported this view. According to this school, Allah who created the world and the laws of nature, also created all properties and actions of man. The predestinarian

view was mainly a reaction against the libertarian or Qadarite school, which suggested that man is naturally free from any predestinarian nature.

2. The neutral view. This view of human nature emerged after the middle of eighth century in response to the predestinarian view. The most representative scholar of this school was Ibn 'Abd al-Barr. (b. 368 AH). The neutralist school suggests that *fitrah* is neutral, neither inclined to *iman* nor to *kufr*, neither good nor bad, but a blank state.
3. The positive view, which suggests that *fitrah* is a state of intrinsic innate goodness and that it is the social environment which cause the individuals to deviate from this state. This school suggests that there is a natural correspondence between human nature and *religion natural*, which is Islam. According to this school, man's nature has inherently within it the potential to know Allah, to love Him, to worship Him and the will to practise His commands and to be a true *hanif.* This school suggests that *tawhid* is integral to man's *fitrah* because Allah, in His infinite wisdom, intended man to know Him, as the one and the God. This is why man was able to acknowledge his Lord before his existence on earth in the state of involuntary submission to Allah and of acknowledging Him (Qur'an.7:172). *Fitrah*, according to this school, which is recognized by an absolute majority of Muslim scholars, has both the normative and the cognitive properties.
4. Dual interpretation. Modern scholars who regard man as innately both good and evil are adherents of the dual interpretation of *fitrah.*

The question of *fitrah* deserves a book of its own. Fortunately there is one by Dr Yasien Mohamed, a valuable work under the title *Fitra.*[14] Yasien Mohamed, in his well-researched work, has explained the common features and the differences of above interpretations as follows:

Interpretations of Fitrah

	Dual	Neutral	Positive
1. Born	With preparedness for both *iman* and *kufr*.	In a state of ignorance and innocence – no *iman* or *kufr*.	In a state of iman and Islam with a potential.
2.Predisposition	Equal innate predisposition to both right and wrong.	No innate predisposition to right or wrong man a blank state.	Innately predisposed to know Allah and to do right.
3. Evil	An external agent of misguidance complements the innate evil in man.	An external agent of misguidance.	An external agent of misguidance.
4. Prophethood and revelation	External divine agents of guidance which complement the good in man.	External divine agents of guidance.	External divine agents of guidance which complement the innate predisposition.

As we have noticed, there are quite a few interpretations of the concept of *fitrah*, covering classical, neo-classical and contemporary theories in Islam. The concept of *fitrah* has been the subject of discussion throughout the history of Islamic thought. One may even detect conflicting interpretations of *fitrah*. But they have all served a valuable purpose. They are all valid insofar as they represent a collective Islamic viewpoint and insofar as they are based on Islamic sources and value system. The majority of Muslim scholars regard *fitrah* as something vested in man's spirit by Allah. *Fitrah* itself is good and must be good, because Allah is good and is the source of all good.

The question and doctrine of *fitrah* has left a great impact on the entire Islamic theology, law, epistemology, philosophy, ethics, psychology, metaphysics, and other fields of Islamic thought. The implications of *fitrah* are thus both qualitative and quantitative, normative and cognitive. *Fitrah* cannot be viewed in isolation from man's mind, behaviour, belief, conduct, and worldview. *Fitrah's* relevance is implicit in all these areas. One cannot, for example, develop a theory of education without certain assumptions concerning human nature.

From another point of view, there have been three major approaches to the question of ethics and moral values and the means to appreciate them: deontological, naturalist and consequential. The Mu'tazilah, their followers and those who support Islamic rationality have generally adopted the first approach, though not exclusively. However, the Mu'tazilah did not deny the role of *fitrah* in this process. The absolute majority of Muslim scholars have supported the second approach by accepting the doctrine of *fitrah*, though they did not reject the role of reason in this process. The consequential approach has been explained in Islam in term of salvation and disgrace, the hereafter and success and failure in this world. Ghazzali may be recognized as one of those who supported the last approach. However we must understand that in Islam these approaches are not exclusive of each other and usually a combination of all three approaches has been promoted by Muslims. Here the question is that of priority of each of the three approaches.

The secularization of knowledge and psychology, however, has led to introducing human primordial nature as instinct or conscience. This can be noticed in modern psychology especially in the post-Freudian development of psychology.

To appreciate the concept of *fitrah* in Islam a brief comparison between the concept of human nature in Islam and in Christianity will help. Religions may be contrasted with secular philosophy in that the former recognizes the transcendent principle of human nature while the latter tend to view man as a material being. This transcendental principle is usually referred to as the spirit or the soul in man. Islam and Christianity both recognize the innate spirituality of man. But they differ in the method by which they attain this self-realization and they also differ in their views of innate human nature. For better understanding of the Christian view about this issue one needs to turn to the doctrine of original sin and natural corruption of man in Christianity and compare it with the doctrine of original goodness and decent nature of man in Islam. Such a comparison would bring into focus the divergent perspectives of human nature of two major religions of the world. According to Christianity Adam's disobedience plunged the entire human race into ruin and fallen man could not of himself do good, please God, gain salvation (Paradise lost). The Christian is thus born in sin and in an impure state and cannot redeem himself by his inner resources. He can only do this through the abstract salvation through Christ. Man is innately incapable of redeeming himself for he does not have the innate potential and abilities to do so. Without the doctrine of original sin there would be no need for salvation and for a saviour and, consequently, the trinity, the crucifixion and the resurrection would become meaningless. Accordingly, not only man is naturally corrupt, the entire nature is corrupt too.

By contrast, Islam recognizes both the innate goodness of human nature and the innate potential of man to earn his own salvation and also regards the entire nature as a divine gift. Islam rejects the concept of original sin, the doctrine of the innate evilness of man and religious and spiritual intercession. This Islamic principle has been explained by Farabi. According to Farabi, evil, as a 'cosmic'entity, is entirely non-existent. Whatever exists in the universe, including man, and is independent of human willing, is wholly good. For once we posit the First cause and the series of entities which result from it in the order and disposition meted out to them, every part of the series exists 'in accordance with that order and justice of merit' pertaining to it, and this is the essence of goodness. The only kind of evil which exists in the world is 'voluntary evil', which consists either in the privation of happiness or the ultimate good, designated in the wretchedness (*al-shaqa*), or in the performance of those voluntary actions leading to this wretchedness. For 'everything natural whose principle is voluntary action, may be either good or bad. Whenever and wherever the will is excluded, evil is excluded too. Everything is good in its original shape and form, until man decides voluntarily to misuse it'.[15] We can understand that Farabi suggested that the entire creation and existence is good and evil is entirely non-existent. Both Farabi and Ibn Sina maintained that the soul has a longing to ascend and love for what is above and yearns thus for its own final absorption into the 'One'. This means that the means and methods (*fitrah*) for this ascent, suggested by Muslim thinkers, do not point to the modern concept and doctrine of humanism. Ibn Sina, in a short essay on "*Ilm al-Akhlaq*' ('Science of Ethics') in his work *Rasa'il fi al-hikmat wa al-tabi'iyyat*, (*Essays on Hikmah and Natural Dispositions*), begins by acknowledging that Allah is the 'one who enriches the soul (*nafs*) of the man who is devoted to His virtues (*fada'il*) and the means whereby he may acquire them for himself'.[16] This idea of Farabi and Ibn Sina set the tune for similar discussions and opinions by their successors, from Ibn Sina (d. 1037) to Moskawayh (d. 1030), al-Tusi (d. 1247), al-Suhrawardi (d. 1191) and others.[17]

Fitrah, human primordial nature, has three major properties:

1. Cognitive properties such as primary, innate, obvious, inherent, non-sensual and unacquired basic knowledge; e.g. the invalidity of vicious circular argument, infinite causal regression, contradiction in argument leading to being and not being of the same thing (everything being considered). These innate non-sensual, non-experimental principles form the basis of human knowledge.
2. Normative, ethical and moral properties such as the sanctity of justice, truth and all universal ethical principles and inborn archetypal axioms.

3. Psychological properties such as love for children, love of arts, perfection, creativity, knowledge, truth, beauty, loving and being loved, etc.

Muslim scholars on the basis of Islamic sources claim that all these (the three types of natural properties of *fitrah*) are universal, absolute, innate, primordial axioms, intuitional, inborn, obvious and divinely bestowed at the time of birth. They are in the form of potential properties until later on at the time when individuals are rationally mature when they become the actual properties of natural man.

Muslims reject Platonic archetypal forms of virtues, which, Plato suggested, existed before man is born and have an independent existence of their own. They suggest, instead, that these properties are given by God as potentials before birth or at the time of birth and are only actualized later on in life when they are given the chance to be actualized. Accordingly, all innate properties (primordial natural properties, *al-Fi triyyat*) are, like natural and instinctive properties and potentials, to be discovered, developed, explored, trained and actualized. Man does not make them. The Qur'an frequently states that it is a 'reminder' and it called itself 'the reminder' (*dhikr*).[18] The Qur'an states that the duty of the Prophets (put) and messengers of God is to remind peoples of their primordial nature and to try to bring them back to it. The main feature of the concept of Islamic primordial natûre and its spiritual, educational, psychological, ethical, epistemological and emotional values is that these values are all blessings from Allah, (swt) and that *fitrah* itself is given by God to man as His blessing.

Many Western philosophers, thinkers and almost all the proponents of the school of Humanism also believe that man has innate values, principles and basic knowledge, but they suggest that they are the products of nature and nature of man and not of God. Earlier in the history of Western thought, Cicero's *De Officiis,* and natural law theory, also discusses justice, one of the major principles of natural law, as grounded in the inner character of man according to the law of nature. Cicero's comments include justice, in which is the crowning glory of the virtues and on the basis of which men are called 'good men'. As was explained in Chapter One, some even suggest that God and belief in God is also the product of man's nature. Some accept that man is a multi-dimensional being, animal and human, spiritual and physical and that man is naturally seeking perfection and believing in moral values. But at the same time they suggest that the spiritual property of man has created God and not the other way round. Islam on the contrary regards Allah (swt) alone as the source and cause of all man's spiritual and ethical properties and virtues and suggests that man's primordial nature is created by Allah (swt). Islam suggests that guidance in general and guidance of humans in particular is of two kinds:

1. Ontological guidance (*al-takwini*) which is somehow related to guidance at the level of primordial nature covering the entire universe (*al-fitri*).
2. Acquired guidance (*al-iktisabi*) which corresponds to educational and cognitive guidance (*al-ta'limi*). The second guidance is the actualization of the first one, without which man would not be able to acquire guidance, knowledge, and perfection and without which it would be impossible for man to recognize ethical values, virtues and salvation. The Qur'an explains this point.[19]

Almost all Muslim sects and Islamic schools have unanimously accepted the principle of the authority of *fitrah* and regard it as the source of both knowledge (*al-fitriyyat al-idrakiyyah*) and ethical virtues (*al-fitriyyat al-akhlaqiyyah*). Some Muslim scholars suggest that human soul is incorporeal and immaterial (*al-mujarrad*) because only an incorporeal entity is able to produce universal, general, absolute and obvious basic principles and general universal knowledge, which are the source of and basic foundation of acquired knowledge. This is because all corporeal and material knowledge is partial, relative, local, exclusive, conditional and particular, and not able to produce logical general conclusions and rationally acceptable results. Partial, particular, and relative knowledge are inconclusive unless they are formulated into general and universal principles, which are acceptable by man's primordial nature and are innately recognized.

It is in this way that we can establish a solid relationship between ethical values and ontological realities. This is because the source of both of them is man's primordial nature, which is reality and is real in its own right in itself. Both epistemological principles and ethical virtues are general, universal, inherent and obvious realities, which cannot be the results and products of a corporeal, physical, material, relative and sensual source, physical experiment and observation. It has been suggested that ontological realities are categorized as descriptive and ethical values as normative and that descriptive categories do not lead to normative-imperative commands. However, this theory does not necessarily mean that ethical values and normative-imperative virtues are relative, temporary, and circumstantial and without a solid base in the reality of man's primordial nature, which is real and a reality in itself. Muslim scholars, in fact, describe ethical virtues in terms of ontological reality by basing man's ethical primordial nature (*al-fitrat al-akhlaqiyyah*) on man's ontological nature (*al-fitrah al-takwiniyyah*). In doing so they suggest that man's ethical primordial nature does indeed fulfil man's ontological needs. The first one in fact follows the second. This is certainly true with human instincts, so much so that human instincts are regarded as human ontological realities. But man, being a rational being with will-power can interfere with his primordial ethical nature and thus ignore its reality. Man even interferes with his instincts to ignore his emotional, psychological and primordial ethical nature. But this interference should not and does not change the reality of either his instinct or his primordial nature. Indeed the belief in *fitrah,* the belief that there is a universal human nature that we all share and from which we can derive the principles of rights, lies at the heart of a very common (the most common) conception of natural law and natural rights. This is because the judgements of human primordial nature are inherent, common to all, and lead to and provide certainty. It has been suggested that deriving ethical norms and human rights from observing nature and laws of nature is deriving an *ought* from an *is.*[20] But this argument is not convincing because inherent moral judgement carries its own certainty and is based on reality as well. Even if we doubt the authority of human reason on the ground that it is impossible to accept the existence of a standard in reason, which is shared by all human beings in similar form, we cannot challenge the authority of certainty produced by human primordial nature.

Fitrah in Islam is thus a multi-dimensional and a multi-functional realistic attribute and property of man. This property is both cognitive and normative. It leads to the recognition of orders and laws of nature, natural law and also to rights, responsibilities, and ethical and spiritual obligations. These functions include the following:

1. The ideological function, which implies that the belief in the divine being is natural for man and that man has always believed in a kind of divine being.
2. The cognitive function, which implies that man has the innate potential to know this divine being by means of acquired knowledge and also by means of intuition. Knowledge is a virtue in itself and ethical virtue, or knowledge of the right, may be both inborn and acquired.
3. The spiritual dimension, which implies that man has always been in need of worshipping the divine being and has been doing it in one form or another throughout human history. The history of ritual practices is very old. [21]
4. The ethical dimension, which implies that man is naturally innocent, in search of perfection, happiness and salvation (*sa'adah*) and that man is naturally inclined to be good, do good and avoid evil.[22] Moral excellence and perfection is a characteristic of human nature because man is innately inclined to virtue. Healthy psychological and social circumstances are required in order to awaken this inherent virtue. The ethical dimension of morality is derived from human nature itself but it is also the consequence of social moral prescriptions. Moral prescriptions based on divine revelation accord with man's *fitrah* and give expression to the virtue within

man. When a person's conduct is in harmony with his inner nature, he is regarded as spiritually, ethically and psychologically healthy.

It should be pointed out that, the animal dimension and that part of man (*gharizah*) that also has its animal desires and needs, which if met in the right manner may help man's desire for perfection, but which otherwise leads to evil. This is termed ' the soul which incites to evil' (*al-nafs al-ammarto be al-su'*). At the same time the Qur'an also refers to the 'upbraiding soul' (*al-nafs al-lawwamah*), that is the soul whose conscience is awakened, and thus blames or upbraids itself for its own transgressions and deviation from its divine natural course. The Qur'an also refers to the 'soul at peace' (*al-nafs al-mutma'innah*). This sanctified soul is the soul in the state of perfection and divine nature and is not subject to vice and imperfection.[23]

In worldwide cultural literature there are some terms and concepts that may correspond loosely with *fitrah* and human primordial nature, unless they are given divine dimension and attributes in which case they may correspond more closely.

Moral feeling is the susceptibility to feeling pleasure or displeasure from being aware that our actions are consistent with, or contrary to, the law of duty. Since any consciousness of obligation depends upon moral feeling to make us aware of the constraint present in the thought of duty, there can be no duty to have moral feeling or acquire it; instead every human being (as a moral being) has it in him originally. Obligation to moral feeling can be only to cultivate it and to strengthen it through wonder at its inscrutable source. It is appropriate to call this feeling a moral sense, for by the word 'sense' is usually understood a theoretical capacity for perception directed towards an object, whereas moral feeling is something merely subjective, which yields no cognition. No human being is entirely without moral feeling, for were he completely lacking in receptivity to it he would be morally dead; and if (to speak in medical terms) the moral vital force could no longer excite this feeling, then humanity would dissolve (by chemical laws, as it were) into mere animality and be mixed irretrievably with the mass of other natural beings.

Conscience is the term loosely employed to denote the ethical and moral sense of individuals. It could be regarded as a secular substitute for *fitrah*. Conscience is really the property of individuals and thus may vary from one individual to another. It may even change in an individual according to circumstances and thus create conflict. However some philosophers of ethics have given conscience a more inclusive definition. As we pointed out before, Kant's idea about conscience is very close to the Islamic concept of human primordial nature. He sugggests that

> conscience is not something that can be acquired, and we have no duty to provide ourselves with one; every human being, as a moral being, *has* a conscience within him originally. To be under obligation to have a conscience would be tantamount to having a duty to recognize duties. For, conscience is practical reason holding the human being's duty before him for his acquittal or condemnation in every case that comes under a law. Thus it is not directed to an object but merely to subject and so it is not something incumbent on one, but rather unavoidable fact. So when it is said that a certain human being has no *conscience,* what is meant is that he pays no heed to its verdict. For if he really had no conscience, he could not even conceive of the duty to have one, since he would neither impute anything to himself as conforming with duty nor reproach himself with anything as contrary to duty. Unconscientiousness is not lack of conscience but rather the propensity to pay no heed to its judgement.[24]

Kant then goes on to explain love of human being and self-respect in the same manner. What is interesting in this respect is that he regards these concepts, principles and ethical rules as innate, subjective and almost as properties of *fitrah*.

However, modern psychology is broadly concerned with the study of individual and group behaviour where thinking, remembering and even intention are forms of behaviour which can be experimented, tested, measured, observed, analysed and evaluated. Furthermore, the definition of behaviour in modern psychology is rather inadequate, as it does not take into consideration the dimensions of faith, spirit, religious intention and metaphysics. Recent developments in psychology have brought it closer to an interest in the cognitive aspect of behaviour and even the spiritual aspect to a very small extent. The discussion of human primordial nature is still left out of the domain of psychology. Religions in general and Islam in particular are behavioural systems too. But they neither start nor stop at behaviour only and they are concerned with faith, intention, and the spiritual, moral and metaphysical dimension of human beings and human behaviour. This is why the question of the primordial nature of man, in one form or another is of importance in religions in general and in Islam in particular.

It would be appropriate to understand what the Western concept of conscience is and whether it corresponds with the concept of *fitrah* or not. (The voice of conscience is the very essence, and sum total, of even secular ethics and the foundation of mainly individual morality.) The complexity, ambiguity and unpredictability of situation in which we often find ourselves sometimes makes it difficult to determine by rational reflection what we ought to do. In a specific context both the appropriate material good to seek and realize, and the morally permissible means by which to realize it, may be unclear. In such a situation – as in those where reflection is not so troubled by obscurity and confusion – we may be told that we ought to be guided by our 'conscience'. If we follow our conscience, it may be claimed, we will do what for us is right. To go against our conscience can never be morally justified, no matter what school of ethics we belong to. But the main question here is: what is meant by conscience? The term may refer to our rational judgement of the situation before us, based upon our apprehension of the factors involved in that situation and the values and principles of conduct which have captivated us as being normative. In this sense the dictates of our conscience are in fact the final conclusion of our understanding of the matter at issue. It is obviously right for us to follow these dictates because they are our rational decisions. They are properly to be treated as authoritative for us since they express what we have decided to be right for us to do in the circumstances. This is really the case even if our judgement may later be recognized by us or by others to have been mistaken. But at the time when they are made they are morally binding upon us.

This view of conscience may be challenged on the ground that the guidance of conscience is immediate. Since, that is, conscience is experienced as telling us directly what we are to do, it may be held that it is wrong to treat it as if it were based upon a process of reasoning and its deliverance as the expression of the conclusions of such reasoning. In answering this objection, it must be admitted that our experience of our conscience is not an experience of an explicit reasoning process leading eventually to a conclusion. Our consciousness of conscience is that as we consider a situation we become deeply and convincingly aware of what we ought to do. The error in this objection, though, is that it assumes that all our reasoning process is conscious and explicit. But it is not so. The reasoning that is most significant for us is not conducted by explicit stages but occurs largely, if not wholly, unconsciously. This is due to our natural reasoning faculty. It is a sort of instinctive perception by means of which we reason without effort and intention. This immediacy in conclusion should not deceive us.

The conclusions thus reached do not only have legitimacy but it is necessary for us to regard them as authoritative for us. They declare what we fundamentally assess to be our duty. At the same time we must not forget that these conclusions are only as sound as the reasoning which produces them. Because that reasoning may be partly based on mistaken principles and values, because it may have misapprehended the situation, and because its connection of items may be faulty, its conclusion in any particular case may be in error, even though it is binding upon us.

Another more widely accepted understanding of the nature and concept of conscience is also put forward. This concept characterizes conscience in a way which, contrary to intention, renders it less rather than more trustworthy than the view which sees it as expressing the conclusion of some unconscious reasoning process. 'According to this view conscience is to be regarded as a form of experience of direct means of perceiving the will of God, a kind of personal revelation. It has been regarded 'as the voice of God in the nature and heart of man'.[25] Although C.C.J. Webb does not regard such experience as being able to provide an infallible insight into truth, he does hold that 'when we judge ourselves what is right we have the living God present within us, speaking to the conscience, supplying grace, enlightening the mind, impelling the charity. It seems that those who hold this idea about conscience have treated it as a form of religious experience.[26]

Fitrah, human primordial nature is more than just a form of religious conscience. The most fundamental property of conscience and *fitrah* is vested in its ability to recognize and distinguish right and wrong, good and evil. It will be explained in Chapter 5 that there are two major schools dealing with the issue of good, truth, evil and falsehood and human ability to appreciate these: the Mu'tazilite and the Ash'arites. The first school suggests that imperative-normative ethical rules (both commands and prohibitions) follow good and evil and are appreciable by man, but the Ash'arites suggest the opposite and that good and evil follow command and prohibitions. On the face of it and at the beginning it looks as if only the Mu'tazilite school supports the doctrine of primordial nature and natural law. But a comprehensive and careful study of Ash'arism shows that the Ash'arites also accept the doctrine of the primordial nature of man. The main difference, here, probably, is that the Mu'tazilites apply primordial nature fully and comprehensively both horizontally and vertically in all spheres of religion, ethics, life and spirit. But the Ash'arites apply primordial nature vertically, starting from the top of the pyramid (the belief in God and His attributes and so on) and leave the rest to the command of Allah (swt) as the direct source of law, virtue and knowledge. I believe that both Mu'tazilah and Asha'irah support the same approach to the issue of ethics and *fitrah*. Although Asha'irah suggest that there is an inclusive relation between divine commands and moral imperatives, at the same time they also suggest that God's commands have moral force, perhaps not in themselves, but because God is perfectly good and benevolent (Merciful, Gracious and Benevolent).

It is thus reasonable to conclude that both the normative and the descriptive, the ethical and the ontological principles are all realities and enjoy being absolute, universal and permanent because both of them derive their value and authority from the same source; the primordial nature of man. The normative principles are based on the descriptive principles and they both lead to the same end; the fulfilment of man's potential, happiness and his salvation. Thus the unity of the source, the means and the end establishes the full harmony between the so termed ontological dimension of man and his spiritual and ethical dimension as well and thus Islam introduces itself as Ur-religion, or *religio naturalis* and the religion of primordial nature, both at the level of universe and at the level of humans and from both the normative and the cognitive point of view.[27]

FOUR

The Major Principles of Islamic Rationality

In the last chapter we dealt with the role of human primordial nature (*fitrah*) as one of means and the basis of ethics in Islam, on which the Islamic concept of natural law can be explained and justified. This chapter and the next deal with another very fundamental issue, namely the role and position of reason in natural law, natural law ethics, ethics in general and the relevant concepts according to Islam. If ethics and the relevant concepts have an objective basis, it must also be because of the role that reasoning can play in them too.

We know that there are quite a few conflicting opinions regarding this point. Hume, for example, rejects the role of reasoning and reason in ethics and replaces the role of reason with that of feelings. He believed that an *ought* judgement cannot be derived from a series of *is* statements'. Hume's view has been challenged by many in different ways. Kant is the greatest opponent of Hume's view of the role of reason in ethics. He suggested the following statement as an alternative to the statement made by Hume, mentioned above. Kant's famous imperative is 'Act only on the maxim through which you can at the same time will that it should become a universal law'. Kant does not wholly reject the role of feelings in ethics, but believes it should be the kind of feeling that all rational beings must have. There are some scholars who believed that intuition is the basis of ethics, such as Henry Sidgwick who suggested that intuitional axioms are self-evidently true. Ludwig Wittgenstein and A.J. Ayer supported logical positivism as the basis for ethics. Ayer's position is regarded as 'emotivism'. Existentialism also rejected the role of reason in ethics. In fact existentialism denied ethical objectives in human behaviour. According to Sartre's existentialism man's being (existence) follows his becoming. Some philosophers are also not so certain about the role of reason in natural law.

We would now like to point out that Muslim philosophers of ethics also suggested quite a few alternatives as the basis of ethics. These alternatives include reason, revelation, intuition, human primordial nature and combination of these. But the majority of Muslim philosophers of ethics support the last alternative, a combination of all.

Islam has developed numerous schools of thought, law, ethics, philosophy and mysticism dealing with legal philosophy, ethical issues, spiritual and theological subjects including the order of nature, primordial nature, human rights and responsibilities, divine will and wisdom, determinism, voluntarism, natural law, man, human society, cosmos etc. The majority of the major schools, scholars, jurists, thinkers and philosophers have in one way or another supported the authority of human reason and human primordial nature (*fitrah*), both in the field of epistemology, education, law and ethics.

It is not our intention to explore fully the rational elements, principles and foundations in Islam, nor to go into the history of Islamic rationality. Our immediate objective here is to explain the historical development of the doctrine of the compatibility and harmony of *Shari'ah* and *hikmah,* which led to the doctrine of the authority of human intellect as an avenue or source of legal knowledge in Islam or vice versa, and as a result the subject of human rights and responsibility and the relationship between Islam and natural law.

Reason and Rationality in Islam

The term rationalism has often been used in this book and by some Muslim scholars. Naturally when non-Western and Muslim authors use it, it is used within the relevant contexts and should be appreciated within its proper definition, which is completely different from that of Western contexts and definition. Islamic rationality is radically different from Western rationalism in many ways: definition, sources, background, bases, implications, goals, history, philosophy, application, justification etc. When we examine, for example, the work of Ibn Rushd, the chief religious Muslim jurist-judge and author from Andalusia , in its original Arabic text, and within its proper Islamic context, we find it completely different from the European Averroes, the arch-rationalist and enemy of revelation.

What do rationality and rationalism mean? There are several definitions for rationality and rationalism proposed by different schools and people. These definitions usually cover a certain dimension of rationality from a specific angle. The nineteenth-century philosopher Nietzsche gave a succinct definition of rationality as follows. Rationality is a matrix of connections, which assigns cause to effect. Looking for the roots of rationality, Nietzsche delved deep into the psychobiological roots of epistemology. He argued that rationality is an inescapable consequence of what he calls man's 'will to power'. Buried in the human psycho, he argued, is a deeply seated, possibly inexplicable, urge to have control over the events of the outer world. This 'will to power' is the psychological mainspring of all creative activities. Rationality is essential for the sublimation of this urge because without it there cannot be any chance for any human to have any control over events or conscious social change. Stripped of this 'will to power', humans become mere buoys that float on the waves.[1]

By causal connection Nietzsche probably means immediate/physical causal connection and by the 'will to power' he means human will to power too. This definition of rationality is very exclusive and includes only limited causal proofs and rationalization. He thus excludes all other forms of intellectual inquiries and rational speculations. According to this definition, Ghazzali's intellectual inquiries into the 'first cause' or the 'cause of the causes' (*'iIllat al-ula, 'illat al-'ilal*) and introducing it as the only cause and also introducing the 'divine will' as the only 'will to power' is not an intellectual inquiry and rational speculation. It will be clear, in the course of our discussion that definitions like that of Nietzsche do not cover all dimensions of rationality. They certainly do not fully cover Islamic concept of rationality.

Readers should take notice that the term 'rationalism' has several different meanings. It is the multivalent ambiguity of rational note that has made the disparate modernist appeal to rationalism. The term rationalism as a label for thought systems normally refers to the seventeenth- and eighteenth- century intellectualism in the West and to modern Western philosophy. Thus it is both a modern and a Western concept, which must be applied cautiously to pre-modern, non-Western intellectual traditions.

Muslim philosophers have produced a more inclusive definition of rationality. Haj Mulla Hadi of Sabzewar in Iran (1212–95/1797–1878) in his famous work *Ghawal al-La'ali* defines and introduces intellectual inquiry and rational speculation as a combination of three intellectual movements, as follows:

1. Movement from intellectual indifference and ignorance, which is the state of questioning about a general subject of study and speculation, (and not particular or trivial subjects only) to the state of interest in the subject of inquiry.
2. The movement from this state to the state of serious inquiry; the state of research and the state of searching, finding and providing solid proofs, preparing logical and rational premises and demonstrative evidences.
3. The intellectual movement from the second state to the final state of conclusion.[2]

(*al-fikru harakatune la al-mabadi; wa men mabadiya ela al-murardi*)

The definitions of reason and wisdom in general and of *aql* and Islamic rationality in particular have been dealt with properly by Karim Douglas Crow as a thesis for his Ph.D.[3] Having said this we will be explaining later on in this section that there are difficulties in finding accurate and precise definitions for reason in general and thus for rationalism as well, and for components of reasoning, and rationality. These difficulties have left their impact on the concept and definition of reason and rationality in Islamic literature. For the sake of convenience we have used the term Islamic rationality for *al-ʿaqlaniyat al-Islamiyyah,* the terms *ʿaql-ta'aqull* and *fikr-tafakkur* for reason and reasoning, and the terms *hikmah* and *tadabbur* for intellection and philosophical activities of the human mind. We would also like, therefore, to make a distinction between philosophy (Western) and *hikmah* and between reason and intellection. Farabi recognized this point in his famous book *al-Fusul al-muntazaʿah* (*Excerpts from the Writings of the Ancients*). Farabi explains this point in section seven of *Fusul* as follows; the major powers (or parts) of the soul are five: the nutritive, the sensitive, the imaginative, the concupiscent, and the rational. The last power has a distinctive ethical function, being the power 'through which man reasons, deliberates, acquires the sciences and the arts, and distinguishes between right and wrong actions'. Its subdivisions are then given as theoretical and practical, and the practical is further subdivided into technical (*mihani*) and reflective or deliberative (*fikri*). The former includes intuition (*al-ʿaql al-fitri*), science/knowledge (*ʿilm*) and wisdom (*hikmah*); the latter includes practical reason, prudence (*taʿaqqul*), keenness (*al-dhihn*), sound judgement, and sound opinion. Only the second group or that of reflective virtue is pertinent to the study of ethics.[4]

The term rationalism has been used since the Renaissance by the majority of Western philosophers as the only method of acquiring knowledge. Western rationalism proposed human reason rather than revelation as a source of knowledge, which was used by the independent man of Renaissance humanism instead of, and against, God. Through the rise of Western rationalism man's reason was declared independent of revelation and man even declared a war against it. Islamic rationality should not and could not be identified with rationalism within Western contexts. By the term rationality in the present work we mean Islamic intellection, the kind of rationality within the Islamic definition of the term. *Al-ʿaql,* or human reason in Islamic literature, applies also to that part of primordial nature that provides man with the insight to follow the right path and is in conformity with reason. The Western rationalism that emerged from the Renaissance in rebellion against revelation is different from Islamic intellectualism and has nothing in common with it except in name.

The word *ʿaql,* which is translated as intellect, reason, wisdom, or intelligence occurs forty-nine times in the Qur'an. Inspecting these verses one finds that the operative notion of *ʿaql* in the Qur'an is neither the Greek *nous* nor the modern Western notion of rationalism, although the meaning of *nous* is certainly closer in meaning to the Qur'anic term than the English rationalism. *'Aql* in the Qur'an is used as the means by which man is also able to recognize the ultimate significance of things *(ayah)* besides the appearance of things. *Aql* was defined in a famous utterance attributed to the Prophet Muhammad (puh) as 'a light in the heart that discriminates between truth and falsehood' (*nurun fi al-qalb yufarrequ bayn al-haqq wa al-batil*). While Western rationalism and empiricism are concerned mainly with the nature of appearance and formulating scientific theories, *'aql*, as introduced in the Qur'an, is concerned with insight. Naturally man must be able to understand the appearance of the things first to be able to discover their spiritual significance. There is not, thus, a contradiction between the reasoning of the scientists and the exercise of *'aql*. In a sense *'aql* is more inclusive than empiricist reasoning.[5]

Having pointed out, briefly, some of the differences between Islamic rationality and non-Islamic rationalism, between *'aql* and *hikmah* and *hikmah* and philosophy (which will be explained further in the course of our discussion), we feel it is fair to point out also that these terms have been frequently used very loosely and interchangeably. The differing contextual employments of the term *'aql* were commonly viewed by classical Muslim scholars to exemplify a form of 'textual polysemy', admitting multiple significance when its meaning is appropriated by different circles.[6] This point will be clarified in the course of discussion too.

The term Islamic rationalism, (instead of Islamic rationality) used by many does not thus seem to be appropriate. We would like to provide, in the course of our discussion, the kind of definition and terms that cover all Islamic and Muslim intellectual inquiries and rational speculation throughout the history of Islamic thoughts, excluding only the Literalists (Zahiris). However, I believe that it is almost impossible to give a comprehensive and inclusive definition of rationalism in general and Islamic rationality in particular. As was the case with *fitrah*, we can appreciate the concept of rationalism and rationality by appreciating the attributes and properties of reason and intellect.

Main Features of Islamic Rationality

By pointing out some of the main features of Islamic rationality we shall appreciate the difference between Islamic rationality and rationalism, Western rationalism included. This will provide us with a clearer picture of the concept of Islamic rationality. Some of the major characteristics of Islamic rationality are interrelated with others. We would like the readers to be patient and forgive some repetitions.

1. Human reason in Western speculation is individual human reason based on the concept of liberty of man and liberalism, which in turn is closely allied with, and is based on, individualism. This rationalism is indeed individualistic reasoning as against the universal human reasoning, human collective reasoning and individuals' reason that is universally shared by all members of humanity, which is suggested by Islam.

2. Western rationalism was also accompanied by scepticism, and most probably was the outcome of it, and this has a long history. The introduction of human reason as the exclusive means of knowledge by Renaissance rationalism and the inability of this means to answer all questions helped the promotion of scepticism too. 'Renaissance scepticism not only affected later European thought, but it helped create a conception of man whose streak of doubt was not about his power to dominate the order of nature, but to know ultimate principles and all that had defined man throughout human history.'[7] This scepticism caused scepticism in the field of human intellection, sacred knowledge and revelation and even scepticism in the ability of reason itself and thus resorting to senses and experience as the only cognitive means (empiricism).

3. Closely related to Renaissance rationalism and scepticism is neo-naturalism, which introduced man as a powerful physical being with only physical properties, nature, needs, pain and pleasure. This naturalism is involved more in the rediscovery of physical pleasure than in the spiritual and moral/ethical significance of the body of nature.[8] This introduces Western rationality as a physical, materialistic property of man. This physical reason is not capable of spiritual, ethical and metaphysical activities.

4. The humanistic Renaissance and rationalism also tended to associate freedom with human reason. A case in point is *De Libra Arbitrus* of Lorenzo Valla, where freedom (inclusive freedom, freedom from religious, ethical and moral obligations) is judged from the point of view of human reason and not religious and spiritual principles. Valla, in fact, insists that reason is 'the best author', not to be contradicted or supported by any other authority whatsoever.[9] Introducing human reason as the only judge and introducing freedom as an inclusive concept contradict the Islamic concept of both reason and freedom. This concept of reason thus excludes what the

Muslim philosophers called ethical reason and was termed as practical philosophy (*falasafeh-e ʿamali*).

5. Renaissance rationalism and belief in the freedom of man not only led to the contrast between faith and reason, it also led to the contrast between becoming and being, between acting and being. The traditional doctrine of man's action depending on his mode of being was reversed and changed to the claim that 'the being of man follows from his doing', thus placing microcosm against macrocosm. Accordingly, man's freedom in fact is issued from the contradictions of his being. From the fact that he does not possess a ready-made nature, a protean one, man must acquire his being without consciousness. This is a complete denial of man's primordial nature and consequently of his reason as an essential part of his primordial nature. The Renaissance rationalist man claimed his full independence from religion, revelation and primordial nature.

6. Western rationalism does not simply mean the use of reason but the exclusive use of reason by individuals, independent both of intellection and revelation. Individual human reason means the reason of man without its relation and connection with metaphysical sources. Islam does not support this concept of rationalism. During the Enlightenment, philosophers such as Descartes, Spinoza and Leibniz taught that reason alone, and not religious faith and knowledge, was sufficient for knowing the nature of existence in the world. In intellectual circles, the Muʿtazilah for instance, would have agreed with some of the principles of Enlightenment rationalism, but not with all it suggested and produced. Even in the West some philosophers had some reservation about the wholesale authority of Western rationalism. The French philosopher Montesquieu, for example, characterized the rational, but still remarkably theological, character of the universe.[10]

7. Modern Western rationalism originated in the seventeenth century where the fathers of Eurocentric Western sciences devised a unique methodology for their sciences. The so-called scientific method introduced other means of knowledge, such as reason, revelation and primordial nature as unscientific. This methodology radically differs from those of non-Western, non-Christian civilizations and cultures. By design, it is exclusively based on the mechanization of nature, on mathematical reconstruction of natural phenomena. And it rests on purging the natural world of its unseen sympathies and spiritualities. It is based strictly on dualism and on the concept of reason as against revelation and intuition, on abstracting the

mind from the body, and the mind from spirit and object from the subject. This Eurocentric mechanistic methodology became identified with reason itself and with the absolute truth. It also became the only lens through which everything including nature could be seen and studied, with all other modes of understanding the truth and thinking disqualified as irrational. This Eurocentric rationalism constitutes an exclusive belief-system that is not compatible with any religion and certainly not with Islam.

8. Enlightenment rationalism is an antidote to Christianity. Islamic rationality, on the contrary, is a product of Islam and has a longer history. Rationality or the use of reason in Islam tends to be associated in the minds of occidental scholars with the study of Greek philosophy in the Islamic world and its partial acceptance by theologians. It is interesting to notice that the orientalists, in dealing with the history of Islamic rationality, tend to transpose the Western, European and Christian approach and experience onto the history of rationality in Islam. For example, H. A. R. Gibb makes the following judgement. If the priests and popes were anti-rationalists and firmly opposed to human reason, then the same case must have prevailed for the scholars of Islam. If the Catholic Church, in their estimation, stifled human thought, restricted human endeavour, and allowed for concessions and favours, then the same must hold true of Islam.

   This is a false impression and is a judgement based on wrong premises. In order to present a complete picture it is necessary to look briefly at the history and development of Islamic rationality and the use of rational methods in all fields of Islamic studies especially in early Islamic theology and jurisprudence.[11] Islamic rationality acquired its legitimacy and foundation from its own original Islamic sources. The history of Islamic rationality goes back to the revelation of the Qur'an, to the life history of the prophet, to the early theological speculations and to the use of *ra'y* (reason)and *ijtihad* (reasoning) in the early history of Islamic law and jurisprudence. The proponents of the use of reasoning in Islamic studies established rational schools, such as the Mu'tazilites, the school of *Ahl/Ashab al-ra'y* against opponents who were called *Ahl/Ashab al-hadith* or *Sunnah* in the early history of Islamic speculation, and Islamic theology and law. Islamic rationality took its primary shape before Muslims came into contact with Hellenistic teachings. This point will be explained later. In the West, even up to the fifteenth century, faith and reason, and philosophy/science and religion, were regarded as antagonistic to each other. Hence the teachings of Aristotelianism and Averroism were banned at the beginning, but were later used, which ended up in producing anti-religious Enlightenment rationalism. Muslim scholars and intellectuals took up the task of developing Islamic rationality and establishing harmony between religion/faith and reason very early. It was later on that the Muslims made use of the thoughts of Plato, Aristotle, Plotinus and other Greek philosophers. By doing this they developed Islamic rationality, philosophically and contributed to the development of rationalism in the West and made it possible for European Christianity to entertain the idea of the harmony of religion and reason, which Western secular rationalism had put an end to.

9. As a consequence of Western rationalism, man emerged as the only measure of all things and hence the rise of anthropomorphism, which introduced man as the sole criterion of everything, including knowledge and even man's perception of God and divinity. In fact man replaced God and introduced himself as God. As a reaction against this extremism another kind of extremism concerning the position of man emerged. All types of reductionism gained ground; reducing man to simply an element in human collectivity and society, according to Hegel and Marx. Man was reduced to an accident in the process of evolution, according to Darwinism, or even reduced to a purely sensual animal according to Freud. Western rationalism and humanism is grounded in anthropocentrism, which is drastically different from the theocentric rationality suggested by Islam. In Islam man is God's vicegerent (*khalifat Allah*), who is endowed and blessed with reason and primordial nature to fulfil a divine duty and respond to his divine responsibility.

10. Human intellect and reason has been introduced in Islamic tradition as an inner divine guide and as the internal messenger of Allah, as the Prophet has been introduced as an outer reason and intellect. An Islamic tradition states that God has provided man with two means of guidance: the external and the internal. The first one is in the form of Prophets and Messengers of God, divinely appointed means of guidance. The implicit, internal means of guidance is human reason and intellect.'*Inna lil al-Allahi hujjatain, Hujjaton zahirah wa hujjaton batinah. fa amm al-zahirah fa al-rusul wa al-anbiya', wa am al-batinah fa al-'uqul.*'

    '*Aql* was defined in a famous utterance attributed to the prophet Muhammad (puh) as 'a light in the heart that distinguishes between truth and falsehood', '*nurun fi al-qalb yufariqu bain al-haqque wa al-batil*'. In another famous utterance, attributed to Muhammad al-Baqir and Ja'far al-Sadiq, '*aql* has been defined and introduced to their disciples as follows:

> Know *'aql* and his troops, and know *jahl* [ignorance] and his troops! Thus shall you be rightly guided. Truly, God created *'aql* and it is the first spiritual-immaterial creature. He created it on the right side of His Throne from His own light. Then He (tested it) ordered it, 'Go back!' And it obeyed and withdrew. Next He said to it 'Come forward!' and it did accordingly and drew near ... Upon this God addressed it and He said 'I swear by my glory, majesty and dignity that I have created you in all your glory and bestowed upon you the honour and preference over all my creatures and I have not created anything dearer to me than you and I have not perfected you except in those I love. I address my commands and prohibitions to you. I reward (by) you and I punish (by) you. I have created you in all your glory and bestowed upon you the honour and preference over all of my creatures.[12]

11. Islamic rationality and Muslim rationalists do not necessarily stand against traditionalism and traditionalists. The conflict that exists between rationalism and traditionalism and between reason and revelation (*'aql* and *wahy*) in the contemporary West does not really apply to Islamic world. The two trends are not mutually exclusive in Islamic society. For example, modern Islamic thought, in the writing of scholars like Muhammad 'Abduh has incorporated elements of both reason and traditionalism. The conflict between the Mu'tazilah and the Ash'arites is not a direct conflict between rationalism and traditionalism in the Western conception of the two terms. We shall return to this point later on. The doctrine of the unity of truth in Islam establishes harmony between the two.

Islamic rationality has gone through phases both at the level of the general public and at the level of intellectual and scholarly speculation. While at the level of the masses it has faced difficulties, sometime drastic, it has continued its progress though with different degrees of development. The Ash'arite, the Hanbalite, the Wahhabis and lately the Salafi movements left some impact on it and hindered its progress at the level of masses. However, the Islamic rational movement was a great revolutionary one within Islam – not outside it or against it. It is mainly for this reason that Islamic rationality has never stopped its progress throughout its history. Because it was in harmony with both Shi'ah and Sunni doctrines and thus comprised both Shi'ah and Sunni alike it enjoyed contributions from both camps in its progress. Opposition to Islamic rationality usually came from conservative elements which, appealed to the masses, such as Ibn Hanbal, a literalist, traditionalist (*muhaddith*) and not regarded even as a jurist. He manipulated the simple masses into a campaign against intellectual inquiry and Islamic rationality. Literalist, traditionalist people like him usually enjoyed widespread sympathy at the level of the masses. The competition between the Muslim rationalists and the traditionalists did not necessarily mean that each group rejected all the doctrines of the other group. The competition was in the field of approach, methodology and epistemology. Muslim rationalists did challenge each other too, as far as conclusions and doctrines were concerned. In fact many conclusions made by Muslim rationalists in the past are not credible any longer, but their rational approach is still appreciable. It is in the light of this point that one may cite Ghazzali, for example, as a scholar who employed an intellectual and rational approach and method, though his conclusions seem to be of Orthodox and conservative nature.

12. As has been pointed out, the doctrine of *tawhid* in Islam is of crucial importance and is a multi-dimensional doctrine. It is an epistemological doctrine as it is a theological one, for example. This leads to the doctrine of the unity of truth and the unity of knowledge. Reason may certainly have its illusions and aberrations as well as its uncertainties. Its capacity for criticism gives it a fair degree of protection; but wherever ultimate truth or reality is concerned, its human predicament leaves it in need of corroboration by the infallible source of revelation. Once the questions of first or ultimate principles are settled, then reason acquires new vigour with which it can overcome the problems confronting it. Its basic presuppositions and premises must all be certain. Some are so by self-evidence; others are the common experience of humanity at large. There are others, however, which are capable of an ought-necessity only; i.e., they are capable of being perceived as true only by those who have the requisite degree of wisdom, or maturity of religious or ethical vision and are on that account expected to see the reality as it is. Hence, recognition of such truths and values may not be mathematically universal, but it enjoys a different kind of necessity, an ought-to-be-necessity. Where reason does not enjoy certainty, the light of faith can provide this certainty and in fact cast illuminating light on all other presuppositions, and support with additional certainty the whole worldview built upon them. This light of faith is definitely epistemological, and comes as a consequence of reasonableness, not its opposite. Between it and the logical certain presuppositions of reason, there is affinity, harmony, correspondence and complementarity. This is the case at least in Islam. Unlike other religions, which are dogmatic through and through, in Islam faith is never irrational in its role and contribution. It does not stand beyond reason. The perception of reason and faith as diametrical opposites, and of man having

to choose between them is not Islamic, but rather the antithesis of the Islamic position.

As far as the theory of knowledge is concerned, the position of Islam may be best described as the unity of truth. This unity devolves from Allah's absolute unity, and is convertible with it. *Al-haqque* (the truth) is the name of God. If God is indeed God, as Islam affirms, the truth cannot be many. God knows the truth and, in His revelation, He tells it as it is. What he conveys in the revelation cannot be different from reality, since He is the creator of all realities as well as of truth. The truth, which is the object of reason, is embodied in the laws of nature. These are the pattern of God in creation. His *sunnah,* or divine orders, which are constant and unchangeable, and hence are possible to discover, are for the benefit of humanity. Besides proclaiming God's existence and creation, revelation instructs about the world, giving the very same laws of nature or divine patterns in accordance with which the universe runs. Obviously, there can be no truer disclosure or rendering of these laws or patterns than by their Maker and Author. Theoretically, therefore, there can be no discrepancy. This logical equivalence of reason, truth and reality with the facts of revelation is the most critical principle epistemology has ever known. This equivalence is based on three principles underlying all Islamic knowledge.

First, the unity of truth prescribes that no claim on behalf of revelation may be made which goes counter to reality. The propositions which revelation is supposed to teach must be true, i.e. they must correspond to reality and agree with it. It is inconceivable that God may be ignorant or that He may seek to cheat or misguide His creatures. His statements, therefore, given expressly to guide and instruct, cannot oppose reality. Wherever such variation from reality occurs, the Muslim is rightly cautioned by the doctrine of the unity of truth to reconsider his understanding of revelation. The doctrine guards him against over-hasty interpretation, exaggerated allegorical interpretation and exegesis, or reading into the material of any esoteric meaning (BA TIN) which is arbitrarily assumed on someone's personal authority.

Second, the unity of truth prescribes that no contradiction, difference or variation between reason and revelation is ultimate. It categorically denies that there is no over-arching principle, fact or understanding which can solve the contradiction. In one's investigation of nature and attempt to discover the pattern of the laws of Creator in the universe, it is certainly possible to make mistakes, to fall under illusion and to think one has grasped the truth while being in error. This would create discrepancy between revelation and reason. The unity of truth rejects such discrepancy as illusory and demands the inquirer to reconsider, and reinvestigate the data. The cause of discrepancy may well be in the findings of science or reason, in which case it would be salutary to send the investigator back to the data for re-examination. And it may be in his understanding of revelation, in which case it would be equally salutary to send him back to the data for review.

Thirdly the unity of truth, or laws of nature with the pattern of the Creator, prescribes that no inquiry into the nature of creation or any part of it may be closed or concluded. The patterns of God in creation are infinite. No matter how much or how deeply we may come to know of them there will always be more of them to discover. Hence, openness to new evidence and persistence of the quest are necessary characteristics of Islamic mind, which accepts the unity of truth. A critical attitude to all human claims and an active search for the laws of nature which is never ultimately conclusive, are at once necessary conditions of Islamic and of genuine science. Under this view, the strongest conclusion is always tentative, valid only until new evidence has questioned, refuted or verified it.[13] Muslim philosophers and theologians did not find any conflict between reason and revelation.

The following case may illustrate what has been suggested. The Ash'arites appealed to human reason to challenge the Mu'tazilah, and Ghazzali also resorted to human reason to challenge philosophers in *Tahafut al-Falasafah,* just as Ibn Rushd did in *Tahafut al-Tahafut*. The reader must therefore realize that both Islamic rationality and Islamic traditionality do not correspond exactly with the same terms in Western contexts and literature. It is thus important to understand that neither the so-called Muslim traditionalists deny that humans are created by God with intelligence, or that humans are expected to exercise their rational faculties, nor do the rationalists deny the authority of revelation and Islamic textual sources. The reason/revelation dilemma does not seem to have a solid ground in Islamic thought, although this dilemma has a long history in human thought. It probably goes back to Greek philosophy.[14] It is the product of Western enlightenment of the last three centuries.

13. The intellectual argument amongst the Muslim intellectuals has been misunderstood by occidentalists. It is important to be clear that the traditionalists, *Ahl al-Hadith*, Ash'arites, Sunnis and other similar schools and groups do not deny that humans were created by God with intelligence and reason. They do not deny that humans are expected to exercise their rational faculties and potentials. Nor do Muslim rationalists, *falasafah*, (plural of *faylsuf*), *Ahl al-Ra'y*, Mu'tazilites, Shi'ah and other schools and groups with similar affiliation deny the authority of revelation, Qur'an and

sunnah. (The Mu'tazilah preferred to call themselves *ahl al-'adl wa al-tawhid*, the people of justice and unity, justice and unity of Allah.) The main issue in question between the two major schools and groups has been the question of priority, the starting point, and the preference. Alfred Guillaume explains this point as follows:

> It must not be supposed that the representatives of these two opposing schools of thought were always divided into two sharply-divided camps. Distinct as their methods were in principle, there were many of the most influential men in the world of Muslim jurisprudence (Muslim world) who sought to confirm the findings of *Ra'y*, (reason) for example, by the traditions of the orthodox, as did al-Shaibani. Moreover, on the other hand, *al-Muwatta'* the law book emanating from the 'home of the *Sunnah*, where *hadith* fails, the author appeals to *Ra'y*.[15]

This does not mean that the two opposing schools did not differ. They did on many issues. For example, the traditionalists/Ash'arites differed sharply with the Mu'tazilites on whether the rules of law (*shari'ah*), which God revealed through His messenger Muhammad, are good because God had revealed it, or whether God had revealed it because they were inherently good. The Asha'irah supported the first view and the Mu'tazilah the second. The Mu'tazilah should not be regarded as 'free-thinkers' in the Western interpretation of this term. In fact, some of the anti-Mu'tazilahs were accused of atheism (*ilhad*). The following short story may explain this point. A great proponent of Mu'tazilah known as al-Jahiz (d. 868) composed a treatise, now lost, titled *Fadilat al-Mu'tazilah* (*The Excellence of the Mu'tazilah*). This work was refuted by a freethinking critic of the Mu'tazilah, Ibn al-Rawandi, (d. 910) in a work, also now lost, titled *Fadihat al-Mu'tazilah* (*The Ignominy of the Mu'tazilah*) in which he refuted the Mu'tazili doctrines. Indeed, Ibn Rawandi, and others like him, was accused of atheism for his attacks on the Qur'an and prophets and Islamic principles. Likewise, the Asha'irah should not be branded as anti-rationality.

It is also important to point out that each of the two major schools and groups gained strength and domination at a certain juncture of the history of Islamic thought in a certain area at the expense of the other school and group. But neither of the two trends of thought and affiliation have ever disappeared or died down completely. Indeed something of both the Mu'tazili and the Ash'ari spirit has survived almost side by side throughout the history of Islamic intellectual activities, for example, something of the Mu'tazili spirit may be observed in modern Islam from Morocco to Indonesia. Some historians of Islamic thought refer to this movement as

'Neo-Mu'tazilism'.[16] The same can be said about the Ash'ari spirit during the Mu'tazili domination.

It must also be pointed out that neither the Ash'ari school of thought fully represent the Sunni school of law (*madhhab,*) nor the Mu'tazili school of thought (*maktab*) fully represent the Shi'ah school of law (*madhhab*). Each school of thought may correspond to some extent or even a great extent to a large section of the respective sect. But neither of them fully corresponds with nor represents the other. The Ash'ari approach, for example, has always had some following amongst the Shi'ah. 'Abd al-Jabbar, the staunch supporter of Mu'tazilism in the middle history of Islamic thought is very much anti-Shi'ah. He even referred to the Shi'ah by the derogatory nickname 'turncoats' *rafiïah* (see *Kitab al-Usul al-Khamsah*). While the majority of Basrah-centered Mu'tazilah held closer to the Sunni political theory, the majority of the Baghdad Mu'tazilah learned Shi'ah doctrines. The Shi'ah also strongly reject that their doctrines fully and always correspond with those of the Mu'tazilah. The same is also true about the relationship between the Mu'tazilah school of thought and the Sunni schools of law. The contemporary Neo-Mu'tazili movement amongst the majority Sunni section of the Muslim community from Morocco to Indonesia explains this point.

What is of special interest here, and must be emphasized, is that both Mu'tazilism and Ash'arism had something in common. They both introduced themselves as *maktab, nihlah* and not as *madhhab* (school of theology and of law and not as sect). They both intended to serve Islam, though with different approaches. It is for this reason that we must interpret Islamic rationality and traditionality in the light of time, space, circumstance, and especially in the light of the commitment of the followers of all schools to serve Islam. This point is fairly true about the contemporary Mu'tazilism of people like M. 'Abduh, the Neo-Mu'tazilism of people like Harun Nasution and also of contemporary Ash'arism and traditionalism, of many versions, in different parts of the Muslim community. The Mu'tazili–Ash'ari or the rationalist and traditionalist trends are not mutually exclusive and they both continue to attract Muslims of different persuasions. Modern Islamic thought, in the writings of scholars like M. 'Abduh has incorporated elements of both rationality and traditionality. The Mu'tazilah were men of faith and religion as the Asha'irah were. As Muslim rationalists, they held that reason could demonstrate the existence of God and the general ethical responsibility that is incumbent upon human beings in society. They also held that the revelation is a divinely provided blessing and advantage above and beyond the human rational faculty, which can by itself lead to the knowledge that God exists.

The greatest challenge to the Mu'tazilah came not from the Asha'irah but rather from Hanabilah/traditionalists who were challenging not only the Mu'tazilah but also other Sunni schools of law such as Hanafis, Shafi'is and Malikis. A great variety of schools of law, theology and other religious disciplines formed the orthodox centre of Islam. But although the Sunni formation and control of Islamicate society was orthodox, it was not monolithic or undifferentiated. The Islamic term that was generally applied to this cluster of traditional Muslim groups within Islamicate society during the first few centuries was *Ahl al-Sunnat wa al-Jama'ah*, the People of *Sunnah* and Community, from which the term Sunni is derived. (probably this was a name adopted to distinguish them from the Mu'tazilah who preferred to call themselves *Ahl al-'adl wa al-tawhid*, the people of justice and unity (justice and unity of Allah). Both traditionalist and rationalist religious leaders belonged to this broad and dynamic Sunni majority, though some Mu'tazilah leaned towards Shi'ah political theology. But both groups functioned as its critics, albeit from different points of view. Even for the traditionalists the independent reasoning (*ijtihad*) of a faithful Sunni Muslim of a sound mind, in interpreting the *shari'ah* was more authoritative than blind acceptance (*taqlid*). For rationalists speculative reason was a tool for bringing rational human beings to Islamic faith, from which they could discover the benefits of accepting God's revealed religious duties. We can thus see how both the traditionalists and the rationalists could meet on a common ground and work towards the same goal. What is intended here is to point out that there has always existed in Islam an approach and a way to legitimize the use of reason and to establish a harmony between reason and revelation, and secondly, that this approach has always managed, in one way or another, to be a rational – revelational and interpretative – approach.

The use of *ijtihad,* which is a combination of both reason and revelation, was approved and even encouraged by the Prophet (pbh). This is confirmed in a tradition concerning one of his companions who was being sent as his emissary, Mu'adh ibn Jabal. *Ijtihad* as an independent strenuous juristic effort to discover or make the right and correct legal decisions was practised by 'Umar, the second Caliph in many occasions. For example, Caliph 'Umar decided to waive the severe punishment in the case of theft due to hunger, because he thought that this would serve better the Islamic and Qur'anic ultimate concern, justice, than following the letter of the Qur'an's ruling. 'Umar's juristic reasoning (*ijtihad*) in this case constituted a precedent, so that thenceforth the punishment (*hudud*) would be waived for theft in periods of famine. It is suggested that 'Umar was inspired in his *ijtihad* in this case by a tradition quoted from the Prophet (pbh). It is reported that the prophet said that the punishments (*hudud)* are waived in cases of uncertainty (*al-hodudo todra'o be al-shobahat*). The heads of the three major Sunni schools of law used *ijtihad* in one way or another with different degree of frequency. Abu Hanifah used it systematically in the form of *ra'y*. Shafi'i used it with reservation and with careful consideration. Malik practised it in the form of juristic principles of *istihsan* and *istilah* (juristic preference and common good). *Ijtihad* was being exercised on a regular basis until the four major schools of law were established. Then for some reasons, mainly to avoid fractions and pressure by the ruling authorities to justify their political power in term of Islamic law, *ijtihad* was abandoned, (the gate of *ijtihad* was closed). This continued until the new reform movement took shape. This movement is really a movement for re-opening the gate of *ijtiha*d.

In Islam, the defence of rationality should be regarded as the projection of Islamic potentials and ability to face, challenge and solve contemporary and future problems of human community. The defence of reason and rationality has never been regarded as the defeat of divinity and revelation. It is, however, very tempting to suggest that Islamic fundamentalism and even traditionalism belong, to a great extent, to a larger discourse of which theological modernism, including Neo-Mu'tazilism is an important part.[17]

14. Intellect and reason along with primordial nature are two key faculties upon which knowledge is based, and are the key terms in the present discourse. These two terms have different meanings in Islamic studies from their meanings in modern Western languages. The main difference between the Islamic term *hikmah* and *'aql* and the Western term intellect is that in modern Western languages, intellect is used as synonymous with and equivalent to reason. The distinction between the two is usually forgotten. Although in Islamic languages and literature a single term, *'aql*, is usually used to denote both reason and intellect, yet the distinction between the two, as well as their interrelation, is clear and has been noticed. The term intellect and reason are both derived from Latin roots *intellectus* and *rationem*. Intellect in contemporary English and French is understood as the human manual faculties or intellectual powers of the mind by which one knows and reasons – excluding sensation and distinguished from *feeling* and *will*. Intelligence (Latin *intelligentia)* now connotes possessing the faculty of understanding, knowledge, and cognisance, as well as sensible, sagacious, having a full measure of understanding. Reason (Latin *ratio*) connotes the act of reasoning or argumentation, sanity, the guiding principle of human

mind in the process of thinking. Both the Latin *intellectus* and *intelligentia* are translation from the Greek *nous* or mind, understanding. They all carry Greek philosophical, Latin cultural and Christian religious connotations and implications.

There are quite a few terms in Islamic literature, which are used to explain human rational, intellectual and intelligent activities. They include terms such as *'aql, lubb, fikr, ra'y, fiqh, fain, hikmah, tadabbur,* and many more. The root of the term *al-'aql* is a/q/l, which means basically, 'to bind'. It is that faculty which binds man to God (the source of knowledge), and at the same time binds him to moral and ethical principles and restrains him from wrong doing. It thus has a double functions and properties: cognitive, means of knowledge and, normative, guidelines for ethical behaviour. *'Aql,* however, is also used to denote reason, intelligence, common sense, foresight, contemplation, investigation, meditation, ratiocination and other concepts of related order. There is thus a harmony between intellect and primordial nature, or *al-'aql wa al-fitrah.* Islam has never seen a dichotomy between these two and has never set one against the other either. There is a marriage between the two and thus also a marriage between intellect and revelation, because revelation in Islam is associated with *fitrah* and with *'aql,* as was explained in the chapter dealing with *fitrah.* In the light of revelation, the intellect functions, not merely as reason, but as intellectual intuition, and thus intellect and intuition become the same and the conflict between knowledge and ethics is also solved. This is because they both derive their justification and authority from the same source but not necessarily by the same means. Even a so-called 'rationalist' school of Islam such as the Peripatetic (Mashsha'i) suggests that one of the means of acquiring both knowledge and salvation is intellectual intuition. Still even this school is not a 'rationalistic' one, as this term is usually understood in Western philosophy.

15. The question of harmony of reason, human primordial nature and intuition is another interesting point in Islam. This can be observed in almost all fields of Islamic studies. The question of rationality in a religious legal system is closely associated with theology, faith and beliefs. We cannot enter into this field here. They are in the premises of philosophy of religion in general and in the case of Islam in the premises of *kalam.* Muslim theologians and philosophers have tried to formulate a kind of rationality that does not contradict other means and forms of appreciating the truth, especially *fitrah.* They have questioned the constitution of knowledge and whether it is relative and conditioned by our faculties or not. (They have even questioned the concept of causality, see Ghazzali, *Tahafut al-Falasafah*).

They also questioned the means of obtaining reliable knowledge etc. Nevertheless, on the whole they agree that absolute truth does exist (at least God) and that man is able to discover and appreciate it by a variety of means. They believe that in the field of theology, law and ethics Islam strongly rejects relativism, mainly because of the absolute properties of *fitrah*, reason and revelation. They suggest that reason, intuition and revelation can support each other in recognizing and appreciating the truth, and that there is not a conflict of authority between reason and intuition, instinct, primordial nature on one side and between them and revelation on the other. They suggest that criticisms of reason and intuition are themselves based on rational arguments. Reason itself involves reasoning and intuition for Muslim theologians and philosophers and includes deductive and inductive methods, the premises of which are intuition. Intuition is the basic component of reason itself. In fact all reasoning processes use intuition in recognizing the truth of their premises. The Muslims, especially jurists and judges use two other types of reasoning, which in some form may be regarded as inductive. These are argument by cumulative reasoning/circumstantial evidence (*amarat*) and argument by converging probabilities. The cumulative reasoning is a combination and collection of proofs and evidences, which collectively produce a solid conclusion. Argument by converging probabilities is the combination of proofs and evidences of different nature but leading to a single conclusion.

The harmony and balance between intellect and intuition is perfected by the founder of the last school of philosophy in Islam, Mulla Sadra of Shiraz (1571/2–1642 AD). It should also be pointed out that heart has also been introduced as the instrument and means of true knowledge thus heart has been introduced as the seat of primordial nature and the seat of intuition.[18]

Islam supports knowledge and morality based on a universal rationality and *fitrah* particularly in the field of knowledge (not sciences) which is beyond cultural relativity. Modern sciences are beyond culture and morality. This can be the case with knowledge as such. We can understand that science is consensual and that scientific knowledge is beyond culture and morality and that it is even and also against them. This may lead one to the idea of the relativity of truth and morality. But one must also understand that the philosophy of science itself is not relative. The relativity of certain cultural values does not necessarily challenge the idea of the absolute character and universality of the actual moral values and truth. However, one can also understand that the authority of knowledge based on certainty can also be a matter of consensus and universality.[19] Islam, thus, proposes major means of acquiring truth and knowledge of the truth, such as revelation, intellect, intuition, primordial nature, experience and sensual means.[20]

Fitrah, like *'aql* covers a large area. It is used as intuition in the field of presential knowledge *(al-'ilm al-huduri)*, in opposition to acquired and attained knowledge *(al-'ilm al-husuli)*, which is attained by means of *ta'aqqul* or intelligence and reason. *Fitrah* has also been used as conscience, in the field of personal moral judgement, as human primordial nature, in a vast area covering all fields. It has been used as intellection, in the field of spiritual aspiration, and even as reason and intelligence, in the field of natural rational potential. There is not, therefore, any contradiction between *fitrah* and *'aql* provided they are both used for the same end and without prejudice. In a world in which intelligence and reason have become synonymous with a purely biological quality concerned only with material gains, worldly success and purely scientific development and in a world where there is no place and room for moral, ethical, spiritual values and principles, and in a world in which intuition is concerned with foretelling, and clairvoyance, obviously there is a conflict between intellect, human primordial nature and intuition (*'aql, fitrah* and *mukashafah*). Islam does not recognize this conflict and difference and thus establishes harmony and balance between sound common sense, *'aql*, and sound universal human conscience, *fitrah*.

We know that a materially clever man is not necessarily a man practising the dictates of his conscience, and likewise a materially and even scientifically clever and successful society is not necessarily a society of conscience and moral standards. But this is because man is a creature of choice and has the ability to interfere with both his rational potentials, his intuitional/conscience principles and with his primordial nature.[21]

16. The importance of reason/rationality and human primordial nature in dealing with the question of human rights and natural law is clear. If reason and conscience were banned we would have no way of discriminating between true and false, between sense and nonsense, between right and wrong, between valid belief and wanton credulity, and between the proper implication of belief and improper ones. The group of people who regard reason as an evil, which seeks to infiltrate into the healthy body of faith in order to destroy it, and the other group which is prepared to base its belief system entirely only on the shaky foundation of feelings, rather than reason, both are doing injustice to God, to man, his faith and to humanity in general. Admittedly human reasoning is sometimes subject to temptation, prejudice, mistakes, misunderstanding, distortion etc. Nevertheless, in spite of its defects, reason is one of the reliable tools which

human beings have for arriving at responsible decisions and conclusions. Certainly more reliable than some other tools. Even Kant's critical examination of reason is done by means of reason. And even Hume's alternative to reason, empiricism, is explained and justified by him in term of reason and by means of reason.[22]

All these criticisms and alternatives to reason are presented rationally and by means of reasoning. This is because they are held to be the results of rational reflection that they are presented as being justified. Consequently, as Ewing points out, the so-called 'revolt against reason' is not logically coherent if it is regarded as a rational revolt against reason as such and not merely as a suspicion as to whether people who pretend to be reasonable are so.[23] In fact the justification of the reliability of reason depends upon the self-critical role of reason, which continuously subjects its methods and its conclusions to critical examination. Consequently, in spite of the qualifications which have emerged since the time of Locke from the study of the use of reason, it is still the case, as Whitehead puts it, that ultimately nothing rests on authority; the final court of appeal is intrinsic reasonableness.[24]

17. There are three major levels of perception: sensory perception, rational perception and spiritual perception. Islamic epistemology recognizes all levels of perception in man in contrast to Western psychology, which recognizes only sensory and intellectual perceptions. The objectives of each of these levels of perceptions are associated with certain levels of knowledge and reality. Through the senses we acquire knowledge of the physical environment. Through the mind we acquire analytical and synthetic knowledge, knowledge through reasoning alone, which includes knowledge of metaphysical and abstract phenomena, e.g. the concept of God. The 'heart knowledge' or the knowledge of the intellect (*hikmah*) involves the experience of spiritual realities. All these levels of knowledge are true and real. The basis of Islamic epistemology concerning Islamic practices is revelation. But man's senses, reason, intellect primordial nature and intuition play a great and crucial role in many fields of Islamic studies such as theology etc. Besides, man's reason helps him to understand, interpret and explain even revelation.[25]

Intellect, as the faculty of spiritual perception, however, transcends the limitations of discursive reasoning when it is guided by experience based on divine revelation. The intellect inherently has a greater affinity to divine revelation than reason and so the latter is necessarily subject to the intellect. Man's nature (*fitrah*) and his relationship with Allah, as *khalifah* (vicegerent of Allah) and as His *'abd* (His obedient subject), cannot be fully understood without an understanding of the meanings and implications of reason. With the help of sensory, rational, spiritual perceptions and with the use of 'heart' (*qalb),* reason (*'aql*) and intellection man is capable of the highest level of consciousness. There is a point of importance with regard to the relation between *'aql* and *qalb* in Islam. *Qalb* or heart is a perfected rational soul. In the modern Western view, rationality and heart are seen as being at odds with one another. In the Western literature, the heart symbolizes the emotional side of man and the head stands for the calculative, rational dimension. This dichotomy is completely alien to the Islamic spiritual tradition, in which the heart is identified with the rational, and rationality is understood as transcending the merely calculative. According to this tradition it is not the soul that contains the heart and intellect, but rather the soul and reason in proper harmony give rise to the heart. This is mainly because, according to Islamic tradition, virtue is knowledge based and Islam derives its appeal from universally available rationality and intellection. A clear distinction should be made between reason and intellect. Reason is limited to the function of analysis and logic. Intellect (*'aql*) transcends this limitation. It is capable of knowing the principles of things.

18. Western rationalism introduces reason, mind and rational perception in contrast to both sensory and intellectual perception. But Islamic rationality supports the belief that there is a harmony between all levels and means of perception. Islam thus suggests that: man is capable of perception from the lowest sensory to the highest spiritual level; truth does have an independent existence of its own; moral values are not subject to man's whims; man is capable of knowing the truth and recognizing moral values; man does have *fitrah*; man's reason, mind and intellect work in harmony with his *fitrah*; and the most important property of human intellectual faculties is the ability to recognize the truth and its attributes and properties.

19. We have been experiencing difficulties in making a clear distinction in English literature between the concept of reason as a logical and deductive approach (*tafakkur*) and intellection as a transcendental, inductive inspirational, intuitional and spiritual process (*al-'aql al-'ali, ta'aqqul, tadabbur*). Islamic philosophical literatures make a clear difference between philosophy (*falasafah*) and intellection (*hikmah*) and between reason and intellection.

The questions regarding the ambiguity of the authority of intellect, reason and alternatives to it, in Western literature, is mainly because, as G.J. Warnock points out, there is 'no universally agreed or uniquely correct sense of reason'.[26] There is no precise definition of the nature of reason. It has been even suggested that reason involves two components, which we may call 'reasoning and intuition'. Quite a few methods such as logic, syllogism, induction, inference, cumulative reasoning and arguments by converging probabilities are proposed to deal with the first of these two, reasoning. As far as the second component of reasoning, intuition, is concerned we would like to point out that the view that intuition is a respectable part of reason might be surprising to some people. In *Reason and Intuition*, however, Alfred Ewing points out that what he calls 'intuition' is an essential component of all forms of rational reflections and arguments. It is that immediate insight which is employed in all reasoning processes. It is by intuition that first we recognize what are valid premises and significant evidence, secondly we perceive the validity of the connections between the different stages in an argument, and that thirdly we judge the strength of the conclusion reached by an argument. All reasoning processes use intuition, in one way or another, in recognizing the truth of their premises, the significance of their evidence, the validity of their logical steps, and the strength of their conclusions. As Ewing puts it, reason includes 'intuition'.[27]

The difficulty we have with not being able to provide a precise definition for reason applies to intuition too. A common objection to intuition is that by its very nature it precedes argument, is therefore unjustified by argument and, in practice, provides a way in which erroneous ideas are foisted on to others. Ewing recognizes that the notion of intuition is 'liable to gross abuse' because people may persuade themselves that their prejudices represent real intuition, or use the appeal to intuition as a way of avoiding the need for a careful examination of what is to be accepted on this basis.[28] It is also unfortunately evident that, with the best will in the world, people have sincerely disagreed about intuition or have come to realize that what was once generally accepted as intuition of the truth is mistaken. Ewing responds to these difficulties by holding that intuition both need to be and can be carefully checked to see if it is justified. This testing and care will never completely eliminate the risk of error but it will significantly lessen it. Included in these tests, that is applicable to intuition, are the extensiveness (ideally the universality) of its recognition, the experience of the persons having it in the kind of material concerned, the clarity of apprehension of what is intuited, the consequences of holding it, its coherence with other things which we claim to know, and the degree of unprejudiced care with which the situation has been considered. Admittedly the results of these tests will itself be finally a judgement of our intuition but by using them we may hope to avoid being dupes of false intuition.

Here again, therefore, we find that it is the reflective, self-critical activity of reason that justifies its use.[29]

Islam, however, does not recognize any conflict between human primordial nature (*fitrah*), intuition (*kashf*), reason (*'aql*) and intellect (*al-'aql al-'ali*). They rather serve as complementary to each other. Islam has created a hierarchy of knowledge and of the methods of attaining knowledge according to which degrees of both intellect and intuition and primordial nature become harmonized in an order encompassing all the means available to man to know. Western rationalism does not simply mean the use of reason, but the exclusive use of human reason independent of both intellection, intuition and revelation and the consideration of reason as the highest and exclusive authority for the attainment of truth.[30] This is certainly not the case with Islamic rationality, which was developed to establish harmony and peace between all of them.

FIVE

Islamic Rationality

Islamic Rationality in the Early History of Islamic Thought

An Introduction to the Concept of Hikmah *and* Shari'ah

At the outset, it would be useful to explain briefly the two major terms we shall be frequently using in this section: *hikmah* and *shari'ah*. This is because it is in the field of Islamic law that the questions of the relationship between Islam and natural law, human rights in Islam and the authority of human intellect may be practically answered.

The word *hikmah*, a derivative of *h/k/m*, literally means withholding, restraining and preventing (almost the same as *'aql*), therefore *hikmat al-dabbah*, the rein used to control animals, because the rein withholds and restrains them, *hikmat al-safinah*, ship's anchor, for it prevents the ship drifting.[1] *Hukm* (pl. *ahkam*), another derivative of h/k/m, literally means to withhold, restrain and prevent. The word *hukm* is used as a technical term both in Islamic philosophy; *hikmah*, for philosophical principles, and in the legal rulings of Islamic law, *shari'ah*. *Hikmah* usually applies to wisdom, science and philosophy. *Hikmah* as a common term amongst Muslim scholars is identified with philosophy,[2] except that *hikmah* covers a wider area and includes more goals than *falsafah* (philosophy), which applies only to mainly non-Islamic and Hellenistic philosophy.[3]

As has been pointed out, the term *hikmah* is almost synonymous with Islamic philosophy. We do not therefore need to repeat here the different definitions given for it by Muslim scholars. Suffice it to quote just some of the important points explained by them concerning *hikmah*. Jurjani defines *hikmah* as 'to set the thing in its proper place'.[4] In another place he defines it as the discipline concerning knowledge, science, the science of religious law and the truth concerning divine essence.[5] Imam 'Ali (puh) gave the definition of justice as 'putting everything in its right place' (Sermon no. 429, *Nahj al-Balaghah*). This corresponds with Jurjani's definition of *hikmah* and thus establishes the relation between *hikmah* and *'adl*. (Imam 'Ali's definition of justice evokes that proffered by Plato in *The Republic*: 'we have laid down, as a universal principle, that everyone ought to perform the one function in the community for which his nature best suited him … that principle, or some form of it, is justice.')

We can therefore see the close association of Islamic philosophy and Islamic law for they are both covered by *hikmah*. Farabi believes that *hikmah* was what Greek philosophers meant when they used the word philosophy.[6] Avicenna introduces *hikmah* as the perfection of the human soul by speculation about the theories and understanding of the truth as far as possible for human beings.[7] Averroes defines it as investigating things in a logical way.[8] Ibn Taymiyyah, (eighth/fourteenth century), who was known for his strong opposition to philosophy, defines it as the knowledge of truth and acting according to the truth.[9] Al-Tirmadhi (Abu 'Abd Allah Muhammad al-Tirmadhi, b. between 205 and 215/820 and 830), dubbed al-Hakim, the Wise, applies the term *hikmah* to esoteric knowledge, in contrast to exoteric knowledge. He suggests that the source of replenishment of esoteric knowledge through *hikmah* resides in God (*Kitab al-Furuq*, p. 97). He also suggests that *'aql* or intellect is the crown prince of *ma'rifah* (gnosis or knowledge) and holds the position of judge. God has created it from the light of awe and glory. He also introduces intellect as *al-lubb* and regards it as the nucleus of the heart's core and the organ of the light of *ma'rifah*. (Termadhi, *Ghawr al-umur*).[10]

The word *shari'ah* literally means 'the road (or path) to the source of water' (water way).[11] It also means straight road, as it is used in the Qur'an.[12] It also means where people drink water, water hole.[13] In its religious or terminological usage it means 'the highway to good life or ordaining of the way'. It has been used in its terminological sense in the Qur'an only once. 'Then We put thee on the [right] way [course] of religion: so follow thou that [course]. And follow not the desires of who know not' (Qur'an, 45:18). Its derivatives have been used more often. Raghib believes that there is a close connection between the literary meaning of *shari'ah* (the path or road to water) and its terminological meaning (the way to the source of good life).[14] The term *Shar'* seems to have been used in the Qur'an to apply to specific religions:[15] and thus, *Shari'atu Musa* (Moses' *shari'ah*), *Shari'atu 'Isa* (Jesus's *shari'ah*), and of course *Shari'atu Muhammad* (Muhammad's *shari'ah*), which means Judaism, Christianity and Islam. (Muhammad's *shari'ah* means the *shari'ah* which was introduced, practised and recommended to be practised by Muhammad and not necessarily made by him; thus the term Muhammadanism for Islam is not correct). But the term *din* (religion, submission, following) has been used in the Qur'an as an equivalent of Islam, to apply to a single continuous religion rather than religions.[16] *Shari'ah* and *din* cannot be therefore taken as synonyms although they are both equally applicable to each other and to religion in the widest sense of the terms.[17] We may therefore conclude that while the Qur'an does not support the plurality of religion (there is only one religion – Islam, submission to God – which has been the real faith of mankind), it frequently refers to various *shari'ah*s. This explains that when we speak of the compatibility and harmony of *hikmah* and *shari'ah*, we mean a particular *shari'ah* or religion, Islam.[18]

The issue of the interrelation between philosophy and Islam and consequently the issue of the harmony of reason and religion in Islam is an interesting one. We do not intend here to enter into this discussion in detail. However, it is important to explain this point briefly. The history of Islamic intellectual discussions goes back to the early years of Islamic theology, the second half of the first century of Islam. Systematic intellectual, theological and philosophical speculations amongst the Muslims started very early, soon after Arabic translations of works of Greek philosophy of the second/eighth century. Quickly this interest developed into a brilliant intellectual and philosophical movement, which produced great philosophers and works of great value and originality from the third/ninth to the sixth/twelfth centuries. This movement came to fruition in the comprehensive works and system of Farabi and Ibn Sina (370–428/980–1037) generally known to the West under the Latinized name of Avicenna.

Some part of the materials from which this philosophical system was made could have been, and probably was, from foreign non-Islamic sources. But the major parts and the actual construction, the system itself, certainly have an Islamic stamp. All along its metaphysical frontiers it reckons with the corresponding religious metaphysics of Islam and consciously tries to create points not only of contradiction but also of coincidence with the latter. This was the first step towards establishing the harmony between reason and religion and *hikmah* and *shari'ah*. Working in the fields of Islamic theology and philosophy, producing works of great value in these fields, and having thus reached a stage of consciousness, where the entire philosophical metaphysic seemed to correspond point by point to theological beliefs of religion but never exactly tallied, Muslim philosophers faced a major problem about the nature of philosophy and religion and their mutual relationship. Either there was a double truth, one apprehended by philosophy, the other by religion, or truth was unitary but appeared now in a rational and again in a metaphorical, imaginative form. The first alternative, that of two truths, did not seem possible rationally and Islamically so the philosophers decided to pursue the latter line of thought. Religious truth is but rational truth, but instead of being expressed in nakedly rational formulas, manifested itself in imaginative symbols – a fact which was responsible for its widespread acceptance by, and effectiveness among, the masses. Thus religion is but philosophy for the masses.

The Islamic doctrine of unity of the only Necessary Being (Allah, *Wajib al-Wujud*) and the unity of His being and His attributes which led ultimately to the doctrine of the unity of truth (*haqq*) helped the development of the doctrine of the harmony of reason and religion and *hikmah* and *shari'ah*.[19] In a highly motivated intellectual community such as that of Islam, it was only natural that the doctrine would be, and was, challenged and criticized in one way or another by some. But even the orthodoxy had to accommodate some of its consequences.

In the course of discussing the doctrine one has to have some idea about what is meant by the components of the doctrine of harmony of *hikmah* and *shari'ah*.

Shari'ah has been used mostly by Sufis as the 'outer law' in conjunction with *al-tariqah* (road, pathway) and *al-haqiqah* (the inner truth). But as has been explained, *shari'ah* literally means *tariqah* and has been applied to *haqiqah* , because *shari'ah* is regarded as the practical truth based on spiritual principles. However Sufis seem to have used *shari'ah* to apply only to the practical side of religion. This obviously does not sound reasonable, for *shari'ah* covers three major areas:

1. spiritual–theological; creed, beliefs and doctrines;
2. moral and ethical codes, values and virtues;
3. legal and ritual matters and code of practice.[20]

It should be noted that although *shari'ah* is more limited and less general in its use than *din* it is used in a wider sense than *fiqh* (law), for *fiqh* does not cover creed and beliefs while *shari'ah* does.[21]

It is interesting to know that *shari'ah* has been defined, by almost all Muslim jurists, as the collection of rules (*al-ahkam*), dealing with human deeds, beliefs, creed and practices. *Shari'ah* can therefore be defined to include legal rulings or *ahkam*, too.

The legal term *hukm* is derived from the same root as *hikmah* (h/k/m). *Hukm* also literally means prevention and control, for the rulings of law control people and prevent them from misbehaviour. We can therefore see that the terms *hukm, ahkam* and *hikmah* (which can be taken as the equivalent of *shari'ah*) are from the same root and have the same literal meanings. We can therefore understand why there is a very close literary relationship between *hikmah* and *shari'ah* (between Islamic philosophy and Islamic law). This is because *shari'ah* is Allah's (swt) commandments, emanating from His wisdom, relating to the activities of man. The Lawgiver and the Lawmaker (*al-shari', al-hakim*,), Allah, is also *al-hakim* (wise). The whole literary analysis and definitions of the terms *hikmah, hukm, hakim* and *ahkam,* on one side, and *shari'ah*, *shar'i*, *shar'* and *shari'* on the other, explain how *hikmah* and *shari'ah* are interrelated, linked together and thus must be understood together.

It has been suggested that the question of the harmony of philosophy and religion had been discussed before Islam. It has been said that Philon of Alexandria (d. 50 BC) tried to harmonize philosophy and Judaism and tried to use a rational and philosophical approach in his commentary on the Old Testament.[22] It is stated that the Church leaders who followed the Platonic and Neoplatonic schools, like Origenes (d. 254 AD), Klementheus (d. 17 AD) and St Augustine (d. 430 AD) also adopted a philosophical and rational approach in their interpretation of Christianity. They explain Christian principles in philosophical terms and this is the approach and the ground for the Scholastic philosophy and school which reached its climax in the thirteenth century.[23] Schuon believes that Christianity had to resort to Hellenism to justify its principles. The Christians finally thought along the lines inherited from philosophy to shore up their theological speculations.[24]

But it is not known whether there had been systematic speculation about the harmonization of religion and philosophy, in general and in the same way, before Islam. Nor is it known whether pre-Islamic speculations in this field had any effect on this question in Islam or not. However, Islam treated the question afresh, established its own basis and introduced its own sources for the doctrine or at least for the question. This question in Islam, as is the case with the Islamic philosophy, took its first explanation and justification from the Qur'an and other Islamic sources. A brief review of the contents of the Qur'an explains this point.

The term *hikmah* (philosophy) has been used in the Qur'an quite a few times.[25] The teaching of *hikmah* has been made the object and aim of Prophethood in the Qur'an.[26] The adjective *hakim* (wise, sage) has been used in the Qur'an many times too and its derivatives more than a hundred times.[27] The word *hakim* has been used as one of Allah's (swt) attributes many times in the Qur'an.[28] This is the case with other sources of Islam. Encouraged by the Qur'an and other sources, Muslim scholars engaged themselves with intellectual activities very quickly. Ghazzali, along with other Muslim intellectuals believed that only Allah (swt) can be regarded as *al-hakim* (the possessor of *hikmah*) for *hikmah* is the perfect knowledge concerning the perfect being and only Allah (swt) can have perfect knowledge of the perfect being (God Himself). Some of the Prophets (put) have been introduced by the Qur'an as *hakim* for they have been given *hikmah*.[29] The Qur'an introduces itself as *al-kitab al-hakim*.[30] It is interesting to notice that while the word *hikmah* and its derivatives have been used in the Qur'an very frequently, tens of times, the term *shari'ah* has not been used in the Qur'an with the same frequency (about ten times). This is in spite of the fact that the Qur'an is basically a holy religious book and not even exclusively a book of Islamic law, theology etc., let alone a book of philosophy. But it is equally wrong to believe that the Qur'an does not contain theosophical and philosophical materials and principles. Philosophy, or *hikmah,* from the Qur'anic point of view starts with metaphysics and ends with it too. The Qur'an establishes that God is the Creator, the world therefore is created. It discusses the world and the things in it, which are physical or natural (philosophy of the world of nature) and authorizes human reason and intellect to investigate the created world and its creatures, and their Creator. Finally it asks human beings to use their intellect too in their faith. Some verses indicate that almost all the Qur'anic verses have philosophical applications.[31] When the Qur'an regards itself as *hakim* (the book of wisdom), it means all its verses have *hikmah* (wisdom).[32]

As has been mentioned, *al- hikmah* is a word that is mentioned twenty times in the Qur'an. On ten of these occasions, the word *al- hikmah* is preceded by *al-kitab* (as an adjective describing of the Qur'an). This is a very powerful indication of the importance of *hikmah* as a value and quality. Let us take a look at some human attempts to define the word 'wisdom'. We are told that 'wisdom consists in the highest use of the intellect for the discernment of the largest moral interest of humanity' (Felix Alder) begging the question of who defines the largest moral interest of humanity. Similar problems arise from other definitions. It is introduced as 'a special knowledge in excess of all that is known' (Ambrose Bierce). It is defined as 'keeping the sense of fallibility of all our views and opinions' (Gerald Brenan). It is introduced as 'the knowledge of things human and divine and of the cause by which these things are controlled' (Cicero). It is introduced as 'a collection of platitudes' (Norman Douglas). It is defined as 'the ability to do good and to abandon sin' (Jonah Gerondi). It is introduced as 'the means of attaining the lasting contentment which consists in the continual achievement of a greater perfection or at least in variation of the same degree of perfection' (G.W. von Leibniz). It has been defined as 'the recognition that there is an original Being ... and that all ... exist only through reality of His being' (Moses Maimonides). It has been explained as 'the faculty of judging from the very viewpoint of ... Creator and father' (Peter Minard). It has been referred to as 'to believe the heart'(George Santayana). In the scriptural Bible that is current, we have the following comments on wisdom: 'The spirit of human love' (*Apocrypha* Wisdom of Solomon, 1: 6), 'The wisdom of this world is foolishness with God' (I Corinthians, 3:19), 'Fear of the Lord is the beginning of wisdom' (Psalms, 111:10). We notice that in the above Biblical sentences there is no mention of man's acquisition of wisdom from God through a learning process, as is the general description of *al- hikmah* in the Qur'an.

This is an attempt to bring together a wide range of statements on wisdom by Western thinkers. And there is no doubt that some of these statements do convey insight, wit and the ability of the human intellect to describe wisdom. But like everything else that is human, the attempt falls short of a total grasp of what wisdom is. But in the Qur'an there is that durable and abiding grip on the word (and its concept). The first outlining of the word *al-hikmah* or *hikmah* is in the ten verses *(ayat)* that have the adjective *al-hikmah* always following the word *al-kitab* (scripture). This is as if to say that *hikmah* is a follow-up or a by-product of the human apprehension and understanding of Allah's scripture, His Book.[33]

The Prophet (puh) also encouraged the use of *hikmah*, *ijtihad* and reason and some of his companions were practising it in their daily religious thought and practice.

Islamic rationality is based on a multitude of bases, sources and principles. The doctrine of the compatibility of *shari'ah* and *hikmah* as a part of Islamic rationality is, therefore, based on quite a few Islamic principles and grounds. It is based on Islamic texts as well as on Islamic thought. There are many verses in the Qur'an asking and even telling people to think, contemplate, meditate, speculate, observe and to use their reason and intellectual potentials.[34] It encourages the seeking of knowledge, natural philosophy, experimentation and learning. These terms are frequently used in the Qur'an.[35]

There are even many more traditions providing materials for Islamic rationality, the compatibility of *shari'ah* and *hikmah* and the authority of human intellect. In fact, there are extensive chapters and sections in all great collections of traditions, as well as widely scattered fragments, concerning these issues.[36] For example, one of the four major Shi'ite collections of traditions (*ahadith*), *Usul al-Kafi* by M. al-Kulayni (329/941), begins in the first section with *ahadith* about the position of reason in Islam (*the Book of Reason and Ignorance*), e.g. a tradition regards human reason as an 'inner Prophet and the Prophet (puh) as an outer, external reason'.[37] Another tradition related to the Prophet states that '*hikmah* is the missing fortune and the lost (intellectual) property of every Muslim which he must look for and take wherever and whenever he can find it'.[38] Some texts go as far as regarding the philosophers as Prophets of God. The Qur'an confirms that some Prophets (put), such as Luqman, were endowed with *hikmah* and were therefore *hakim*.[39] Mulla Sadra, a great Muslim philosopher, describes at length how Seth and Hermes (corresponding to the Qur'anic Idris and the Biblical Enoch) were given the responsibility of spreading the study of *hikmah*. (Mulla Sadra's view on the concept and doctrine of Prophethood will be discussed later). Many traditions regard man as answerable and responsible for his actions, on the grounds of his intellectual potential and faculty.[40]

In addition to the Qur'anic verses and traditions that deal directly, in one way or another, with questions such as the authority of human faculty, the encouragement of man to use his reason for obtaining *hikmah*, to seek knowledge and so on, Islam and the Qur'an provided Muslims with many rational principles/basis and allowed them freedom and responsibility to investigate questions and subjects of dialectical, ideological and theological nature. From the earliest days of its rise, Islam engaged itself with intellectual discussions and dealt with philosophical subjects. Along with *hikmah* and speculation, the encouragement to learn and seek knowledge is another important characteristic of Islam. Educational terms such as learning, teaching, science, pen, book, writing and reading are used in the Qur'an hundreds of times. In fact the first revelation (the first *surah*) dealt with subjects such as knowledge, reading and the pen.

In the early phase of the history of Islamic intellectualism and rationality and in the pre-speculative and pre-controversy period, reason (*'aql*) and revelation (*wahy*) were regarded as complementary. 'There is no doubt that in the early history of Islamic Thought reason and revelation or *hikmah* and *shari'ah* were not used against each other.'[41] It was later on (second/eighth century) that the distinction between them was made. The Mu'tazilah are to be credited for initiating systematically the rationality movement in Islam. They also initiated the idea concerning the relation between reason and revelation in a positive way. They accepted, in general, the authority of revelation and text (*nass*, *sam'*, *shar'*) in legal and ritual matters. But they declared both theology and ethics to be under the authority of human reason and objects for the human reason to investigate. Good and bad, they held, were not *shar'i* or ordained by divine law but were *'aqli* or rational. (Cf. the Stoics who made a distinction between that which is by nature and that which is ordained). God has forbidden killing, for example, because it is bad; it is not bad because God has forbidden it. The Mu'tazilah did not question the binding and divinity-ordained character of the law but advocated almost without restriction freedom for human reason in the field of theology and ethics and they did not see any conflict between the two. They strongly supported the universality of rationalistic ethics and strongly protested against the denial of universality of rationalistic ethics proposed by Ash'arites.[42] We shall deal with these questions later on.

Islamic rationality which led to the doctrine of harmony of *hikmah* and *shari'ah* has been explained in various terms and based on a few foundations: the Qur'an, traditions, Islamic principles; theological and intellectual, logical, philosophical and rational. The source, the objective and the means of *hikmah* and *shari'ah* are basically and fundamentally the same. The source of *hikmah* is Allah (swt), its means is human intellect and its method is rational reasoning.

The source of *shari'ah* is also Allah (swt) and its means are basically the Qur'an, Islamic traditions and human intellect for three reasons:

1. Revelation does not come to man without reason and for no reason.
2. Revelation and traditions cannot be understood without the help of human intellect.
3. The authority of human intellect has been approved in Islam by the Qur'an and traditions.

The methodology of Islamic law is legal reasoning (jurisprudence), which is based on rational/intellectual analysis. There is not, therefore, any contradiction between *hikmah* and *shari'ah*, neither as far as their sources are concerned nor in their methodology nor objectives. They only differ in their subject. The subject of philosophy is existence/being, and its objective is understanding existence, reality and truth, but the subject of *shari'ah* is human beliefs and behaviour and discovering divine rules dealing with beliefs and behaviour, which is also the truth (practical truth) and its objective is human salvation. There is thus harmony of the source, objectives and approach of *hikmah* and *shari'ah*. The teaching and learning of *hikmah* has been stated as the goal of religion and the prophet's mission in the Qur'an, too.[43]

One definition of *hikmah* and wisdom, in Islamic literature, is the knowledge of what is right or true coupled with just judgement as to action, i.e. sagacity, discernment or insight. But who is to say what is right or true and what is wrong or false? If this is left entirely to humans, there will never be a uniform and universal definition or concise explanation of right and wrong and thus the whole question of right and wrong is meaningless. If the answer is a deity or divinity then we would have to execrate God-given mind and intellectual potential.

Of course there has always existed a group of scholars who thought that there was a conflict between religion and philosophy. Probably this is why religious dialectical logic (theology – *'ilm al-kalam*) came into existence in all religions to defend them. But the actual existence of this dialectical logic showed that there have always been many groups who believed in the harmony of religion and philosophy. Indeed, this is very true of Islam.

In addition to establishing a new kind of legal discipline (Islamic jurisprudence), Muslim philosophers gradually changed the course of their intellectual activities from the Greek philosophy in their efforts to create general Islamic philosophy. This was mainly because they thought Greek philosophy was not able to adjust itself to religious objectives and vice versa and was not fully equipped to cover all the subjects of religious interest. They therefore intertwined the general philosophy with theology on one side and dialectical or logical theology on the other. The development of the features of Islamic philosophy and its whole history is a continuous effort towards the establishment of the doctrine of the compatibility of *hikmah* and *shari'ah*.

Muslim scholars relied mainly on the Qur'an and Islamic sources and traditions in their effort to establish the doctrine of harmony. They found it more convincing to adjust and explain philosophical principles in terms of Islamic texts and vice versa. That is why Muslim philosophers usually explain their views in terms of the Qur'anic verses, Islamic traditions and principles.[44] Some of them even quote traditions from the Prophet (puh) to prove his encouragement of the study of philosophy. For example, Farabi collected some of the Prophet's (puh) sayings in approval of logic and his encouragement of the learning of logic. This book is called *The Prophetic Traditions Concerning the Discipline of Logic.*[45] Mubashir ibn Fatik, who is said to be the first Muslim historian of Greek philosophy, starts his book with the traditions related to the Prophet (puh) in praise of *hikmah* and his encouragement of its study.[46] This is the approach frequently employed by Farabi, especially in his book *Tahsil al-Sa'adah* (*Earning Salutation),* and by Avicenna in most of his books. This is because the 'book' (*kitab*/the Qur'an) and '*hikmah*' are usually mentioned together in the Qur'an and they both form a single gift.[47] It is thus natural for Muslim philosophers to explain philosophical concepts, opinions, terms and principles with Qur'anic verses. The term *hakim* (the possessor of *hikmah*) has been used in the Qur'an many times as one of the Attributes of God. Ghazzali believes that God is the only *hakim*. It has also been applied to four Prophets (put) by Muslims, because in the Qur'an, *hikmah* has been granted to David, Jesus, Luqman and Muhammad. [48]

It is therefore natural to associate *hikmah* with *shari'ah* and *hukama* (Muslim philosophers) with the Prophets (put).[49] We can thus see how the Qur'an and Islamic traditions closely associated themselves with *hikmah* in contents . Furthermore, discussing the harmony of *hikmah* and *shari'ah* we would like to refer to the efforts made by some Muslim thinkers to reconcile these two by way of establishing that the aims and objectives of the two are the same. Al-Kindi believes that the aim of philosophy is the discovery of the truth and the goal of religion is also to lead man to truth. Shahristani explains that salvation and happiness are what human beings seek and cannot be reached except by way of philosophy, which is of two kinds: speculative philosophy and practical philosophy. They both lead mankind to an understanding of the universe, which in turn leads them to God, and this is exactly what religion does. The objective and task of philosophers and Prophets (puh) is therefore the same: to guide man to reach the truth, to the understanding of God and the way to salvation and happiness of mankind. [50]

This has been explained by a Muslim scholar as follows: 'God has sent down two books: one created, which is nature, and one which is revealed, the Qur'an. The latter encourages us to investigate the former by means of intelligence which has also been given us by Allah.'[51] Furthermore Muslim intellectuals used rational methods and approaches (such as logic and demonstration, syllogism, etc.) in dealing with *shari'ah*, law and jurisprudence.

Development of the Doctrine of the Harmony of Hikmah *and* Shari'ah

The Qur'an and Islamic rational materials engaged the mind of Muslim thinkers early and swiftly. The first signs of this influence may be detected in the way they questioned whether the right of command belongs, directly and exclusively, to the will of God and the commandments and *shari'ah* rules are right by virtue of being God's commands, as the Kharijites, at the beginning, and later the Ash'arites, put it; or whether the commandments and prohibitions are based on the wisdom (*hikmah*) of Allah and thus their inner quality and because the acts they refer to are good and bad in themselves; and whether only revelation is the avenue to knowledge or whether reasoning can be so too. This seems to be the first form of the questions concerning the doctrine of harmony of reason and revelation. Later on the Murji'tes, Qadarites and Jabarites also discussed these questions. By the time of Abu Hanifah (the beginning of the second century AH), a group of Muslim thinkers took a systematic affirmative attitude towards the question and suggested the authority of *ra'y* as a source of law. It is interesting to note that the first systematic legal attitude towards the question was jurisprudentially initiated by Abu Hanifah, as well as the philosophical, dealt with by the early Mu'tazilah. Abu Hanifah should indeed be credited for initiating the authority of human reason in the field of law. The Mu'tazilah suggested that religious rules (commands and prohibitions) do inhere in the nature of things and ultimately in God who determines that nature. They also suggested that God, before making us a gift of His revelation, had already given us a gift of reason; both gifts came from God. There could therefore be nothing in right reason that would contradict revelation, since they both came from the same divine source.

Opposite to this movement by Abu Hanifah and Mu'tazilah were, of course, the Hanbalite and Ash'arite movements who represented the opposite stand in law and philosophy. However, this is only one of the many factors helping the establishment and the development of the doctrine of harmony. The most important factor is in fact the attitude that Muslim scholars adopted in dealing with Islamic rationality, which in turn helped the establishment of the doctrine of harmony of law and reason.

In the field of jurisprudence and its method, early in the history of Islamic schools of law, in the interest of consistency and coherence the use of reason and reasoning became more systematic, and arbitrary opinion, or *ra'y,* gradually gave place to analogical deduction, or *al-qiyas al-fiqhi* with the help of syllogism.

In the field of theology there were Muslim theologians and schools that favoured determinism, for example Ash'arites and their sympathizers. But on the whole, the majority of Muslim theologians, philosophers and schools rejected both absolute determinism and absolute free will in favour of the middle course. In this way they somehow found what seems to be the solution to the problem of some inconsistency, on the surface, of some Qur'anic verses and some Islamic traditions that support one or the other extreme. The answer to this question and the solution of this problem helped Muslim scholars and prepared the ground to develop the responsibility and authority of human reason in understanding and discovering the truth and in implementing what is right and avoiding what is wrong.

As far as the question of harmony of philosophy and religion is concerned, Muslim intellectuals and rationalists can be divided into three groups:

1. those who believe in the complete harmony of philosophy and religion, such as al-Kindi, Farabi and Averroes;
2. those who believe in the partial compatibility of the two, such as Ghazzali, in spite of his open attack on philosophy and philosophers in his book *Tahafut al-Falasafah* (*Contradiction of Philosophers*);
3. those who reject the doctrine of harmony between philosophy and religion, such as the Sunni Ahl al-Hadith and the Shi'ite Akhbaris.

As far as the question of the harmony of *shari'ah* and human reason is concerned, even Ibn Taymiyyah (1262–1328 AD/728 AH) does not seem to have rejected it openly. 'Ibn Taymiyyah's programme fundamentally consists of restatement of the *shari'ah* and a vindication of religious values. For him *shari'ah* is a comprehensive concept and includes the spiritual truth (*haqiqah*) of the Sufi, the rational truth (*'aql*) of the philosopher and the theologian, and the lawyers. This inclusiveness is not formal and aggregate but points to a religious quality which is the source of these three.'[52] According to Ibn Taymiyyah, textual authority and reason may, indeed, be distinguished and even opposed, but *shari'ah* and reason cannot be meaningfully opposed. 'The fact that a proof is rational or is based on authentic textual sources is not in itself an object of condemnation or appreciation, or itself a guarantee of truth or falsity. Authentic textual sources and reason are only avenues of knowledge although traditional authority can never be divorced from reason. But the fact that something is a *shari'ah*-value cannot be validly opposed to something being rational.'[53] Ibn Taymiyyah wrote books under the titles of *Muwafaqato Sarih al-Ma'qul li Sahih al-Manqul*, and *al-'aql wa al-Naql* which can be roughly translated as 'The harmony of explicit and absolute rational rules and principles with authentic textual conclusions' and 'The harmony between the authentic tradition and evidence of reason' which are completely devoted to promoting this theme (harmony).

Ibn Taymiyyah argues that since the signification of an utterance (*al-sam'*, *al-nass*) is intentional, and since utterance cannot communicate *per se*, but mean what speakers want them to mean, it follows that in order for communication to be successful, one must know the speaker's intention.

Working through this chain of arguments, Ibn Taymiyyah reaches the conclusion that knowing an utterance is not sufficient to understanding it successfully. Instead two thing should be considered, namely knowing (*al-sam'*, *al-nass*) and reasoning (*al-'aql*) and that using both these means and capacities in understanding is to use *fiqh*.[54]

In his other book, *al-Ihtijaj bi al-Qadar* he also states 'Sometimes by *shari'ah* is meant that which the lawyers of *shari'ah* say on the basis of their own efforts of thought, and by the *haqiqah* is intended what the Sufis find by direct experience.' Ibn Taymiyyah also wrote a book titled *Ta'arud al-'aql wa al-naql* (*The Inconsistency of Reason and Text*). But what he expresses in this book must be understood in the light of his other books.

Contrary to what has been said about Ibn Taymiyyah's anti-rationalist and anti-philosophical position, he always proceeds to examine the religious issues and questions philosophically and rationally. He examines, for example, the arguments of Ibn Rushd one by one and refutes them philosophically and rationally.

He suggests: 'Uundoubtedly, all these groups just mentioned are seekers of truth. Sometimes they are right and sometimes they are wrong but neither of them wishes to contravene the prophet. If the findings of both agree well and good, otherwise neither of them has an exclusive claim to be followed, except by a clear proof from the *shari'ah*.' Ibn Taymiyyah even praises the Mu'tazilah for promoting the idea of good and evil, of divine Commands and prohibition as a live religious force. He suggests that the truth does not belong to one party exclusively but is accessible to all seekers of it.[55]

The case of Ibn Taymiyyah is very special, for he is presumed to be the man on whose opinions Wahhabism, the most anti-rationality *madhhab*, is based. But as has been explained, an analysis of his works proves not to be so. Ibn Taymiyyah disagrees with the Ash'arites on almost all the major issues especially on the issue of good and evil (*al-husn wa al-qubh*). He suggests that

Muslims, both Sunnis and Shi'ah, differ among themselves on the question of the determination of good and evil according to two opinions. The first opinion is that of Ash'ari and his followers, and also of many jurisconsults of the Maliki, Shafi'i and Hanbali schools. According to this opinion good and evil may not be known through reason, but only through revelation.

Opposed to this is the second opinion, according to which good and evil may be known through reason. Ibn Taymiyyah then points out that though this opinion is generally, known to be that of the Mu'tazilah, it is also that of several other groups, namely, the Karramiyyah, the generality of Hanafi jurisconsults, and many jurisconsults of the Maliki, the Shafi'i and the Hanbali schools. He then goes on naming quite a few jurisconsults of each school. He even cites by name two Hanbali jurisconsults, Abu al-Hasan al-Tamimi and Abu al-Khattab (al-Kalwadhani) adding that Kalwadhani (who was a contemporary of Ibn 'Aqil) stated that this opinion was also that of most of the *'ulama* (Muslim scholars).[56] Ibn Taymiyyah in this passage does not say to which of the two opinions he adheres, but it is clear that he is in sympathy with advocates of reason as the source of determining good and evil. That he favours this opinion is made explicit in another passage, in connection with the legal qualifications of acts. The truth of the matter, he says, is that the legal qualifications of acts do not belong to the category of necessary attributes, rather they are accidental attributes applying to acts in accordance with whether they are to be done or avoided. Good and evil are understood in the sense of a thing being desirable or reprehensible, beneficial or harmful, and so on. They are real attributes of the thing qualified, varying with variations of circumstances, but are not their necessary attributes. He goes on to say that the generality of Muslims who affirm the nature and properties of substances, affirm also the good and evil in acts with respect to their being done or avoided. He then quotes the following Qur'anic verse (7:157): 'He commands them that which is right and prohibits them that which is wrong. He allows them as lawful what is good and forbids them what is bad. ' This indicates, he says, that an act in itself is right or wrong. And this is where Ibn Taymiyyah makes clear his opinion that good and evil are not dependent upon command and prohibition. He says that if there were no qualities in substances or acts except by virtue of their connection with commands and prohibitions, the implied meaning of the Qur'anic verse would be, 'He commands them what He commands them and forbids them what He forbids them'. But God is far above this kind of discourse. Ibn Taiymiyyah in another work says that the qualifications of good and evil may be known through reason (*'wa inna dhalika yu'lamu be al-'aql'*, Ibn Taymiyyah, *Kitab Nubuwat*, pp.163,117). A famous disciple of Ibn Taymiyyah, the jurisconsult Ibn Qayyem al-Jauziyyah, in his book *Miftah dar al-Sa'adah* (pp. 11, 45), asserts that reason knows the distinction between good and evil prior to the promulgation of the revealed law, and independently of it. Ethical values are not based on the law, but also on reason.

Another famous scholar, whose opinion in this respect should be taken into consideration, is Ibn 'Aqil. He deals with the issue as follows: if the knowledge of good and evil through reason did not precede our knowledge of the revealed laws, the revelation's reprimand and censure for an act would not be possible. He supports this point by quoting many Qur'anic verses and concludes that all of the Qur'anic censures are apprehended through reason; thus the revealed law censured those endowed with reason in which there is a prior knowledge of good and evil.[57]

However, Fazlur Rahman suggests that 'to the right wing traditionalists, *Kalam*-theology itself had become suspect because of its very *rapprochement* to philosophy. This traditionism found its monumental expression in the eighth/fourteenth century in the prolific work of Ibn Taymiyyah, which was destined to be of lasting importance. Especially in his important work '*The Harmony between the True Tradition and the Evidence of Reason*' he severely criticized the thesis of both the philosophers and the theologians.'[58] But as we suggested, Ibn Taymiyyah's opinions, like those of Ghazzali's, should be treated in the light of their overall approach.

It is noteworthy that another group of Muslim philosophers also tried to establish harmony between Islamic mysticism (in which the source of knowledge is only intuition and insight, neither revelation nor reason on their own) and Islamic philosophy. This group made some efforts to reconcile religion, philosophy, mysticism and gnosis parallel to the first groups mentioned above. They not only present us with an Islam which is at once rational but also present us with a mysticism which is also rational. Suhrawardi, Mulla Sadra and even Farabi, Averroes and, recently, M. H. Tabataba'i can be included in this group. As for the jurisconsults, *Us ulis*, of course they must all be categorized as the Muslim intellectuals to whom the most original Islamic philosophy of law, that is Islamic jurisprudence, owes its actual existence and development. The *usulis* are the group of Muslim scholars who should therefore be recognized as those who created the Islamic discipline of jurisprudence to explain the harmony of *hikmah* and *shari'ah*, in an Islamic way.

It was only natural that the Muslim scholars should produce the harmony of *hikmah* and *shari'ah* as the first and the most obvious and important result of Islamic rationality and its rational elements, principles and materials. However, the question of the harmony of *hikmah* and *shari'ah* in a precise, systematic and developed way did not arise until the middle of the second century AH. Although the main and basic principle of Mu'tazilism was this doctrine, the early Mu'tazilah did not discuss it as an independent question. They usually dealt with it indirectly. It was during the Ash'arite anti-Mu'tazilah period of activities and during the period of antithesis to Mu'tazilism that the doctrine and question began to take shape. The question was not dealt with systematically before this period either because intellectual and purely philosophical and rational questions had not yet been formed, though they were discussed unsystematically, or because nobody challenged the harmony of *shari'ah* and *hikmah*, for it was accepted indirectly from the beginning.

The Mu'tazilite philosophers certainly are to be credited for preparing the ground for the doctrine of the unity of truth and thus for the doctrines of the authority of human reason and the harmony of *shari'ah* and *hikmah*. The Muslim scholars who came after them developed these doctrines. Al-Kindi (*c.*185–252/801–73), the Latin Alkindus, is reported to have written a book entitled *Al-hathth 'ala Ta'allum al-Falasafah* (*Exhortation and Encouraging the Learning and Study of Philosophy*). Al-Kindi did not confine the function of philosophy to purely abstract thought. Instead, as a good Muslim he believed philosophy to be the 'handmaid' of religion. He believed that the truth the philosophers seek was not different from the truth to which the prophets have summoned humankind. In fact, for al-Kindi the truth to which Muhammad (puh) was summoned, and to which he invited people added to what he had received from God Almighty, is such that it can be demonstrated by recourse to rational arguments, which only a fool can question. According to al-Kindi, to understand the intent of the prophet in the Qur'an, it is necessary to resort to interpretation in the manner of 'people of sound religion and intelligence'.[59] It seems that al-Kindi was one of the earliest advocates of rational/philosophical and allegorical interpretation of certain verses of the Qur'an and also the supporter of the doctrine of harmony of reason and religion.

Furthermore, he wrote a short treatise entitled *Maqulat fi al-'aql* (*Essays on the Intellect*), which became the prototype of subsequent treatises by Farabi (*Risalaton fi ma'ani al-'aql*) and Ibn Rushd (*Fasl al-Maqal*), and similar titles by others. In this treatise Al-Kindi distinguishes between four different types of intellects as follows: the intellect which is always in action, *'aql al-fa'al*; the potential intellect, *'aql bi al-malakah*, the intellect which has passed from the state of potentiality to the state of actuality; *'aql bi al-Fi'l* or the acquired intellect; and finally the manifest intellect, *'aql al-mustafad*, whose function is to abstract the universal forms embedded in matter.[60] Al-Kindi was truly a champion of his period, of the doctrine of harmony of religion and philosophy and reason and faith. He believed that a higher divine wisdom, imparted to mankind through revelation did not contradict philosophy, but rather supported, supplemented or reinforced it. Al-Kindi's influence lasted for a long time. As the first major philosopher within the world of Islam, he believed quite strongly in the compatibility, indeed solidarity, between philosophy and revelation or *hikmah* and *shari'ah*.

The issue, nevertheless, was seriously discussed and even challenged when the instinctive suspicion of the masses about philosophy, a foreign importation to Islam, was raised. Coupled with this was the serious but subtle reservation of such eminent scholars as Sajestani and al-Tawhidi, who were not innocent of philosophical culture. These reinforced popular belief in the hazard inherent in philosophical discourses. Philosophy and religion, according to Sajestani and al-Tawhidi, stemmed from two different sources and were therefore impossible to reconcile. Al-Tawhidi believed that others, more competent than the Brethren of Purity (Ikhwan al-Safa), had attempted to reconcile the two without success.

The Mu'tazilah championed the cause of the reconciliation. But their attempts at reconciliation were dashed after the death of Ma'mun, their patron. Upon the accession of al-Mutawakkil in 847 AD, the theological policies of the state were reversed and the stage was set for the rise of the first major post-Mu'tazilite movement of Ash'arism. But even Ash'ari himself in his famous treatise, *Istihsan al-Khawd fi 'Ilm al-Kalam* (*The Vindication of Use of Science of Kalam*), approved of the use of logical deduction, *qiyas* (syllogism). He even suggested that its use had been even recommended by Qur'an and that the prophet had practised it. He suggested that it is the duty of every reasonable Muslim to refer in matters where the Qur'an and *hadith* are silent to the body of principles consecrated by reason, sense-experience or common sense.[61] On the whole, on the more substantive issues that the Mu'tazilite theologians had raised, Ash'ari tended to tread a milder course between the traditionalists and the rationalists.[62] However, Ash'arism is supposedly regarded as the school that did not promote and support rationalist movement. This may be detected in the works of almost all the leading Ash'arite scholars from the time of Ash'ari onwards. Nevertheless, even Ash'arites did not directly challenge the doctrine of harmony of *hikmah* and *shari'ah*, because the doctrine had not been formed properly by the time of Ash'ari to be challenged. But it should be borne in mind that this does not mean that the concept and material for the doctrine did not exist or that the doctrine was not discussed at all, even indirectly and unsystematically.

It seems that the question of harmony, like many other questions, was first discussed in a proper scholarly manner directly and as a philosophical subject by al-Kindi. But he did not coin the doctrine of harmony between *hikmah* and *shari'ah*, though later scholars believed that al-Kindi did use the term 'harmony of *hikmah* and *shari'ah*'.[63] Nevertheless he held that whatever had been approved by *shari'ah* could be understood and explained by human reason and intellect. He went on reasoning intellectually and philosophically for the rules of *shari'ah*.[64] He believed that the validity of any kind of knowledge (including religious) can be measured by rational means.[65]

He was followed by Abu Zaid al-Balkhi (second/eighth century). It is said that he believed that 'either philosophy (*hikmah*) or Islamic law (*shari'ah*) is the product of the other and thus the mother of the other. Their relationship is thus that of a mother and child.'[66] A Shi'i philosopher, Abu Tammam al-Nayshaboori, also helped the development and establishment of the doctrine.[67]

Another Persian scholar, 'Imad al-din 'Abd al-Jabbar (323/4–415 AH) also contributed to the development of the doctrine of the harmony of reason and revelation. He strongly advocated the authority of reason in ethical and legal issues.[68] 'Abd al-Jabbar believed that revelation does not necessitate the evilness or goodness of anything. It only uncovers the character of the act by way of indication, just as reason does. He differentiated between the command of the Exalted and that of another being, by His wisdom, for He never commands what is evil to command.[69] He thus explains the doctrine of harmony of revelation and reason this way, and thus justifies the harmony of *hikmah* and *shari'ah*. He categorizes the rulings of *shari'ah* into two groups: first, all those rulings, *ahkam,* that are made by human reason, which are called rational rulings even though they are also made by revelation; and second, the rulings which are based wholly on revelation.[70] He therefore openly introduces the authority of human intellect as a source of law and therefore finds a rational and religious foundation for the doctrine of harmony of *hikmah* and *shari'ah*. It is suggested that he believed, like other Mu'tazilites of his period, that 'God's purpose is a rational one; to bring about the maximum objective good in the world, in the same sense of good that man understands. Thus, even when man cannot see by his natural reason what is good in detail, God's prescriptions to him do not go beyond what he can understand in principle. This fact guarantees the harmony of reason and revelation,'[71] and therefore the harmony of *hikmah* and *shari'ah*.[72]

Abu Bakr Muhammad ibn Zakariya al-Razi (c. 6865-925), born in Rayy, near present-day Tehran and known to the Latin scholars as Razes, also supported the doctrine. He produced great works in the fields of contemporary sciences. He is known in the West for his achievements in the fields of sciences, especially in the field of medicine. His philosophical works and thoughts are distinctive, original and controversial. He is accused of holding the view that reason enjoys preference over other means of knowledge, including revelation. His philosophical works have survived in fragmentary forms. His love and appreciation of reason made him the subject of criticism by his opponents. But a careful study and analysis of what he said about reason proves that he came to his conclusion about reason with his commitment to his faith intact. The following extract may explain this point.

> I say that, the Creator, His name be exalted, gave us reason and favoured us with it solely in order that we may be granted, and attain by means of it, benefits in both this world and in the next. To the furthest extent of that, the bestowal and attainment lies in our essential nature. Reason is the most magnificent of God's favour to us and it is the most useful and advantageous of divine gifts and objects for us.

He goes on to explain the use of reason in all fields of knowledge. He then states:

> By reason we arrive at knowledge of the Creator, He is mighty and glorious, who is the loftiest of our contemplation and the most beneficial object of our striving. In sum, reason is a divine gift without which our state would be the state of beasts, of unreasoning infants and of the insane. Reason is something by which we form a mental image of our intellectual activities before they are manifest to the senses, for we see them as though we had already perceived them sensorial.[73]

Islamic Rationality in the Middle History of Islamic Thought

By the time of Farabi, the Latin Alpharabius, (*c.*258–339/ 870–950), Islamic philosophy had developed greatly and consequently the doctrine of harmony was firmly established. But Farabi helped its elaboration.[74] His special interest in the doctrine is reflected in his book *Risalaton fi Ma'ani al-'aql* (*Discourse on Human Reason*).[75] Farabi established himself as the 'Second Teacher', the first having been Aristotle. He was the second outstanding philosopher after al-Kindi. His commentary on Aristotle's *Metaphysics* helped Avicenna understand that work. He was a practising Sufi and the spirit of Sufism runs throughout his work. Probably this state of mind helped him in his effort to establish harmony and consistency between the Platonic and the Aristotelian approach in his famous work *al-Jam' bayn Ra'y al-Hakimayn Aflatun wa Aristo* (*The Harmony between the Opinions of the Two Sages, Plato and Aristotle*).

Farabi's account of the relation between religion and philosophy is interesting. Religion, we are told by Farabi, consists of two parts, creed and action. These two are similar to the two parts of philosophy: theoretical and practical. They seem to be compatible and even interchangeable. For him the practical things in religion are those universals in practical philosophy. The demonstration of the theoretical things in religion is to be found in theoretical philosophy. Accordingly the universals of religion depend upon the universals of philosophy.[76] Farabi believes that Islam supports the idea of universals.

However some contemporary commentators on Farabi's works suggest that he was not a natural law theorist. Christopher Colmo, comparing Farabi's idea about the prudence of founders of states in the *Book of Religion* with that of Machiavelli's in *The Prince*, suggests this.

> J. Parens has written at length on the relation of al-Farabi's teaching to doctrine of natural law. He finds, as we do, that Farabi cannot be taken to be a natural law theorist. Parens supplements this interpretation of al-Farabi with the theory that, while there are no universal rules of action, al-Farabi does admit, indeed, insists upon, a 'permanent hierarchy of ends'. The ends are permanent, even if the rules of actions leading to those ends cannot be fixed since rules of actions must adjust to infinite variety of circumstances.[77]

This interpretation of Farabi does not really correspond with Farabi's overall approach to religion and philosophy.

After Farabi a group of Muslim philosophers worked together to develop and prove the doctrine of unification and harmony of *hikmah* and *shari'ah*. The Sincere Brethren or Brethren of Purity, lived around the middle of the fourth century AH. It seems that not only did they contribute a great deal to the development of the doctrine by explaining it, but they also applied it to many other fields besides Islamic law. In their books called *Rasailu Ikhwan al-Safa* (*Tracts of the Brethren of Purity*), which were widely read, they frequently discussed the harmony of *hikmah* and *shari'ah*. It is presumed that Zaid ibn Rafa'ah, Abu Sulaiman Muhammad ibn Ma'shar al-Basti al-Magdisi, Abu al-Hasan ibn Harun al-Zanjani, Abu Ahmad al-Nahrjuri and al-'Ufi were some of the members of this philosophical circle. Ikhwan al-Safa believed that *shari'ah* had been soiled and misunderstood and could not be cleansed except by *hikmah* (Islamic philosophy). They held that all rulings of *shari'ah* are in complete harmony with the dictates of reason (*al-aql*) and philosophy (*hikmah*). A small minority disagreed with them vigorously, amongst them Abu Sulaiman, Muhammad ibn Sajestani and Abu Hayyan al-Tawhidi. Ikhwan al-Safa's ideas, doctrines and books spread throughout the Muslim world and they became very popular. They obviously had a great influence on Muslim intellectuals. It is said that Avicenna read their books and probably was under their influence. The doctrine of the harmony of *shari'ah* and *hikmah* was thus widely accepted and publicized after Ikhwan al-Safa.[78]

Then came Avicenna, the great Muslim philosopher, who developed the doctrine more systematically and philosophically than before. He established a close connection between revelation and reason. Avicenna wrote a book on *'aql* (*kitab al-'aql*) which is included in *Opera* (*Majmu'ah,* Collections) translated by John of Seville and published twice in Venice in 901/1495 and in 906/1500).[79]

He suggested that *al-'aql al-fa'al* or the active intellect which is universal and independent of the individual, and is divine, which illuminates the mind through the act of knowledge, was created by God (divine intellect). The function of *al-'aql al-fa'al* is to provide and pour out *ifadah*, knowledge, both to the Prophets (put), who are endowed with Prophetic intellect, by the intermediary of angels, such as Gabriel, and to ordinary man who is blessed with human intellect (*al-'aql al-insani*). This takes place by way of realization of potential intellect (*al-'aql bi al-quwwah*), through universal intellect (world soul, *al-'aql al-kull*) and by way of habitual intelligence (*al-'aql bi al-malakah*), and the acquired intellect (*al-'aql bi al-fi'l*). He thus suggested that human intellect should be regarded as an inner Prophet, as a Prophet is an outer intellect (compared to the human soul).[80] This establishes the full harmony of *shari'ah* and *hikmah*.[81] (Mulla Sadra's opinion concerning the concept of prophecy will be discussed later.)

This approach became known as the Farabi–Avicenna approach as against the approach adopted by al-Kindi. While al-Kindi tried to interpret religious principles and texts in philosophical and rational terms, Farabi and Avictried to establish a rational basis and grounds for religion and its principles, especially the doctrine of Prophethood (*al-risalah*) as was pointed out earlier. However, they did not reject al-Kindi's approach.

It should be remembered that Muslim philosophers were not the only people who helped the development of the doctrine of harmony. Along with them on a parallel line, two other groups of Muslim intellectuals, theologians and jurists, contributed towards its establishment. Islamic theology has always supported the authority of reason in a way. That is to say that since the Mu'tazilah had a great influence on Islamic theology, Muslim theologians, even those who sympathized with the Ash'arites, mostly accepted the harmony of *hikmah* and *shari'ah*, at least in the field of theology. Imam al-Haramain al-Jowaini, Ghazzali and Imam Fakhr al-din al-Razi, (Imam al-Shakkakin) are good examples of those Muslim scholars who, though they did not approve of Greek philosophy, accepted the doctrine of harmony in this context.[82]

The orthodox refutation of philosophy, formulated by Ghazzali in his classic work *Tahafut al-Falasafah* (*The Incoherence of the Philosophers*, 1095 AD), argued against the philosophers' position with regard to some of their doctrines, although it should be taken as his stand on Islamic theology and not as his opposition to the doctrine of harmony. His opposition to philosophers is a very particular subject, for he defines their purposes and objectives in his other famous book, *Maqasid al-Falasafah* (*The Objectives of Philosophers*) and thus justifies them to a certain degree in a special way. The most crucial basis of the orthodox dissatisfaction with the philosophers' stand concerned the nature of religion itself. The philosophical theory of the prophetic revelation, which saw in the Prophet an immensely endowed intellect and spirit, capable of coming into contact with the universal intellect or the Archangel, was not completely rejected. But the character of revelation, as being essentially intellectual, was rejected, especially the idea that religion is but a symbolic form of rational and intellectual truth.

It is said that Ghazzali accepted the authority of human intellect as a source of law.[83] He regards *'aql* as one of the main principles of *usul al-fiqh,* whose main function, he believes, is to establish legal freedom from obligation, prohibition and freedom from liabilities in the absence of *shari'ah* rulings.[84] Ghazzali certainly retained the right of reason to arbitrate in theological discussions. He distinguished between those parts of philosophy which clash with fundamental principles of religion and those that do not, such as logic, ethics and others. An ignorant friend of Islam who is worse than the enemy, he argued, could only question the latter. He therefore definitely accepted the doctrine of harmony at a certain level and in certain fields.

Ghazzali may at first appear to be one of the opponents of the doctrine of harmony because of *The Incoherence of Philosophers*. But an analysis of his entire works and a review of his whole approach shows his great efforts to harmonize or reconcile, philosophy (*hikmah*), law (*shari'ah*) and gnosis (*'irfan*), which is far more than the attempts made by Muslim scholars, who tried to establish harmony only between the first two. We are told in the preface to *Tahafut al-Falasafah,* that his objective of writing *Mi'yar al-'Ilm* and *Maqasid al-Falasafah* was simply to lay down the groundwork for the refutation of Aristotelianism, or rather, Neoplatonism (in fact the refutation of Aristotelian rationalism), as interpreted by Farabi and Ibn Sina and probably not the refutation of philosophy as such. In *Tahafut*, Ghazzali distinguishes between four different parts of philosophy and he only rejects that part of philosophy which contains the bulk of the philosophical errors, namely physics and metaphysics.[85] Ghazzali in *Tahafut* was not attempting to refute philosophy as a way of reasoning and as a topic or a set of topics for reflection and investigation, but to refute only specific doctrines associated with the mix of neo-Platonic and Aristotelian thought. As far as method and subject matter are concerned, Ghazzali was no less a philosopher and supporter of rational reasoning than Ibn Sina or Ibn Rushd. What Ghazzali and Jalal al-Din Mawlavi were challenging was the denial of the position and authority of revelation and more direct form of knowledge through illumination by some philosophers.

It is suggested that the criticism of philosophy amongst Muslim thinkers should be viewed within the consideration of two factors. First, what are generally criticized are the specific ideas stemming from the works of certain philosophers and thus leading to alternative philosophical proposals. So the second factor is the readiness of many critics of philosophy to elaborate philosophical and rational theories of their own. The classic example of this movement is Ghazzali's refutation of philosophy and his own philosophical elaboration of his creed replete with rational proofs for the existence of God, for His uniqueness and for various divine attributes. Even the Sufi tradition of Ibn al-'Arabi has entered into a philosophical dialogue with Peripatetic philosophy in which they have offered their own way of thought as a rational alternative to that of philosophers, while retaining the method of demonstration and many of the concepts employed by their opponents.[86]

In contrast to what has been said about Ghazzali's anti-rationalism, he was not in principle opposed either to reason or to logic. Ghazzali suggested that the *adillah al-shar'iyyah* (the sources and principles of Islamic law) are on the whole in harmony with reason. This will be clear from the fact that the *shari'ah* in all its parts is addressed to the *mukallaf* (the people to whom *shari'ah* is addressed), that is, the competent person who is in possession of his faculty of reasoning. The *shari'ah* as a whole does not impose any obligation that would contradict the requirement of *'aql.* Since the criterion of obligation (*taklif*) is *'aql,* and without it all legal obligations fall to the ground, it would follow that a *hukm al-shar'i,* which is abhorrent to *'aql,* is of no consequence.[87] Furthermore, as Islam introduces itself as an inclusive, universal and the last religion of mankind throughout the ages it has to establish a legal system to suit and fit its set objectives and gaols. This legal system has no choice but to benefit from and base itself on a rationalistic legal approach.

However, mainly for fear of being attacked as a follower of Aristotle, Ghazzali was somewhat equivocal on the subject. He thus employed an ambiguous title for his book on logic in order to avoid using the term *mantique* (logic). Muhammad ibn Tuwlus, who had also written about logic, defended himself by calling upon the authority of Ghazzali, saying that 'Abu Hamid al-Ghazzali altered the title of his book as well as the technical terms employed in them to avoid misunderstanding. In place of the terms ordinarily used by the representative of the field, he used technical terms familiar to the *Fuqaha'* [jurists] and frequently used by the *'Ulama'* [Muslim scholars] of his time. This he did to protect himself and to escape what other scholars had experienced who came forward with strange and unusual things.'[88] It is somewhat paradoxical that Ghazzali spearheaded the attack against the freethinkers and the proponents of logic, but in doing so he had to use the weapon of his adversaries. This explains the point that Ghazzali was in fact against certain ideas of the philosophers and not against *hikmah,* reason and logical reasoning.[89]

We may be able to understand the attitude of Ghazzali towards philosophy and its relation with religion from the approach adopted by one his admirers, Ibn Tufayl (the Latin Abentofel, born in Guadix, Spain, educated in Granada,

d. 1185 AD). Ibn Tufayl was basically a follower of Avicenna. He probably inspired him in choosing the title *Hayy Ibn Yaqdan* for his famous book, because Avicenna had already written a book under this title. However, Ibn Tufayl was also a great admirer of Ghazzali. So he admired the philosophy and approach of the representatives of the two supposedly opposing extreme tendencies in Islamic thought. Ibn Tufayl also admired Ibn Rushd although at the same time he expressed some reservations about certain points made by Ibn Rushd. This can explain by the fact that Ibn Tufayl, like many other Muslim scholars, did not think that Ghazzali was against philosophy as such or that there was a conflict between the two trends in Islamic thought.

The position of Ghazzali with regard to *hikmah*, *'irfan* and *tariqah* can be appreciated in the light of the çircumstances of his time. The phenomenon of Sufism and *'irfan* is a very complex one. Immoral, emotive and cognitive or speculative aspects can be distinguished clearly enough. The moral drive with which the Sufi *movahed* started as a method of self-discipline to realize the religious values of Islam in their fullness, however, soon gave way to and was submerged under the strongly favoured ecstatic impulses and the attraction of a privileged type of knowledge.[90] The Orthodox synthetic reform movement that came to a head in Ghazzali was a sustained endeavour to curb the ecstatic extravagances of Sufism on one hand and to limit its cognitive claim on the other. Speculative Sufism, however, like neo-Platonism and to some extent under its influence, is, in fact, a definite type of idealistic philosophy and hence a liaison between philosophy and Sufism and *'irfan*. Sufi intuitions, therefore, in the hands of speculative Sufis is a mode of philosophic thought, except that it seeks to back itself up by a theory of *kashf.* While orthodox speculative Sufi thinkers retained the theory of *kashf*, nevertheless it brought about important changes in the content of the Sufi speculative system. The most important development is that this produced a kind of synthesis of the traditional orthodox *qualm* – theology based on the Qur'an and Islamic doctrine with the purely speculative theology of Sufi theosophy and also produced a kind of harmony between Tiara, *'irfan*, Sufism and philosophy. This was, we think, what Ghazzali tried to establish. Thus, even Sufism took a positive position with regard to Islamic intellectualism and rationality. With this approach intellectual Sufism emerged and thus the deliverance of *kashf* and intuition were brought to the level of sound intellectual processes. This was truly an Islamic Sufism.[91] Ghazzali had a great influence on the Islamic intellectualism which developed by scholars after him. Averroes, the greatest of the believers in the doctrine of harmony and a staunch supporter of Islamic rationality, was influenced by him in his approach, though he repudiated Ghazzali's stand in *Tahafut al-Falasafah* and expressed this by writing *Tahafut al-Tahafut* (*The Incoherence of the Incoherence*). It was Ghazzali who initiated the theory, which was later used by Averroes in his book, *Fasl al-Maqal*, that there are five possible levels of interpretation and meaning for scriptures, thus opening the way for and establishing a systematic approach to reconcile and harmonize philosophical principles with scriptures and traditions.[92] Ghazzali certainly accepted the authority of reason and distinguished between those aspects of philosophy which are compatible with the *shari'ah* and those which are not. He repudiates those philosophers who, he believes, do not understand either *hikmah* or *shari'ah*. Even in his book, *Tahafut al-Falasafah,* he openly suggests that logic (the rational/philosophical approach) should be employed to answer both philosophical and jurisprudential questions.[93] There is no reason to believe that Ghazzali's argument was anti-rational/philosophical and that his arguments should be construed as such. It.has been suggested that his arguments inhibit the mental universe of traditional/classic logic and syllogism.

Averroes suggested that although Ghazzali was regarded as an Ash'arite by the Ash'arites, he was a philosopher with philosophers. Ghazzali regards *'aql* as the highest faculty of *qalb*; its relation to the *qalb* is similar to that of the light to the sun, or of the vision to the eye. We believe that by *qalb* Ghazzali meant *fitrah* and he thus introduces *'aql* as one of the means by which *fitrah* functions. For him knowledge has two aspects, formal and existential. The former is the knowledge of self-evident principles. Such knowledge, though it begins with experience, is more than what it actually contained in experience and as such is not based on experience; it is *a priori*. This is because in such propositions as 'A person can not be in two places at the same time', we make a statement which is true for all time, though our observation is limited to the present time.[94] Formal knowledge is innate while existential knowledge is acquired but both occur and work together. He suggests that man possesses two qualities that distinguish him from animals and enable him to attain spiritual perfection. They are *'aql* and *iradah* (intellect and will). Intellect is the fundamental rational faculty in man. Intellect is the basis of *'ilm* (knowledge) which includes the knowledge of self-evident truth. Knowledge can be acquired only through the intellect.[95] Ghazzali met the philosophers on their ground and made concessions to philosophy in general and to logic in particular and thus accepted the doctrine.[96] For him, intellect or reason is considered to have two aspects, viz. theoretical/pure, *al-'aql al-nazari,* and practical/applied, *al-'aql al-'amali*. Theoretical reason includes intuition.

In short, Ghazzali was opposed not to *hikmah*, science and reason *per se*, for he himself used reason to refute philosophers. He opposed certain issues and aspects of philosophy as expounded by some Muslim philosophers like Farabi and particularly by Ibn Sina. This was because of their certain highly unorthodox metaphysical views such as the eternity of the world, the purely symbolic nature of the prophetic revelation and the rejection of physical resurrection.

Ghazzali's contemporary, M. A. K. Shahristani (464–540 AH), the author of the well-known book *al-Melal wa al-Nihal* (*Religious Sects and Philosophical Schools*), contributed a great deal to the doctrine of harmony by trying to harmonize *shari'ah* and *hikmah*. He is, however, introduced as a follower of the school of Ash'arism. Shahristani, nevertheless, believes that philosophy and religion share the same objectives and follow the same purpose.[97] His position with respect to the question of the harmony of *hikmah* and *shari'ah* may be explained in the same way as Ghazzali's was explained.

The influence of the doctrine on Muslim scholars was so widespread that a group of commentators on the Qur'an established a rational and intellectual approach in their commentaries called *The Philosophical and Rational Commentary*. Under the influence of the doctrine of harmony of *hikmah* and *shari'ah* they interpreted the Qur'anic verses philosophically and rationally. A good example of this kind of commentary is that of Zamakhshari's *al-Kashshaf*. Al-Farabi and Avicenna also adopted this approach of interpreting the Qur'an in their philosophical works. The philosophical commentary was usually done in two ways: employing philosophical principles in interpreting the Qur'an, and interpreting the Qur'an philosophically. These commentators contributed a great deal to the doctrine of harmony of *hikmah* and *shari'ah*.

The efforts made by the great commentators, Fakhr al-din Razi (606/1149–1209), known amongst the Muslims as *Imam al-Mushakkekin*, the leader of sceptics, exemplify the approach adopted by rational commentators to develop the doctrine of harmony. He succeeded in applying his unique method to establish the doctrine of harmony of the rulings of the *shari'ah* and rational principles. In his philosophical commentary on the Qur'an, *al-Tafsir al-Kabir*, he tries successfully to explain the Qur'anic verses, Islamic teachings and rulings of *shari'ah* by philosophical, intellectual, rational and Gnostic approaches and means.[98]

It is interesting to know that as the Islamic rational movement progressed in the East of the Muslim world, it also developed at the same pace in the West of the Muslim world. In Andalusia (Muslim Spain), where anti-rational tendencies in the form of literalism (Zahirism) were strong and where the Zahiri school was established by Davood al-Zahiri, the Islamic rational movement had its many well-known supporters. Ibn Bajjah (Abubakar Muhammad ibn Bajjah, born in Saragossa, Spain, d. 533/1139), known in the West as Avempace, took up the cause of Islamic rationality in the Western Muslim world, probably under the influence of the rational movement in the Eastern Muslim world championed by many including Farabi, Avicenna and Ikhwan al-Safa. Ibn Bajjah believed that knowledge is not acquired by the senses alone. According to his view universal and necessary judgements, the predictive and explanatory meat of science and the foundation of all forms of knowledge about nature, are reached only with the aid of the active intellect, the governing intellect of nature. He believed that intellect can reach truth, even by itself and that revelation is a manifestation of the intellect. He was the teacher of Ibn Rushd and greatly influenced him. Ibn Rushd and Ibn Tufayl followed him and his approach. In his book *al-Ittisal* (*Conjunction with Divine Reason*) Ibn Bajjah supported Islamic rationality in the face of common opposition. Ibn Tufayl in the introduction to his book, *Hayy ibn Yaqzan*, pays tributes to Ibn Bajjah and thus indirectly admits his indebtedness to Ibn Bajjah, though he does criticize Ibn Bajjah on many issues. Ibn Bajjah has been regarded as a link between Muslim East and Muslim West and also as a link between the East (Islam) and the West.

The doctrine of harmony of *shari'ah* and *hikmah* was dealt with systematically, independently and exclusively by Averroes (520-95/1126–98) in his books *Fasl al-Maqal*, and *al-Kashf 'an Manahij al-Adillah*. But as shall be explained later, some other great Muslim intellectuals contributed towards its development. Ibn Tufayl, a contemporary of Averroes, and his master, should be especially brought to attention in this context. Ibn Tufayl (the Latin Abubacer or Abentofal) is known in the West for his criticism of Averroes' commentary on Aristotle's *De Anima* (*On the Soul*). But he supported Averroes' position with regard to Islamic rationality. He was a great admirer of Avicenna. He compiled his famous work of philosophical fiction in a book known as *Hayy ibn Yaqzan (Living, Son of the Awoke, The Self Taught Philosopher)*. This book must not be confused with a similar work by Avicenna under the same title, in which he explains that man's reason and intellectual faculty can lead him to reality and truth, which is compatible with and corresponds to religious principles and doctrines.[99]

In Ibn Tufayl's book he shows that even without the help of tradition and revelation man is able to attain the knowledge of nature and through that to the knowledge of God. This remarkable work was first translated into Hebrew, and Moses of Narbonne wrote an excellent interpretation of it. It was translated from Arabic into Latin by Edward Pococke Junior under the title *Philosophus Autodidactus si Epistola Abu Ja'afar ebn Tophail de Hai ebn Yakdhan* and published together with the Arabic text in Oxford in 1082/1671. It was then translated into most of the European languages. The large number of these translations explains the impact of his philosophical thought and work on Western thought. Ibn Tufayl's approach to the doctrine of harmony was more mystical than epistemological and could appeal only to certain people. It is also the quest for knowledge through union with the active intellect, which is the message of the book. Externally, it resembles Defoe's *Robinson Crusoe*, which, in fact, it inspired. It also inspired Rousseau in writing *Emile*. Ibn Tufayl provided the link between Averroes and the philosophic tradition which culminated with him.[100] This is why Averroes tried to present a more popular approach for the doctrine, which could be used logically, and systematically, that of logic and syllogism.

As we mentioned before, Muslim jurisconsults also contributed to the doctrine of harmony of *hikmah* and *shari'ah*. In fact, the practical dimension of the doctrine is dealt with in the field of Islamic law. The doctrine has been applied in Islamic jurisprudence. Muslim jurists and jurisconsults established a special method and approach for Islamic law (*fiqh*) called *Usul al-Fiqh*, (Islamic jurisprudence), in which Islamic philosophy and rationality is properly reflected, incorporated and implemented. They have also used logical principles in Islamic law, such as analogy by the Sunni schools of law, and syllogism by the Shi'ite school of law. But the most significant contribution towards the development and application of the doctrine has been made by a particular group of jurisconsults, namely the jurist-philosophers who combined law and philosophy. A good example, and in fact the best representative of this group, is Averroes. His book *The Decisive Word on the Harmony of Philosophy and Shari'ah* truly represents a precise picture of the attitude of this group of Muslim scholars towards the doctrine.[101] He supported his argument about the doctrine with Qur'anic texts, traditions and with reason, which he believed was, clearly in turn, authorized by the Qur'an and traditions.[102] Not only did he believe that the use of human intellect was recommended by the Qur'an and traditions, but he also suggested that its use is mandatory, necessary and commanded. [103] He thus concludes that the study of philosophy is one of the necessary qualifications and religious duties of Muslim scholars specially the lawyers.

We do not wish to enter into the background of *Fasl al-Maqal* or the conditions, which led Averroes to deal with such an important subject. He was probably trying to explain the already well-established doctrine, or perhaps trying to justify it in the face of resistance to the doctrine put up by traditionalist theologians or others. We are concerned here only with the contents of this short treatise, which is of great significance to the history and development of the doctrine of harmony of *hikmah* and *shari'ah*. He was both a well-respected qualified philosopher and a practising judge and jurist, *qadi*. He had thus combined law, theory and practice, and therefore represented the actual living circumstances of, at least, the Western part of the world of Islam and the Muslim West.

In dealing with the question of whether the learning of philosophy is commanded by *shari'ah* and the doctrine of harmony, Averroes is decisive, bold, authoritative, logical, rational and progressive as well as orthodox, traditional and religious. He has a great respect for the authority of the Qur'an and authentic Islamic traditions, and he often quotes them to prove his. He did not therefore try to establish the doctrine of harmony at the expense of *shari'ah*. He is regarded as a very devout Muslim scholar, whose efforts in this field were based on his loyalty to his faith and Islam. He should not therefore be regarded as a free thinker in the Western sense of the term.

He therefore explains and justifies the doctrine of harmony on two bases: on Islamic sources such as the Qur'an, traditions etc. and on rational, logical and philosophical grounds.

This is because he believes that since Islam is true and commands us to search for the truth, it cannot contradict and oppose the truth obtained by other means such as philosophy and a logical and rational approach, but accords with it and bears witness to it.[104] The truth is a single entity and not a double one and thus harmonious. *Shari'ah* and *hikmah* are both reliable sources of a single truth, which is in this context the doctrine of harmony.[105]

In dealing with the doctrine of harmony he even finds himself defending pre-Islamic philosophy and philosophers and justifying their contributions towards a better understanding of Islam. In his treatise he frequently tries to reconcile the scripture and philosophical principles in order to solve the problem of occasional and superficial contradiction between the two.[106] In doing this he employs allegorical commentary of the Qur'an and traditions and philosophical principles to fit the scriptures. He therefore believes that philosophy does not and cannot contradict *shari'ah*.

We are not in a position to review and analyse the entire contents of *Fasl al-Maqal* in detail. It needs a careful and exhaustive study. Those interested should really read the text and its critical analysis (see G. Hourani, *Islamic Rationalism, the Case of Averroes*). But he stated with certainty that demonstrative reasoning cannot possibly lead to contradiction with *shari'ah*, for truth attained by one reliable means can never contradicts truth attained by another equally reliable means, but confirms it and testifies to it.[107]

Averroes tried to explain the harmony of *hikmah* and *shari'ah* in all fields of Islamic studies, especially in the field of jurisprudence, (in *Fasl al-Maqal*); in the field of theology, (in *al-Manahij*), and in other fields.

The equally important book concerning the doctrine of harmony, *Tahafut al-Tahafut* (*The Incoherence of the Incoherence*), is obviously an answer to Ghazzali's book *The Incoherencies of Philosophers.* It is Averroes' reply to Ghazzali's attack upon the philosophers. In this book Averroes tries to defend the philosophers against the accusations made by Ghazzali against them. Averroes believes in the value and authority of science, which provides scientists with true information.[108] He believes that philosophy is a branch of science.[109] He believes that the demonstrative scholars (*ahl al-burhan*)[110] or philosophers have the right and are qualified to understand scripture because of their demonstrative and scholarly qualifications and approach, and because they are 'people of firm knowledge' a term borrowed from Qur'an).[111] This term is applied in the Qur'an to the only people who have the right to understand, comment on and interpret the Qur'an, the right and qualification which others do not have.[112]

It is only fair to say that it was Muhammad ibn Muhammad (597–672/1201–74), also known as Nasir al-Din al-Tusi who really took up the challenge of Ghazzali. It was al-Tusi's work, more than the *Incoherence of the Incoherence*, that exerted a lasting influence in the Islamic world of philosophy. Nasir al-Din al-Tusi is regarded as second only to Avicenna in the field of Islamic philosophy. He revived the philosophy of Avicenna by answering the attacks made against him and produced his famous commentary on Avicenna's work *al-Isharat wa al-Tanbihat* (*Remarks and Admonitions*). His commentary is known as *Sharh al-Isharat.* The existence of a rational soul according to Tusi requires no proof, insofar as the most manifest or self-evident entity for a rational being is his own essence or reality, known intuitively without intermediaries. Its independence of sense organs is demonstrated by the fact that the soul knows itself and knows that it knows itself, whereas the sense organs are not capable of knowing themselves, but know corporal objects only. Sense organs, like other parts of the body, are only used by the soul as instruments. He suggests that practical philosophy, of which ethics, household management, and politics are the principle parts, is concerned with the knowledge of voluntary activities or skills insofar as they conduce to human felicity. The principles of such activities or skills are either natural or conventional. In the first case, they are arrived at by human insight or sagacity, the prerogatives of the philosophers or sages. The second arise either from the consensus of the community and are called manners or conventions (*adab wa rosum*), or from the injunctions of a great man favoured by divine support (*ta'yid-e-ilahi*) who is the Prophet or Imam, and are termed divine laws, *nawamis-e-ilahi* or divine orders (natural laws).[113]

It is noteworthy that since the doctrine of harmony was an attempt to solve a basic problem in Christianity as well, both Ghazzali's efforts to harmonize philosophy, religion and gnosis and Averroes' attempt to harmonize the first two attracted the attention of non-Muslim, especially Christian, scholars. This is not the place to explain in detail their influence on Western philosophy and thought generally and their vast contributions to the solution of the problem of the contradiction of philosophy and religion in Christianity in particular.

It is not accidental that followers of St Augustine were to rally around the teachings of Ibn Sina once his works were translated into Latin and that a school was developed which owed its origin to both of them.

Averroes left an impact on Christian scholars who were trying to find an answer to the question of the harmony of Christianity and rationalism. It is even suggested that Averroes had a greater effect upon the Christian world than upon the Islamic world and that he should be studied as a great member of the tradition of Western philosophy rather than as an integral part of Islamic intellectual life. St Thomas called Averroes 'the commentator' (on Aristotle) and Dante referred to him as 'he who made the grand commentary'. According to H. A. Wolfson, Averroes is one of the leading authorities on medieval philosophy and particularly on commentaries on Aristotle.[114] It is suggested that Averroes became more famous in the Latin world than in the Muslim world mainly because very few copies of his books had been made and circulated in Muslim lands, perhaps because of the destruction of his books in Spain by Ximenez' order. In pursuance of this order, eighty thousands manuscripts in Arabic, including those of Averroes and Ibn Tufayl, were burnt in the squares of Granada. In *c.*900/1600, Scaliger, while searching for new manuscripts in Spain, could not find even a single original copy of Ibn Rushd's works.[115]

St Thomas Aquinas, the thirteenth-century master of Christian philosophy and the champion of Christian rationalism should be mentioned here in this context, the question of the harmony of religion and philosophy. Having absorbed the thoughts of Islamic Peripatetic philosophers, especially Ibn Sina and being influenced by Averroeism he tried to answer the questions facing Christianity. Another Christian philosopher, Erigena, stated that philosophy stands supreme in that it is with the direct attainment of God. In his *Annotations* he made his famous assertion *Nemo intrat in caelum nisi per philosophiam* (no one can enter Heaven except through philosophy). He thereby identified philosophy, which as *sophia* exists at the heart of religion, in a manner very similar to numerous Muslim philosophers, specially Averroes (Ibn Rushd), who identified true philosophy with *al-haqiqah* or the truth lying at the heart of the divine law or *al-shari'ah.* It is suggested that the later openness of the Western Christian world to philosophy took place under the influence of Muslim philosophers. 'One of the major factors contributing to this change of attitude (towards philosophy and its harmony with religion in the Western Christian world) was the influence of some important Islamic thinkers, especially in Spain. Probably the most important of these was Ibn Rushd, who actually became more influential in Western Europe, through the translation of many of his books into Latin, than he was in the world of Islam.'[116]

However, we must make it quite clear here that the Muslims' understanding of Islamic rationality supported by Averroes is quite different from the Western and European understanding of Averroeism. Averroes, the chief Muslim religious authority of Cordoba, was completely different from the Averroes of the European Averroists, that arch rationalist and enemy of the authority of revelation. The real Averroes is quite different from his Latin image. He strongly believed, like many other Muslim philosophers, that both reason and revelation are sources of the truth and lead to the same ultimate end as affirmed by his book *On the Harmony between Philosophy and Religion*. Averroes provided the answer to Muslim philosophers who sought to modify Aristotle as well as the challenge of Ghazzali against the philosophers. His book, *Tahafut al-Tahafut*, explains this point. He was to have, perhaps because of this fact, a greater influence in the Christian world than in the Islamic world. However, he was misintroduced in the West. Having said this, it would be fair to point out that unlike Avicenna and other famous Muslim philosophers, Averroes' thoughts remained much more rationalistic than intellectual. This helps us with the point we intended to explain at the beginning of this chapter; that Islamic rationality should be defined within the context of Islam and not within that of Western rationalism. It is reasonable to suggest that neither was Averroes the supporter of rationalism in the Western and modern sense of the term rationalism, nor was Ghazzali the anti-rationality in the Islamic sense of the term rationality.

Having explained, briefly, the issue of the impact of the doctrine on Christianity, we must go back to our main issue.

A contemporary of Averroes, who lived in a different part of the Muslim world, but also a philosopher-lawyer, Abu al-Qasim Husain ibn Mufadal al-Raghib (fifth century AH), also adopted the same approach to develop the doctrine of harmony. This shows that the doctrine was accepted almost at an international scholarly level in the Muslim world, and had established itself firmly.

It is tempting to suggest that from a century after Averroes until the establishment of the Isfahan school of philosophy in the fifteenth century, Islamic philosophy did not make much progress. But his efforts in establishing the doctrine of harmony can be considered very fruitful and long lasting in the Muslim world up to modern times. In spite of the occasional disagreement amongst Muslim thinkers about the doctrine, the majority of scholars have always accepted it in one way or another. The doctrine of harmony of *hikmah* and *shari'ah* and even the unification of the two grew stronger.

It should be borne in mind that some Muslim philosophers and intellectuals have always accepted syncretism in a special Islamic way based on the unity of Truth. Islam supports the unity of religions (revealed ones) and the unity of the source of knowledge: we can find many Qur'anic verses stating that there has always been one single religion, Islam, or submission to God, which is the Natural religion. The unity of God and the unity of truth meant the unity of the message of God and thus the unity of revealed religions though in different expressions. This syncretism also helped the doctrine of unity of all philosophies and all philosophical schools and the harmony of *hikmah* and *shari'ah.*

To the problem of how the rational potentialities of human beings are to be fulfilled without leading them into mazes of subjective and anti-social error, most philosophers (*falasafah*, sing. *faylsuf*) had long since found a solution on the practical level. To begin with they minimized the differences of opinions among philosophers. We have noted how in ancient philosophy the standard philosophic curriculum was based on both Plato and Aristotle, in different respects, despite the well-known contradictions between their views. Although the differences among the old masters were not ignored, *philosophia* was felt to offer a single orientation and purpose, and hence at least potentially a single doctrine as far as truth and the source of truth was concerned. Explicit harmonization between Plato and Aristotle was furthered in two ways. Plato's logical method, for instance, was interpreted by way of Aristotle. Some humanization of philosophies and the views of the philosophers were in direct response to the need to justify *philosophia* as not contradicting revealed religious dogma. The teachings of Aristotle that seemed inconsistent with immortality of the soul and with a temporal act of creation were interpreted by way of Plato, sometimes with the aid of a Neoplatonist booklet early translated into Arabic and mistitled *The Theology of Aristotle.*

Generally speaking there has been attempts by many Muslim philosophers to present a holistic view of philosophy in the Islamic world. This movement started fairly early in the history of Islamic philosophy. The main, and probably the first, exponent and champion of this holistic view of philosophy was Farabi. He held that there is a unity of philosophy. It really is all one school or discipline. He ascribed the differing schools, such as the Peripatetics, Stoics and so on, to the fanaticism of their followers who stressed points of divergence instead of trying to bring about harmonization. He suggested that the philosophical method involves the use of logic, which deals with structures of human mind, which in turn is everywhere, the same. On this basis Farabi considered that philosophy and religion were also in harmony, if each is properly understood. They exist in parallel. He suggested theories reconciling the two traditions, including a theory of prophecy.[117] We may also point out that the holistic view of philosophy in Islam was developed further and more methodologically by Mulla Sadra of Shiraz. He established the school of Transcendental Philosophy to promote reconciliation between the Peripatetic school of philosophy and the Illuminationist school of philosophy, the two supposedly conflicting philosophies. At the centre of this genuine effort was the unity of truth and thus the unity of reason and revelation, the unity of the objective of philosophy and religion, the unity of philosophers and the unity of *hikmah* and *shari'ah*.[118] According to this view, complete and inclusive harmony of knowledge, truth, human primordial nature, natural laws and basic ethical and moral principles are a matter of timeless concepts and free from changes.

A good example of the attempts made in this field is the work of Farabi, *al-Jam' bayn Ra'y al-Hakimayn* (*The Reconciliation Between the Opinions of theTwo Great Philosophers* – Plato and Aristotle).[119] This is probably why some critics of Muslim philosophers have regarded even Avicenna's philosophy as the philosophy of Illumination.[120] Out of this movement grew the support for the doctrine of harmony of *hikmah* and *shari'ah*, too, because all philosophical systems and all religious doctrines express only a single truth. This philosophical movement took the form of reconciliation between philosophy and gnosis on one side, and was called *falasafat al-iaque*, and harmony of *hikmah* and *shari'ah* on the other side.[121] This movement gained support amongst Muslim intellectuals very early on.

One of the conclusions that were made at the end of the last chapter, was that Islam developed and promoted its own epistemology. The main feature of this epistemology was the cognitive trinity of the authority of revelation, reason and human primordial nature. We also suggested that this cognitive trinity forms a unity based on the unicity of truth. The difference between schools of Islamic thought is not based on whether they accept or reject the authority of all the three or one of the three means of reaching the truth. The difference was really based on the question of the priority of each of these means of cognition. While the Peripatetic school believed that reason enjoyed priority, the Illuminationist school suggested that intuition and human primordial nature enjoyed priority. Suhrawardi, head of the Illuminationist movement, suggested that knowledge (*'ilm*) is a light (*nur*) by which the essence of the things (*haqiqat al-ashya'*) are manifested. Neither of the schools completely rejected the authority of either revelation or of the other two means of attaining the truth. The term used to designate the Peripatetic school in Islamic philosophy is Mashsha'i which literally means treading along (the road of reason towards the truth). And the term used to designate the Illuminationist school is Ishraqi, which means being illuminated with the light of the truth. They are both called by the title *hikmah* (*Hikmat al-Mashsha and Hikmat al-Ishraque).* Neither of the two schools, thus, challenges the actual doctrine of the harmony of *hikmah* and *shari'ah*. Each school challenges only the priority of the means claimed by the other school to enjoy priority.

Let us explain this point by referring to the stand adopted by the prominent scholars of the two schools, Ibn Rushd and Ibn al-'Arabi (and we shall return to the issue of the two major schools of Islamic philosophy). It is suggested that Ibn Rushd established an important principle, the principle that it is possible to come to the same truth in a variety of different ways. Ibn Rushd argued that religion and philosophy, by which he meant rational way of establishing truth, which is not based on revelation, are two paths to the same destination. They are two different ways of doing the same thing, as it were, and the differences are important in that they are appropriate to different kinds of people. According to Ibn Rushd, it is possible to get to the same truth in two different ways (rational and revelational). However, Ibn Rushd points out that religion is available to everyone while philosophy is available to a minority.

We tend to identify this sort of argument with Ibn Rushd, but in a different form it was also used by his philosophical opponent, Ibn al-Arabi. The latter argued that we tend to think of the notion of *Tawhid* in ways which do not really make it impinge on our lives. But if the notion of *Tawhid* is taken seriously, it implies that we do not really exist apart from God, that there is not really any 'us' at all, there is just God. Ibn Arabi goes into great detail to explain how we might acquire the ability to see both ourselves and the rest of the world as part of God. So we can see world both as it normally appears (separate from God), and as an aspect of God. Both ways of seeing the world are correct, in the sense that there is truth in both these positions.[122]

What both Ibn Rushd and Ibn al-ʿArabi were trying to establish was the unity of truth and its accessibility by different ways. This point has been and is being explained further in the course of our discussion. Having made this point, we must return to what we were discussing earlier.

Shihab al-din Yahya al Suhrawardi, known as Shaykh al-Ishraque (killed 578/1191) was the first official head of the Illuminationist school. We cannot go into his philosophy in detail here but his contribution to Islamic intellectualism was so great that after him Islamic philosophy developed along two completely independent courses: Peripatetic philosophy, known as *Falasafat al-Mashsha* and Illuminationist philosophy known as *Falasafat al-Ishraque*. Suhrawardi is officially recognized as the head of the second Islamic school of philosophy.[123] However, his contribution to the doctrine of the harmony of *hikmah*, *shariʿah* and *ʿirfan* is beyond doubt. The doctrine on harmony was therefore advocated henceforth by Peripatetics as well as Illuminationists (two supposedly opposing groups of philosophers) as well as by other scholars. Ghazzali, also adopted the same approach, but Ghazzali's attitude towards the philosophers, reflected in *Tahafut al-Falasafah*, did not let him establish himself as a follower of this approach or as the author of the doctrine of harmony of *hikmah*, *shariʿah* and *ʿirfan.*

Suhrawardi questioned neither the doctrine of harmony nor the right of reason to investigate the most complicated religious subjects. His prime objective is the truth and its unity especially the unity of religious and philosophical truth.[124] But, nevertheless, he challenges the priority of the means to the truth suggested by the other school. It must be pointed out that there were other differences between the two schools, such as the question as to whether existence or essence is a mental consideration (*'itibari*) or *a priori* (*asli*). But these other differences do not concern us here.

Suhrawardi discussed at length the question of knowledge, ultimately basing it on illumination. But he combined the way of reason with that of intuition and human primordial nature. He regards the two as necessarily complementing each other. Reason without intuition and illumination is, according to Suhrawardi, puerile and half-blind and can never reach the transcendence source of all truth and intellection. Intuition without a preparation in logic and the training and development of the rational faculty can be misled and furthermore cannot express itself succinctly and methodically. This is why his book *Falasafat al-Ishraq (Theosophy of the Orient of Illumination)* begins with logic.[125] We may thus understand how even the heads of all major schools of philosophy have been working in the spirit of harmony and reconciliation and tried to establish harmony between reason, revelation, intuition and Islamic tradition.

While the Islamic Peripatetic school of philosophy (Mashsha'i) relied most heavily upon the rational, logical and syllogistic methods of discovering the truth and sought to reach the truth by means of rational arguments based on reason, the Illuminationist school (Ishraqi) supported intellectual intuition and illumination as the main means to be adopted, side by side with the use of reason. Contrary to what is sometimes suggested, the Illuminationist school did not reject the authority of reason. This school combined the method of ratiocination with that of intellectual intuition and illumination. This combination of the two trends of thought and methods is also true of the Islamic Peripatetic school. Avicenna, who is regarded as the most representative of this school, combined the doctrines of Aristotle with certain elements from the Neoplatonists. He was one of the precursors of the metaphysical school of Illuminationism, whose greatest exponent was Suhrawardi.[126] We have already pointed out that Farabi also produced a valuable work on the consistency of and the harmony between the opinions of the two great philosophers, Plato and Aristotle. It was an established philosophical tradition amongst the Muslims to see and explain doctrines and methods in the light of harmony, rather than conflict.

Having explained briefly this point about the unity of truth and its source we believe that Ishraqi philosophy of Suhrawardi is of special interest with regard to nature, natural law system and human rights. For this school, as for other schools, nature is regarded as a symbol of the higher order of reality. Nature is regarded as a book, whose inner meanings can be understood only by symbolic interpretation (*ta'wil*) and not by literal observation. Especially the Sufi and 'Arif Ishraqis attached a spiritual significance to the study of nature.

After Ghazzali, philosophy developed in a new important direction, which may be called a purely religious philosophy or philosophical religion. This new philosophical tradition began with the work of Shihab al-Din al-Suhrawardi and reached its final formulation, under the influence of Ibn al-'Arabi, with Sadr al-Din of Shiraz (1571/2–1641/2 AD), as *hikmat al-muta'aliyyah* or the transcendental philosophy, in his monumental work known as *al-Asfar al-Arba'ah*.

The fundamental doctrines of this school are, first, the principle of the unity of existence (*wahdat al-wujud*) and hence the second principle of grades of being (*tashakukiyat al-wujud*, modules of existence). The third principle, another grand theory closely connected to this principle of grades of being, is that of cognition that asserts the identity and the unity of thought and being (*ittihad al 'aqil wa al-ma'qul*), and the fourth principle affirms a realm of similitudes (*'alam al-mithal*). Suhrawardi developed the first two doctrines. He criticized Avicenna's thesis of the distinction between essence (*mahiyyah*) and existence (*wujud)* and thus he removed the distinction between God and the existence of man. Further, he attacked the idea of duality between matter (*maddah*) and form (*sorah*) and formulated the doctrine of pure existence and being, which tolerated the only distinction within itself of 'more or less', or more perfect and less perfect. (The theory of the priority of existence, *wujud*, over essence/whatism, *mahiyyah*, the unity of existence with perfection, *kamal* (*al-wujud 'ain al-kamal*), and the theory of grades/modulation of existence and perfection play a very important role in the position and concept of man amongst Muslim philosophers and philosophers of ethics. It thus plays an important role in the concept of human primordial nature too amongst Muslims.) Consequently, for Suhrawardi, reality (existence and being) was one homogeneous continuum punctuated only by 'more or less' or 'grades of being': the whole God is being and the whole of being is God.

The discovery and development of existence enabled Mulla Sadra, in his philosophical school of *falasafat al-muta'aliyyah*, to articulate a line of causality deeper and more primary than the horizontal causality of motions between creatures. He explored the vertical line of existence from God to creatures and their return to Him. His famous book, *Al-Asfar al-Arba'ah,* which may be literally translated as *The Four Journeys*, was written to explain the four stages of the development and movement of man. The first journey is the journey from himself to God, or the journey from creation to the Truth (*al-safar men al-khalq ila al-haqq*). The second journey is the journey through the Truth in the Truth, or the journey from God to God (*al-safar be al-haqq fi al-haqq*). The third one is the opposite of the first, and it is from the Truth to the creation, or the journey from God to true self (*al-safar men al-haqq ila al-khalq be al-haqq*). The fourth one is the opposite of the second one and is the journey by the Truth in creation, and is the true discovery of oneself (*al-safar be al-haqq fi al-khalq*).[127] Mulla Sadra had the four spiritual journeys in mind. But it is suggested that this idea of Mulla Sadra, however, urges the question of the reality of the horizontal causal line, of the human and of one's interaction with other persons and with nature. Today these are the issues of social justice, human rights, and the protection of the environment; they are the special human concerns at this juncture.[128]

Suhrawardi also developed a theory of knowledge according to which cognition came about by a direct awareness or immediate presence (*hudur*) of the object. He upheld the phenomenon of self-awareness as the primordial characteristic of all knowledge and declared this awareness to be the fundamental self-luminosity of being. Thus, as the stream of being processes from the ultimate reality by emanation, so does the stream of light or immediate consciousness from its ultimate source. Consciousness itself is, therefore, a continuum differentiated at various points by the only category of 'more or less'. This trend of thought produced in Islamic speculative school a characteristic quality of what might be termed a subjective humanism with regard to the universe and its constitution. The human cognitive faculties are projected into the ontological structure of the reality, which appears as a person. Just as a man has sense perception, imagination, rational thought and spiritual intuition, so is the universe objectively invested with these faculties. The mystic Ibn al-'Arabi (560–638/1165–1240) developed the idea of the universe as the macro-anthropos (*al-insan al-akbar*) or macro-persona (*al-shakhs al-akbar*). Man is called micro-anthropos (*al-insan al-saghir*). This doctrine is the reverse of the idea of the macrocosm and microcosm. Where the former patterns the universe on man, the latter patterns man on the universe.

Going back to the main theme of our discussion, we are tempted to suggest that the doctrine of harmony, however, was challenged by some Muslim scholars. We can even state that the majority of traditionist Sunni Muslim scholars have rejected it. But it is equally true that almost the absolute majority of Muslim philosophers, jurist-philosophers, rationalists and many Muslim intellectuals have accepted it. Indeed, groups of Muslim scholars have always supported the doctrine in all periods of the history of Islamic intellectualism up to the present time.

Let us now continue with the history of the doctrine of harmony. As we have already pointed out Khajah Nasir al-din al-Tusi, philosopher and astronomer, adopted Avicenna's attitude towards the doctrine of harmony of *hikmah* and *shari'ah*. In his commentary on Avicenna's *Al-Isharat*, in *Sharh al-Isharat*, he explains his views on the harmony of revelation and reason.

Although he rejected some of the philosophical opinions of his time, e.g. the doctrine of the eternity of the world, he can be regarded as one of the jurist-philosophers for he also left us some works on Islamic law) who supported the doctrine.[129] His student, Hasan ibn Yusuf, known as 'Allamah Hilli (647–726 AH), one of the greatest jurisprudents and Shi'ite scholars, also followed his master and accepted the doctrine of harmony. He is regarded as one of the Shi'ite jurist-philosophers, for he has left us works of great value in both fields. We shall have some quotations from his writings later on in this chapter.

'Abd al-Rahman, known as Ibn Khaldoon (732–808/1332–1406), the very well-known Muslim philosopher of history, is another scholar (jurist-philosopher) who supported the doctrine of harmony. Among many disciplines he perfected were logic, philosophy, history and Islamic law. He can be truly regarded as one of the Muslim scholars who advocated and applied the doctrine of harmony of reason and revelation and of *hikmah* and *shari'ah*. As he was equally at ease with both philosophy and law, though he owes his fame to neither, his approach to the application of the doctrine of harmony always remains of special interest. He was the author of the first work on the philosophy of history in Islam. He is known for his approach to philosophical history reflected in his introduction to his world history.[130] On occasions he even criticizes philosophy (see the chapter on 'repudiation of philosophy' in *Al-Muqaddamah*).[131] But his criteria for evaluating philosophy are essentially religious. He suggests the use of logical method in solving crucial problems affecting man's ultimate destiny and salvation. But he only permits the use and study of logic after one has become fully proficient in religious disciplines, especially Qur'anic studies and law and jurisprudence.[132] Ibn Khaldoon divided the sciences into rational, traditional and linguistic, in a manner reminiscent of Farabi in his work, IHSA AL-'ULUM (*Enumeration of Sciences*). The first division, rational, which he calls natural, includes the philosophical sciences such as logic, physics, mathematics and metaphysics. The second division includes religious sciences grounded in the Qur'an such as the sciences of exegesis, transmission of Islamic traditions (*hadith*), jurisprudence, and theology (*kalam*). Ibn Khaldoon recognizes that philosophy has some positive advantages. It at least sharpens the mind and enables us to formulate arguments in accordance with the rules of logic. However, he makes the study of jurisprudence and *shari'ah* a pre-requisite for the study of logic and philosophy. His approach, therefore, in solving and explaining scholarly problems is rational, but in a very refined academic and scholastic form.

Islamic philosophy, intellectualism and rationality, along with other Islamic disciplines, suffered greatly during the Mongol period in which interest in the development of the doctrine of harmony consequently declined and suffered. This lasted until the late sixteenth century. In the seventeenth century the classical division of schools of philosophy into two main schools of Peripateticism and Illuminationism was weakened. A third school of philosophy, which later came to be known as the Isfahan school of philosophy, for its founders and developers lived mainly in Isfahan, was established. The harmony and balance between intellect, reason and intuition is perfected by the champion of the last school of philosophy in Islam, namely Mulla Sadra of Shiraz.[133]

We can define the philosophers prior to Mulla Sadra in Isfahan as the initiators and founders of the school of philosophy that is referred to as Transcendental philosophy, and define those after him, as the developers and expanders of this school of philosophy. Mulla Sadra was a student of Shaykh Baha' al-din Husein al-'Amili (d. 1631), and Sayyed Abu al-Qasim, known as Mir Finderski (d. 1640), all in Isfahan and the recognized founders of this school of philosophy. Some of Mulla Sadra's many great students are Mulla Muhsin Fayd Kashani, 'Abd al-Razzaque al-Lahiji and Qadi Sa'id al-Qummi.

Some of the main features of this school (concerning our purpose), which were of great importance to later philosophers, are as follows. The followers of this school believed that philosophy conjoined with revealed truth as imparted to the Prophets (put) and the sages were the highest expression of truth, the identity and unity of the aims of philosophy and theology/religion is complete. They cited various Qur'anic verses and traditions in support of this thesis. Mulla Sadra believed that the sages (for whom he had a very high respect) have been the carriers of the light of knowledge and are the beacon of prophecy.[134] He therefore firmly believes in the unity of truth, the harmony of *hikmah* and *shari'ah*, and in the compatibility of the aims and objectives of philosophy and religion and the unity of the source of *hikmah* and *shari'ah*.[135]

The doctrine and concept of prophecy (*al-risalah wa al-nubuwwah*) among the Muslims is of importance in this context. Earlier Muslim philosophers such as Ibn Sina and Farabi explained it in their Peripatetic philosophical terms and way, treating prophecy in the context of rational understanding of man's cognitive faculties. They traced both human intellect and prophetic intellect to the same source, i.e. the divine intellect. While Mulla Sadra in his philosophy employs the same model and many of the same technical terms, he diverges from his philosophical predecessors, presenting philosophy not only as a perfection of perceptual faculties, but as perfection in being (*wujud*), the Prophet being the most perfect of creation through which creation is ordered and maintained. The Prophet is thus the summit of creation and only by understanding the prophetic function can man understand himself. As an Islamic tradition maintains, 'philosophy issues from the niche of prophecy'. In Sadrian philosophy, philosophy and Prophethood have the same fundamental objective: 'to know things as they are in themselves'. In the beginning of *Asfar* Mulla Sadra writes, 'Know that philosophy is the perfection of the human soul to the extent of human possibility through perception of the realities of existing things as they are in themselves and judgement of their existence verified through demonstration, not derived from opinion and tradition.' He then relates this to the famous prayer of the Prophet Muhammad, 'Lord, show us things as they are' and to the prayer of Abraham 'Lord, give me wisdom'.[136] For Mulla Sadra the objective and the final end of prophethood and philosophy is thus the same. On the highest level, that of intellect (*al-'aql*), the prophet and the philosopher perceive intelligible realities without intermediary. But in his other work, *Al-Shawahid al-Rububiyyah fi Manahij al-Sulukiyyah* (*The Divine Signs Concerning the Paths of Saintliness and Salvation*), Sadra provides important information on the other dimensions of prophecy, which establish a clear break between prophecy and philosophy. The true philosopher participates in the perfection of intellect, but unlike the prophet his faculty of imagination (*khayal*) is not perfect. Through the perfection of intellect and the faculty of imagination the prophet is a means whereby intelligible realities are transferred into imaginal representations which reveal the true nature of reality for all human beings. The philosopher, however, has only the perfect intellect by which he witnesses the true nature of reality. The prophet is thus a vehicle for revelation (*wahy*), whereas the philosopher can only partake of inspiration (*ilham*) and hence of sanctity (*wilayah*). Mulla Sadra's most focused treatment of prophecy is found in the last chapter of *al-Shawahid al-Rububiyyah*, entitled 'On the Prophethood and sainthood'. This book is considered by many to be his last philosophical work and therefore his most mature philosophical expression.[137] It should also be pointed out that Mulla Sadra places a great importance on the issue of *fitrah* in this process.

The champions of this school of thought, like the forerunners of this approach such as Ghazzali and Suhrawardi, not only believed in the harmony of *hikmah* and *shari'ah*, but also in the harmony of these two and that of Islamic gnosis. They were not only philosophers. Some of them were jurist-philosophers, like Kashani, a very well-known member of this school. His combined legal-philosophical work, *Mahajjat al-Baida*, stands as a good example of the efforts of this school and the approach it adopted to explain the harmony of *shari'ah* and *hikmah*. Legal rulings of *shari'ah* are explained by him in rational and philosophical terms and principles in a refined and subtle way.

It must be pointed out, however, that the tension between the traditionists and the philosophers (rationalists) in one way or another continued. From time to time it even erupted into fierce discussions and arguments. But the struggle in defence of the doctrine of harmony also continued. The harmonization of *hikmah* and *shari'ah* indifferent ways and with different speeds by Muslim philosophers, jurists, jurist-philosophers and thinkers has continued and doctrine of harmony has been supported in the history of Islamic intellectualism. It prepared the ground for the reconstruction of religious thought in Islam, and particularly for Islamic legal reform. We are not concerned here with the complex question of this reconstruction and legal reform. This issue deserves to be treated independently. Our task is to follow the destiny of the doctrine through the modern period and see how later and contemporary Muslim thinkers have treated it.

Islamic Rationality in the Modern History of Islamic Thought

Jamal al-Din, known as Asad Abadi/Afghani (1839–1897), seems to be the unanimously proclaimed initiator of reconstruction of Islamic thought and of the modern rational reform movement in Islam. We leave his life story to his many biographies. His efforts would not have borne fruit were it not for his great disciples, particularly Muhammad 'Abduh. They have both left a great impact on Muslim intellectuals in all parts of the Muslim world in modern times. Their main concern seemed to be the revival of Islamic rationality, harmonization not only of *hikmah* and *shari'ah*, but also of *shari'ah* and even modern sciences.[138]

Jamal al-Din believed that Islam was a rational system and that its superiority lies in the fact that it commands its followers to follow reason and not to submit to anything irrational or without proof. Islam always addresses reason and bases its ordinances upon it. Its sources clearly confirm that human felicity is the product of reason and insight and that misery and perdition are the outcome of ignorance, disregard for reason and the extinction of the light of insight.[139] Jamal al-Din is very open, frank and even extravagant in his rationalization of Islam and thus in his support for the doctrine of harmony of *hikmah* and *shari'ah* and sciences. He believed that the mark of the superiority of Islam over other religions lay in that its fundamental principles can be fully rationalized. Jamal al-Din is wholly progressive in his conception of the rationality of theology.[140] Both the rational and the cultural–political dimensions of Islam (initiated through a modern approach in modern times by Jamal al-Din) have become dominant themes in the modernists' interpretation of Islam in the twentieth century' and so is, therefore, the doctrine of harmony of *hikmah*, *shari'ah* and science.[141]

His greatest disciple and life-long associate was Muhammad 'Abduh (1849–1905), who certainly played a crucial role in the modernization and rationalization of Islamic thought on one side, and its renaissance. He was appointed Grand Mufti of Egypt and was regarded as one of the Muslim jurist-philosophers and thus practically demonstrated the doctrine of harmony in the same way that the early Muslim jurist-philosopher, Averroes, did in his period.[142] 'Abduh believed that 'reason is the ultimate arbiter of truth and that reason and religion (*hikmah* and *shari'ah*) marched in unison for the first time in the Qur'an'.[143] He made efforts to explain the harmony of Islam and even modern sciences in his book, *al-Islam Din al-'Ilm wa al-madaniyyah* (*Islam, the Religion of Science and Civilisation*). It has been suggested that 'Abduh's theological departures amounted implicitly to a revival of Mu'tazilism, the systematically rationalist school of the early Islamic period, neo-Mu'tazilism.[144]

One of 'Abduh's most constantly emphasized themes is the essential harmony of reason, revelation and individual moral temperament.[145] In his two significant works, *Risalat al-Tawhid* and *al-Islam wa al-Nasraniyyah Ma'a al-'Ilm wa al-Madaniyyah*, he successfully deals with the harmony of *hikmah* and *shari'ah* in Islam (in the first) and the harmony of *shari'ah* and science (in the second work). He regards Islam as the true friend of science.[146] He states that 'Muslims agree that if religion can reveal certain things to us that exceed our comprehension, it cannot teach us anything that is in contradiction with our reason"[147] He gives human reason complete authority to discover legal rulings in the absence of religious texts and revelation.[148] If then a thinker succeeds in understanding and discovering the truth about God, his attributes, his faith, articles of faith etc. by the sole force of his reason, without the benefit of revelation, as has been the case for certain people then who is to prevent him from setting forth the rules that he judges good and calling other men to share his beliefs and to act as he does? All this is permissible as long as there is no provision in the revealed law to contradict it. Rational knowledge is a full representation of truth as is intuition or knowledge through revelation in practical matters.[149] (We pointed out earlier that Ibn Rushd also suggested this idea long before 'Abduh.) 'Abduh thus believed that there is a full harmony between decisive and absolute rational reasoning and authentic traditions.[150] Here the major role and authority is given to certainty.

'Abduh's theological views are explained in his major work *Risalat al-Tawhid* (*Treatise on Monotheism*). In this treatise he suggests that theological discussions and discourses were not unknown to pre-Islamic times, but theologians in those days tended to support their arguments by appealing to para-natural or miraculous phenomena instead of rational proof. With the rise of Islam, that picture changed completely, and reason was set up as the ultimate arbiter of moral and religious truth. Thus reason and religion coalesced for the first time in a sacred Book revealed to the prophet Muhammad (puh).[151] 'Abduh is of the opinion that the Ash'arite–Mu'tazilite argument is really a verbal one. This is because both groups agree that God's action, with regard to the questions of

His justice and man's free will, exhibit His wisdom and that caprice or folly cannot be attributed to Him.

Indeed 'Abduh emphasizes that Islam not only is not incompatible with reason but is also the only religion which religiously calls upon man to use his own reason and investigate nature. In this context he cites those numerous verses of the Qur'an which enjoin upon man to think intelligently and to study nature, God's creation, as the signs, (*ayat*) of God. Thus although 'Abduh in the actual materials of his reinterpretation of Islam introduced no new ideas into the body of traditional Islamic ideas, his position, nevertheless, present an advance on the pre-modern reformers on two important points. One is his great emphasis on the position of reason in Islam, i.e. the idea that although faith and reason operate on different spheres, they must not and cannot contradict each other, but must positively co-operate in human advancement.[152] And the other, which seems to be his fundamental concern, is to restate the basic ideas of Islam in such a way as to open the door for the influence of new ideas and for the acquisition of modern knowledge in general.[153]

What is interesting at this juncture of the history of Islamic rationality is that parallel with the harmony of *hikmah, shari'ah* and gnosis, Muslim modernist scholars have tried to extend the harmony of those three with science, especially modern sciences. While 'Abduh placed his idea of the harmony of Islam and even modern sciences on concepts and general principles of Islam, later proponents of the idea have adopted a more practical approach towards the issue. Muhammad Legenhausen explains the harmony of Islam and sciences as follows.

'After Renaissance, when European thought was seeking to escape the structures and strictures of Scholasticism, two prominent modes of philosophical thought began to take shape: rationalism and empiricism. The rationalists proposed to limit the notion of rationality to its more calculative aspects and restricted the self-evident to the most subjective certainties. The empiricists, who were less interested in reason as such emphasized the role of sensory in the acquisition of knowledge. Empiricist philosophy comes in all shapes and sizes, religious as well as atheistic, extreme and moderate. Empiricism, however, which is fundamentally neither an ethical nor a political philosophy, is often described as founded on two basic principles: first, that all ideas are derived from experience, and second, that proper judgement must be supported by experience. However, Locke, as well as Berkeley and Hume, held that we have two kinds of experience: sensation, or external experience, and reflection, or internal experience. These two kinds of experience were held to provide the foundations of all knowledge. Knowledge of necessary truth, such as the truth of logic and mathematics, were held to derive from inner experience of the relations among ideas, while empirical knowledge of contingent truth was held to derive from the outer experience of the senses of vision, hearing, smell, taste and touch. If we define empiricism as the doctrine that all ideas and knowledge are derived from both inner and outer experiences, it is difficult to see what is objectionable about this from the viewpoint of Islam."[154]

While empiricism (the kind which is based on the outer experience) concerns itself with the nature of appearances, *'aql* (Islamic rationality) is concerned with seeing things through the appearances to the deeper reality behind them, with insight and disclosure. We do not, thus, find a direct contradiction between the reasoning of the empiricist and the exercise of *'aql*. The Qur'an introduces the things we see and sense as the outer signs (*ayah*) for coming to an inner spiritual experience. This leads us to believe in the harmony of these two experiences. Empiricism is flawed by its unduly restrictive view of rationality. If this view is modified to allow for the rational appreciation of symbolic signification, nothing of essential value in empiricism is thereby lost and the conflict is solved. In this way a satisfying approach to the fundamental problem of the philosophy of Islam, identifying the scope of Islam and its implications for the science and humanities, and particularly for philosophy can be found. Thus, although Islam (not Muslims) cannot be said to contain its own particular microbiology, for example, and for the most part neither contradicts nor implies particular claims in the natural and human sciences, it does present man with various ideas and concepts which proponents of sciences or some new philosophy would supplant by those of their own theories.[155]

Having explained this point we would like to go back to the issue of the history of the doctrine of Islamic rationality. 'Abduh's student, disciple and lifelong associate, Muhammad Rashid Rida (1865–1935 AD), followed his master. But he seemed to be more interested in reviving the old Islamic political system, and recommended *al-salaf*, or early Islamic doctors and Muslim scholars as the people to be followed. In a way Rashid Rida led the Salafi movement in Egypt which in turn moved steadily towards a type of fundamentalism closely akin, and admittedly so, to Wahhabism, the most anti-rational movement in the contemporary history of Islam. His great work was *Al-Manar* (*The Lighthouse*) which replaced '*al-'Urwat al-Wuthqa*' (*The Firmest Bond*), by Jamal al-Din and 'Abduh. Rashid Rida's main concern seems to be the application of the doctrine of harmony of *hikmah* and *shari'ah* in the field of politics, and not law or theology. In fact *Al-Manar* was recognized as the journal of the Salafi movement of Egypt. Although insisting on social and political reform of the Muslim society, its temper steadily moved towards anti-intellectualism. Having said this about Rashid Rida, we must point out here that as far as the actual Islamic law is concerned, he seems to be a revivalist with rational inclination and attitudes. It seems that in Egypt this attitude and this approach can be traced to Rashid Rida . He contended that, for example, even many traditions (*hadith*) of sound *isnad* (transmutation of *hadith)* should still be submitted to criticism of their content. Consequently he rejected traditions if they appeared to him to be rationally or theologically objectionable.[156] His approach and attitudes in this context seems to be similar to that adopted by Sayyed Ahmad Khan and Shibli Nu'mani on the Indian sub-continent, of which more below.[157] They all seem to have appealed to the discipline of *'ilm al-dirayah* in their criticism of traditions, though with different objectives and intention. They suggested that, in addition to the application of the stringent rules of transmission (*'ilm al-rijal*), traditions should be subjected to a system of internal criticism, called *'ilm al-dirayah. 'Ilm al-dirayah,* or the discipline of criticism of the text (*matn*) of traditions, involves judging whether a report or tradition is consistent with reason, with human nature, with common sense, with the Qur'an, with other sound traditions and with historical conditions. N. Coulson in his series of lectures on the conflict and tensions in Islamic law (published by the University of Chicago Press, 1968) explains how the harmony between text/tradition and reason was established early in the history of Islamic law and that this harmony continues to work in solving so-called tensions up to modern times.

At the same time that Islamic rationality was being developed in Egypt by Jamal al-Din and his followers, another Islamic rationalist movement developed in the Indian sub-continent. Sayyed Ahmad Khan (b.1817), Amir 'Ali (d. 1928), Iqbal (b.1876), and Shibli Nu'mani are the prominent figures of this movement. Ahmad Khan, the founder of the University of Aligahr, believed in the complete conformity and harmony of religion and reason (*hikmah* and *shari'ah*). His commentary on the Qur'an is an example of a philosophical and rational commentary. His criteria for religious truth were its compatibility with reason and nature. Amir 'Ali followed Ahmad Khan's path and explained Islamic and Qur'anic tenets in philosophical and scientific terms. He tried to show the compatibility of Islam and modern enlightenment and thought and that the spirit of Islam is compatible with the core of contemporary Islamic intellectual and political freedom.[158] But Iqbal's approach seems to be the most significant attempt to interpret Islam not only in philosophical terms, in general, but to interpret it in terms of modern philosophy in particular. He tries to extend the doctrine of harmony of *hikmah* and *shari'ah* to the doctrine of harmony of *shari'ah* and Western philosophy of knowledge and science. Iqbal was a lawyer and a philosopher.[159] His attempt in the field of harmonization of philosophy and Islam is therefore of a special value and interest. He suggested that because Islam is a temporal as well as spiritual holistic system and because Islam is a rational as well as an ethical and practical religion, it does not and would not contradict philosophy. They are both compatible and harmonious.[160] As we pointed out before, he believed in the harmony of Islam, philosophy and science. He thought that because Islam approved an inductive approach as well as a deductive one, it was in complete harmony with modern scientific thought and approach. He even believed that Roger Bacon received his scientific training and approach through Muslims in Spain (this was also suported by M. 'Abduh). He used philosophical and scientific principles and approaches to explain Islamic beliefs and Qur'anic verses.[161] However, Iqbal was against wholesale Westernization of the Muslim world. The tension between Westernism and Islamic fundamentalism in India produced Iqbal (1876-1938). The contents of his philosophy apart, Iqbal is a synthetic figure in his mental veneer and basic spiritual and mental character. Fazlur Rahman suggests that: 'a serious intellectual and genuinely perceptive mind, Iqbal denounced Western intellectualism and reason as hollow and insisted on faith as the sole guide.'[162] Fazlur Rahman presents a clear picture of Iqbal in this respect:

> Iqbal stresses faith and intuition, sometimes rather than reason and sometimes at the expense of reason, depending on the context he is speaking in and the kind of audience he is addressing. There are three types of positions which Iqbal takes with regard to the relationship between intuition and reason:
>
> 1. that intuition and reason pull in different directions;
> 2. that reason is subordinate to intuition or wisdom and, in a way, leads towards the latter; and
> 3. that there exists between the two an organic relationship and thus neither can dispense with the other.[163]

Iqbal, however, believed that religion goes beyond philosophy and not against it and that reason was born from within a religious sense of life. Fazlur Rahman suggests that:
'it is thus clear that the main body of the Muslim philosophers, intellectuals, lawyers and theologians rejected the idea that there was a double truth, one apprehended by philosophy, reason and science, the other by religion. They held that this did not seem possible rationally so they pursued the idea that the truth was unitary but appeared now in rational, and again in a metaphorical imaginative form. They suggested that religious truth is but rational truth, but instead of being expressed in nakedly rational formulas, manifested itself in imaginative symbols, a fact which was responsible for its widespread acceptance by, and effectiveness among, the masses. Thus, religion is but philosophy for the masses, and, once accepted, is philosophy of the

masses, having as its primary function and objective their moral state and mental and spiritual purification and salvation. i.e. instead of saying 'If you pursue moral good, your mind shall attain the real spiritual freedom which is bliss', the prophet said, 'If you are virtuous and perform these specific acts, you shall enter Paradise and will be saved from the flames of Hell and you shall obtain the pleasure of your Creator, God', etc."[164]

We cannot deal with the development of the doctrine of harmony of *hikmah* and *shari'ah* and the authority of human intellect without referring to those who strongly opposed these ideas. We cannot, however, here, deal with the history of Ash'arism, Hanbalism, traditionalism and literalism and Salafism in details. The seeds of non-rationalism or misology in Islam were sown by Asha'irah. Hanbalism was so strongly associated with traditionalism that many scholars like Tabari, Maqdesi, Ibn 'Abd al-Berr and many others did not regard it as a school of jurisprudence.[165] They regarded the head, Ibn Hanbal, only as a traditionalist or as an specialist in the discipline of Islamic traditions. Soon after the establishment of Hanbalism in the centre of the Muslim world, literalism came into existence, both in the Eastern and Western parts of the Muslim world. In fact anti-rationalism almost always has taken the form of Hanbalism, which rejected all philosophical, rational, and even theological, methods of discourse and clung to the text, literally interpreted.

Of course there have been other anti-rational approaches too. The Shi'ite Akhbari movement is very similar to the Sunni Hanbalite movement in approach. Literalism *(al-daheriyyah)* was initiated by Dawood ibn Khalaf al-Isfahani (d. 883 AD), father of the official head of the Daherite School, Ibn Dawood al-Isfahani (d. 909 AD) in the East. It was followed and developed in the West by Ali ibn Ahmad, better known as Ibn Hazm (born in Cordoba, Spain, in 994 AD, 384–456 AH). His book repudiating the use of a rational approach in law, *Mulakhas Ibtal al-Qiyas*, stands as a good example to show the Zaheris' attitude towards the use of reason and the incompatibility of *hikmah* and *shari'ah*.[166] However, rationalism and philosophy in Islam never completely stopped developing, nor did anti-rationalism. Although the Zaherite school disappeared after a while, anti-rationalism has always had adherents and sympathizers. There have, therefore, always existed scholars who rejected the doctrine of harmony and the authority of reason. In fact, Muslim scholars and intellectuals have never been so greatly divided on any subject of importance, as they have on these doctrines, though not always equally. The main controversy between Mu'tazilah and Ash'airah, it could be said, is based on their different views concerning these doctrines. It seems as if this has been the case with almost all the opposing intellectual groups in Islam ever since. The vast literature on both sides explains this point.

After Ibn Hazm there were many important scholars who followed the same line and at times managed to establish their own movements, which have lasted up to the present time. The followers of Ibn Taymiyyah (d. 1320 AD) of Damascus, Ibn Qayyim al-Juziyyah (d.1350 AD), a disciple of Ibn Taymiyyah, and Muhammad ibn 'Abd al-Wahhab (d. 1792 AD), the founder of the Wahhabi movement, are some of the people who kept Islamic traditionalism, literalism and misology alive and active up to the present time.[167] There are many more traditionalists but these seem to be the most outstanding anti-rationalist figures in the history of Islamic intellectualism. We can even find elements of traditionalism in Ghazzali's works. However, at the beginning, it was some of the early orthodox Ash'arites scholars who rejected the doctrine of harmony and after that there have always existed some people who followed them and their approach. My concern here has been to trace the history of Islamic rationality and the development of the doctrine of harmony. Its interpretations, concepts and application should be dealt with separately. Nevertheless, it must be explained here that the doctrine of harmony of *hikmah* and *shari'ah* or reason and revelation implies that reason and revelation are not to be assigned to separate spheres, but are to be recognized as complementary sources of knowledge within the same sphere and without conflict. Reason and revelation form an integral combination. This can be understood from the early Mu'tazilite[168] and from the latest movements.[169] The obvious implication of the doctrine of harmony is that reason is capable of identifying and distinguishing good and bad, which requires its potential to recognize in turn that things are harmful or useful, which in turn gives reason the authority to regard them as commanded or forbidden by *shari'ah.* It should be pointed out that according to the Maturidite school, good and evil could be understood by right reasoning, though the obligatory character of virtue could only be known from revelation.[170] But the scholars who accepted the doctrine of harmony submitted to its jurisprudential implications too. It is in fact put in legal forms as the principle of *talazum* or the principle of the consistency and compatibility of reason and revelation in the legal field. Some jurists believe that human reason has been authorized to make legal rulings independent of revelation, in the absence of definite authentic text. These groups of legal rules are called *al-mustaqelat al-'aqliyyah* or rules made by human reason alone. Another group of legal rulings is the semi-independent rational rules. These are the rules made by sound human reasoning or *al-'aql al-salim. Al-'aql al-salim* is not and cannot be based on individual reasoning, but must be in accordance with the universal sound human reason, law and general will, which a person shares with the whole human community; that is the rational community and not the section of the community that acts according to its own vested interests and desires. An ethical, rational community is the community that performs good acts and duties for their own spiritual and moral sake. These, in the case of Islam, are the religious obligations that are performed solely to please Allah. The central issue here is the rational duties in accordance with *shari'ah* which are based on good intention (*niyyah*).

We would like to explain the doctrine of harmony and its implication and application in the field of Islamic law with, almost direct, a quotation from a classic source, by 'Allamah Hilli, jurist-philosopher (647–726/ AH, d. 1320 AD). This will help, we hope, to illustrate how the principle of *mulazamah* (correlation) works, how the doctrine of harmony functions and how reason, primordial nature, and *shari'ah* interact. A passage in section four of his book, *Bab al-Hadi 'Ashar*, reads as follows: 'Reason [*'aql*] of necessity and naturally passes judgement as to what actions are good [*hasan*], such as the return of a trust, and doing good [*ihsan*] and veracity and as to what are evil [*qabih*], such as injustice and harmful lies. This is because those who do not believe in any systems of law, like the unbelievers, [*mulahidah*], and the wise men of India, judge good and evil this way. And moreover if they are denied by reason they would also be denied by tradition, because of the denial of the evil of lying in this case by the Lawgiver [*al-shari'*].' Hilli regards justice as one of the attributes of Allah. He thus states that the meaning of justice is that the Most High is free from every and any evil act and from being remiss in what is incumbent. Justice depends on the knowledge of good and evil as determined by reason. He then goes on to say, 'An act the conception of which is necessary [*daruri*], either has a quality in addition to its origination [*huduth*], or it has not. An example of the latter is the movement of one who acts thoughtlessly [*al-sahih*] and of a sleeper [*al-na'im*]. And as for the former, either reason hates that addition or it does not. If it does, that is evil [*qabih*], and if reason does not hate it, it is good [*hasan*]. That is to say, an act which one can know of necessity, such as the things we see and hear, either has a moral quality in addition to its occurrence, or it has not. If it has a moral quality, and reason does not hate it, it is good – otherwise it is evil. However, this is further qualified as follows:

1. If doing and not doing are equal then both are permissible (*mubah*).
2. If doing and not doing are not equal:
   a. if not doing is commanded, doing is forbidden (*haram*);
   b. if not doing is preferable but doing is not forbidden, then doing is permissable but abominable (*makruh*);
   c. if doing is preferable and leaving it undone is forbidden, then doing is obligatory (*wajib*);
   d. if doing is preferable but leaving the act undone is permissible then doing is recommended (*mustahab*).

Explaining this point, 'Allamah Hilli states that good and evil are used in three senses: first a thing's being a quality of perfection, such as our saying that knowledge is good, or that ignorance is evil. Second, a thing's being agreeable to nature, as pleasure, or disagreeable to nature, as pain. Third, good is that thing, the doing of which deserves praise in this world and reward in the world to come; and evil is that thing, the doing of which deserves blame in this world and punishment in the world to come. He goes on to explain why there is no difference of opinion as to the first two being determined by reason and human intellect. But the scholastic theologians, *mutakalimun*, have differed regarding the third sense. The Ash'arites say that there is nothing in reason which can lead to a knowledge of good and evil in this sense; divine law (*shari'ah*) must be the guide, and whatever it calls good is good, and whatever it calls evil is evil. The Mu'tazilites and Imamites (*Imamiyyah*) say that there *is* something in reason which can guide to it, and that good is good in itself and evil is evil in itself, whether the Lawgiver (*al-shari'*) pronounces it as such or not. And they reply to Ash'arites as follows: First, we know of necessity and obviously that some actions are good, such as veracity, fairness, doing good, honesty, returning a trust, rescuing one who is in serious danger and other such things, without needing law to tell us so. We also know that there are other actions that are evil, such as a harmful lie, injustice, tyranny, and doing harm to one who does not deserve it and other such things, without any doubt at all about it. For this judgement is inherent (*markuz*) in human nature. For when we say to a person, ' If you speak the truth you will get a *dinar*', (unit of currency) and he being unprejudiced, by reason alone he will recognize the truth and desires to speak it. Second, if that which recognizes good and evil were only law and nothing else, it would follow that they could not be known apart from it. (But this is not necessarily so. For they could be known apart from it). The explanation for this is that those who do not believe in a law, like the unbelievers (*mulahidah*) and the wise men of India, do affirm that some actions are good and others are evil without hesitating in the matter. For if this knowledge consisted in what is learned from law then they would not have pronounce an opinion. Furthermore, if rational good and evil be denied, then it becomes necessary that legal good and evil will be denied also. But all agree that this necessity is false. Hence that which necessitate it is also false. And the reason for this necessity (for the denial of legal good and evil), is the denial, in this case, of the evil of a lie on the part of the Lawgiver, when reason does not pronounce it evil, so that He gives the lie to himself. And when the evil of a lie in Him is denied, then the trustworthiness of what He tells us regarding good and evil must be denied also,(that is, till reason teaches us that a lie is evil, we cannot trust the Lawgiver – for He may be lying to us).

In this process the role and position of intention, *niyyah* should not be underestimated. The importance of intention in Islam is the key issue which changes a rationally good action into spiritually rewarded one. (Immanuel Kant expressed this issue as follows: 'Act only on that maxim through which you can at the same time will that it should become a universal law'. The only form this law can take is the universal principle of reason.)[171] The position of Islam with respect to deontology (ethical duties, responsibilities and fulfilling them for any other end other than goodness's sake and the pleasure of Allah) and with respect to teleology (observing ethical principles because they serve multi-purposes (heaven's sake, one's own sake) is the middle course, for there is a harmony and balance between acting for goodness's sake (pleasure of Allah), and for heaven's sake (one's personal salvation, *sa'adat*).

As we are coming to the end of our discussion we would like to re-emphasize some of the points. Although a multiplicity of factors helped the development of the doctrine, it could be stated that the doctrine of harmony was originally based on Qur'anic verses and Islamic tradition and principles. Its seed was sown very early in the middle of the first Islamic century. Later on the Mu'tazilah prepared the ground for it for the first time. It was officially introduced by early Muslim philosophers such as Al-Kindi, Farabi, and later revived by 'Abd al-Jabbar. The Brethren of Sincerity proved it. Jurist-philosophers utilized and put it into practice. Ghazzali approved it. Imam Fakhr al-din al-Razi explained it. Avicenna extended it. Other later Muslim philosophers developed it further and perfected it. Sufi intellectuals extended it to include the harmony of *hikmah*, *shari'ah* and gnosis. Modern Muslim thinkers extended it to the harmony of philosophy, law and science and politics. Many Sunni intellectuals helped the development of the doctrine, but the Shi'ite and Mu'tazilite scholars, schools and thinkers are to be recognized as the people who established it and developed it systematically and continuously.[172] However, it seems that the idea was first initiated systematically by the early Mu'tazilah and was last used in a systematically new approach by the neo-Mu'tazilah (if we may use this term) or the most recent followers of the Mu'tazilah school, Jamal al-Din and his followers.[173]

The doctrine of harmony of *hikmah* and *shari'ah* was established very soon in Islam, probably by al-Kindi after the Mu'tazilah prepared the ground for it. But the subject has divided Muslim intellectuals. While the majority of those jurists and theologians who adopted al-Ash'ari's teachings have rejected it, all Muslim philosophers and the jurists and theologians who followed the Mu'tazilah School accepted it. The traditionalists, whether Sunnis or Shi'ites, have almost unanimously rejected it. So did the other groups following the same line, such as the literalists. But the philosophers on the other side seem to have unanimously supported it.

The main contribution to the development of the doctrine was made by the jurists/philosophers of all sects and schools. The doctrine has affected all fields of Islamic disciplines, but Islamic law and jurisprudence have benefited from the doctrine more. Shi'ite jurisprudence in particular, seems to be based on it. The attempts to establish the doctrine of harmony of *hikmah* and *shari'ah* have gone through various phases and covered even the extremes; from harmonization of Greek philosophy and *shari'ah* to the harmonization of Western philosophy, science and *shari'ah*.

The striking results of the doctrine of harmony seem to be:

1. Islamic law in general and Shi'ite jurisprudence in particular are in harmony with natural law through the authority of universal human primordial nature and intellect as a source of law.
2. It has made Islamic law a dynamic law and jurisprudence, except in rituals, for Islamic rationality and the doctrine of harmony require dynamism and change.
3. Jurists-philosophers and *usuli fuqaha* use logical and scientific as well as rational approaches and principles in Islamic jurisprudence and legal matters as the result of the doctrine of harmony.

Islam on the whole and the Islamic legal system in particular have become rational as the result of the doctrine. Some European scholars firmly and properly explain rationality as the main feature of Islam as follows: 'Islam is a religion that is essentially rationalistic in the widest sense of this term considered etymologically and historically. The definition of rationalism as a system that bases religious beliefs on principles furnished by reason applies to it exactly. It is true that Muhammad brought forward his reform as revelation, but this kind of revelation is only one form of exposition, and his religion has all the marks of a collection of doctrines found on data of reason.' He then goes on rationalizing all Islamic fundamental doctrines and proves that Islam is rationalistic in all senses of the term, and that there is a complete harmony between reason and revelation and *hikmah* and *shari'ah*.[174]

Respecting and accepting divinely gifted human reason as the source of knowledge and identifying it with human nature (*fitrah*), Islam has been able to provide a solution to the problem of misintroducing nature and man as gods, with the authority to make law with no internal power of implementation (the two sources of the Universal Declaration of Human Rights). It is quite reasonable to suggest that the idea that religion and reason are irreconcilable is indeed based on the experience of Western intellectual rationalists drawn from the relationship between Christianity and reason. This theory later was generalized to cover all other religions including Islam. It is indeed introduced, projected and exported to Islam by orientalists. The criticism against Islam concerning this point came with a double force from certain Western critics like E. Renan and Sir William Muir. They saw Islam as a religion with Bedouin characteristics alien to reason. It should be realized by now that the idea of irreconcileability of religion/Islam and reason in its Western form is alien to the history of thoughts in Islam. As we have discussed, even the most traditionalist Muslim scholars such as Ash'arites, Ghazzali, and Ibn Taymiyyah cannot really be regarded as anti-rationalists.[175]

APPENDIX

The Concept of Human Rights: a Comparative Analysis of the Universal Declaration of Human Rights and the Constitution of the Islamic Republic of Iran

Introduction

In the course of our discussion, we have dealt with the concept of natural law, human rights, both in the West and Islam, and the means of discovering and establishing the foundation of absolute universal ethical values on which we can base universal human rights. In this appendix we intend to show the reservations of Muslim community about the United Nations UDHR and how a modern Muslim country has approached the issue of human rights.

The Muslim student of human rights certainly accepts the Islamic concept of human rights. He may accept a large part of the contents of UDHR without any reservation and the rest of it with some reservation. But he does not look favourably upon its philosophy and specially its approach. We must understand that different approaches and philosophies may produce different conclusions. Muslims have certain reservations about specific aspects and features of the Western-oriented UDHR. They do not challenge the idea that there are universal, absolute and natural rights, ethical values and moral standards. They certainly cannot be accused of not supporting human rights. The fact that quite a few Islamic 'universal human rights declarations' have been declared and promoted explains this point.

The Islamic reservation about the Western concept of human rights and certain parts of the UDHR is based on this principle. It is in the question of the basis of the rights and the approaches to these rights that the problem lies. What do rights rest upon? This point is also true of other different religions and schools that support human rights in one way or another but justify them differently and base them on different philosophical foundations. For example the Roman Catholics, worldwide, have reservations about abortion, homosexuality and divorce. Liberalism, to take a Western school for example, also challenges the philosophy of human rights of communitarianism and vice versa. What is important here is that the notion of coming to the construction of values and rights out of an initial absence of absolute values and sound basis for the rights is futile. Muslims suggest that religions in general and Islamic spiritual, ethical and theological value system, in particular, provides humanity with a solid basis on which the notion of human rights can be based.

Contrary to what the secularists suggest, the majority of the world population are either following religions or identify themselves with religious cultures and thus share, more or less, these reservations about the contents, philosophy and the basis of the UDHR.

Background to the Concept of Human Rights

The origin of the concept of human rights in general is usually agreed to be found in the Graeco-Roman natural law doctrine of Stoicism, especially neo-Stoicism, which held that a universal order pervades all creation and that human conduct should therefore be judged according to the law of nature. This is why the terms 'human rights' and 'natural rights' are often used to express the same concept.

The expression 'human rights' in the West is relatively new, having come into everyday parlance only since the Second World War and the founding of the United Nations in 1945. It replaced the phrase 'natural rights', which fell into disfavour partly because the concept of 'natural law' (to which it was intimately linked) had become a matter of great controversy. The term 'natural rights' itself is a departure from natural law theory, which taught 'natural duties' as distinguished from the rights of men. The shift from natural law to natural duty and from natural duty to natural rights, and from natural rights to human rights is due to many philosophical, social, political and religious factors. An unfortunate by-product of the modern concept of human rights and welfare state has been the encouragement of a sense of 'right' to the virtual exclusion of the sense of obligation. Any scheme of justice and right is likely to turn sour if nurtured on ideas of 'right' alone.[1] The idea of human rights as natural rights has not been without disagreement mainly because of its association with religious orthodoxy, which has become less acceptable to contemporary secular philosophy, politics and law.[2]

The writings of St Thomas Aquinas, Grotius, Descartes, Leibniz, Benedict de Espinosa, Bacon, Locke, who was perhaps the most important natural law theorist of modern times, Diderot, Voltaire, Montesquieu and Rousseau in one way or another contributed to its development.

Human rights are not always associated with natural law even by the supporters of natural law. Edmund Burke, for example, a believer in the natural law, in his *Reflection on the Revolution in France* (1790) denied that the rights of man could be derived from it. It is only fair to suggest that modern *jus natural* (human rights) derive from many sources rather than solely from the doctrine of natural law. On the other hand, some of the contemporary proponents of human rights have even expressed hostility or ridicule towards natural law. Some proclaimed that both natural law and natural rights are not real. They believe that they are both imaginary. The German jurist, F. Karl von Sauvigny, and some other jurists, such as Englishman Henry Maine, rejected the doctrine of natural law and rights. Some rejected the doctrine of natural rights completely. For example, conservatives Hume and Burke united with liberal Jeremy Bentham in insisting that natural law and natural rights are unreal metaphysical phenomena. The conservatives did this out of fear that natural rights would lead to social upheaval, and the liberal out of concern that natural rights could substitute for effective legislation. Bentham, the founder of utilitarianism, wrote: 'Rights is the child of law. From real law comes real rights, but from imaginary laws and from the law of nature, comes imaginary rights; natural rights is simply nonsense.' The jurist, John Austin (1790–1859), insisted that the only law is the 'command of the sovereign'. In his work *The Province of Jurisprudence Determined* Austin tried to clarify the distinction between law and morality, which he considered to be blurred by the doctrine of natural law. He defined law as a species of 'command'. Commands are orders whose disobedience deserves punishment. Commands are laws and are 'set' by the 'sovereign'. This is what distinguishes 'positivist law' from both the fundamental principles of morality, which is the 'law of God' and from positive morality or man-made rules of conduct, such as etiquette, conventional morality and international law, which do not emanate from a sovereign.

Desacredization of the cosmos, nature, man and law, and the secularization of life, politics and even ethics and religion (in a secularized environment religion has to be secularized first), as the results of biocenterism, scientism, historicism, individualism, utilitarianism, and also as the results of other products of modernism, such as materialism, empiricism and physicism have produced a quantitative kind of human rights which are empty of quality, depth, spiritual, ethical and religious values and dimensions. This process is originally based on the doctrine of the conflict between spiritual, religious and ethical values and principles, on one side and between the corporal, physical, temporal and material dimensions of life and man on the other.

While it is a highly controversial concept, and its meaning has shifted historically, liberalism based on individualism seems to have contributed to the modern concept of human rights and the UDHR. Gradually, liberalism became associated with the doctrine of freedom of choice and suggested that it should be applied to matters as diverse as marriage, religion and even subjects concerned with human spirituality and conscience, and in fact to everything that affected daily life physically, materially and spiritually. Liberalism upheld the values of reason and toleration (which is understandable on its own) in the face of tradition, religion, and absolutism of ethical principles and often even at their cost. Later on, liberal democracy extended its domain and covered also political and social fields of human activities. In this view, the world consists of free and equal individuals with rights. Everything should be about the defence of the rights of these individuals. While liberalism celebrated the rights of individuals, it should be noted from the outset that it was generally and basically the secular individual who was the focus of attention, and the new freedoms and rights were first and foremost for the individual people of Western culture, tradition, history and background. Islam also places man's focus on his habitat and society because a healthy psychology cannot prosper and grow in an unhealthy ecology and social environment. There is an exchange of character between individuals and societies. The individual gains (consciously and unconsciously) some traits of the society he is in. Societies also gain some features of individuals who have the power to influence them. Islam looks at both these ends and properties, individuals and societies, and tries to establish a balance and to cure them of their excesses and perversions so that all can return to the state of nature that Allah meant them to be in.

It is clear that the major codes and generations of human rights bills, which are accepted internationally, have largely emerged from within the traditions and cultures of Western countries. The reference here is to the International Bill of Human Rights (adopted and proclaimed by the UN General Assembly, Resolution 217 (III), 10 December 1948) and the European Convention on Human Rights (Council of Europe, 1966). The same applies to other main UN documents dealing with human rights which are in force. They include the Convention on the Prevention and Punishment of the Crime of Genocide (1951), the Convention on the Suppression of the Traffic in Persons and of the Exploitation of the Prostitution by Others (1951), the Convention relating to the Status of Refugees (1954), the Convention on the Political Rights of Women (1954), the amended 1926 Slavery Convention (1955), the Supplementary Convention on the Abolition of Slavery, the Slave Trade and Institutions and Practices similar to Slavery (1957), the Convention on the Nationality of Married Women (1958), the Convention relating to the Status of Stateless Persons (1960), the Convention on the International Right of Correction

(1962), the Convention on Consent to Marriage, Minimum Age for Marriage and Registration of Marriage (1964), the Convention on Racial Discrimination (1966), the Convention on the Non-applicability of Statutory Limitations to War Crimes and Crimes against Humanity (1970), the Convention on the Reduction of Statelessness (1975), the International Convention on Civil and Political Rights (1976), the International Covenant on Economic, Social and Cultural Rights (1976), the International Convention on the Suppression and Punishment of the Crime of Apartheid (1976) and the Convention Against Torture and other Cruel, Inhuman and Degrading Punishments. (1986). It is thus more appropriate to speak of a family and generations of human rights.

Human rights in contemporary period are claimed to represent the following five major properties.

1. They represent demand for fairness and justice in sharing power, wealth, basic necessities of life, respect etc.
2. They refer to a wide continuum of value claims and express both the 'is' and the 'ought' in human affairs.
3. They are quintessentially general, universal in character possessed by all human beings irrespective of geographical, historical, cultural religious, political and other circumstances.
4. They are accommodating, harmonious and reconcilable, so much so that, for example, the right of the freedom of one individual or community cannot be at the expense of the right of the freedom of another individual or community.
5. They are 'fundamental' and distinct from 'non-essential' claims. This is why some have reduced and limited their number to one or two rights, for example 'the right to life'.

An Islamic Analysis of the Concept of Human Rights and the UDHR

The term 'rights', as it is used in contemporary Western literature in the context of women's rights, children's rights, animal rights, human rights etc., is not used in the Qur'an. The term *haqq* (plural *huquq*), which is being used as the translation for the term 'right', is used in the Qur'an to denote the truth, correct, proper, real, just, befitting, what is due to one, duty and other similar concepts. The word *haqq* and its derivatives have been used in the Qur'an some 227 times in these contexts, e.g. 'the truth [*haqq*] is from thy Lord, so be not of those who doubt' (Qur'an 2:147; 3:60). However, the concept of 'rights', as such, has been expressed in the Qur'an, e.g. the rights of children to inheritance. In this case even the parents have no power to deprive their children of their inheritance. It is the right of children to inherit and the responsibility of parents to respect and implement this right. In Islamic traditions (*ahadith*) and in Islamic law the term *haqq* and also the concept of rights have been used to denote deserving, what is due, rights, and obligations to be fulfilled and respected by others. In a directive issued by Imam Ali ibn Abitalib, on the occasion of appointing Malik Ashtar as the governor of Egypt, he clearly defined and explained the rights and responsibilities of both the authority and the subjects. In a short article, supposedly produced by Imam Ali ibn al-Husein under the title of *Risalat al-Huquq* (*Treatise on Rights*)[3] the term *huquq* closely corresponds with the term 'rights'. In Islamic law the term *haqq* is used to correspond with the term 'rights' and the concept of rights, as such, has been employed, e.g. *haqq al-nas*, (people's rights), *haqq al-'ubur* (the right of passage), *haqq al-shuf'ah*, (the right of first refusal for partners in properties and businesses). Ibn Taymiyyah wrote a treatise under the title of *Fi Huquq al-Ra'i wa al-Ra'iyyah* (*On the Rights of the Authority and the Subjects*). We may conclude that although the term *haqq* used in the Qur'an does not correspond with the term 'right', the concept of 'rights' was brought up in the Qur'an. Both the term and the concepts of *haqq* corresponding to the term and concept of 'rights' have been employed both in Islamic traditions and Islamic law. However, as far as the term and concept of 'human rights' in particular in Islam are concerned, it is appropriate to suggest that they are supported by Islam on different philosophical, religious, ethical and spiritual ground, basis and with different approaches and sources than those of Western ones.

There are two conflicting approaches and attitudes towards the issues of natural law and human rights in their modern context, in Islam and amongst scholars of human rights:

1. Those who argue on philosophical and conceptual grounds reject the idea that they correspond exactly with their Islamic concept. This is because Western contemporary concepts of natural law and human rights are based on different secular and liberal foundations and approaches and are from sources which are completely different from those of Islamic ones. Muslims tend to conform to human rights because this is required of them by Islam and Muslims regard them as their religious duties and their intention is spiritual and divine. By contrast, the contemporary Western concept of human rights are secular, liberal and individual. According to this notion, individuals seek to advance their interest by means of human rights. Jack Donnelley and M. Legenhausen support this view.[4]

2. Those who base their judgement and argument on the basis of 'the end result' suggest that although the Islamic concepts of natural law and human

> rights are conceptually, philosophically, historically and spiritually different from those of modern ones, they all promote the same objectives and produce the same end result. Some Muslim supporters of human rights suggest that Islam supports human rights both conceptually and practically. This is because even if the modern concept of human rights is not to be found in medieval formulation of Islamic law, this does not mean that a contemporary jurist will not be able to derive an Islamic concept of human rights consistent with the religious sources. The Organization of Islamic Conferences (OIC) in its Universal Islamic Declaration of Human Rights and many Muslim scholars of human rights support this approach. (OIC ratified an Islamic Declaration of Human Rights in December 1989 in Tehran and finalized it in Cairo.) However, the reservations expressed by Muslim scholars of human rights are based mainly on conceptual grounds.

In the introduction to this appendix, we explained very briefly the Muslims' reservations about the modern concept of human rights and the UDHR. Here we expand on that point. Although generations of human rights bills emerge from international bodies on which non-Western countries are believed, to some extent, to be represented, the framing and formulating of the codes have been based on Western culture, thought, and politics and the lawyers and politicians of the Western world have mainly been the instrument of its formulation. This raises the question as to whether Western cultural biases have affected the contents of the human rights codes and instruments, and whether their impact in the non-Western world would be greater if the perceptions of non-Western peoples had been given some attention. This is not to say that their contents and objectives should be completely rejected. But room for conceptual variations of human rights should be allowed. Islam and the Muslims have the right to present their own concept of human rights and consequently their reservations about certain aspects of Western-designed human rights and their application should be respected. It would be more appropriate to speak of a family of concepts of human rights, because moral and political theorists in the West have developed differing concepts of rights about which there is considerable controversy. The major reservation that the Muslims have, with regard to the present form of Western-designed human rights, is indeed that of its concept, philosophy and approach, and that it is used and exploited politically with double standard against Muslims. The problem is not with the bulk of its contents. It is even suggested that some judgements made on the basis of an unIslamic system of thought may be in agreement with Islam. The criticism that is sometimes placed against the Islamic concept of human rights, is that because it is spiritually, morally and ethically founded it lacks enforcement. But Islamic law has made provision for both new concepts and for the enforcement of the new concepts. It is a fact that almost all rights, including human rights, in Islam are introduced as divine responsibilities and religious duties. But this does not mean that they are left at the mercy of individuals to be viewed and implemented. It rather provides it with double enforceability. To honour rights, as distinct from just conforming to them, one must be conscious of rights not just as rights but as responsibilities, and divine responsibility is the strongest and the safest kind of responsibility.

The reason for Muslims' reservations about theUDHR is not just based on the fact that they were not asked to be involved and participate in its formation. There are other more serious reasons for these reservations. The UDHR is based on, beside liberal individualism, the concept and approach of relativism and the relativist interpretation of rights. This does not correspond with the approach adopted by major religions, especially with the Islamic concept of absolute and primordial values. One of the major problems of the UDHR is that it promotes ethical absolutism (absolute human rights) on the basis of philosophical relativism and hence contradictions in its concepts and philosophy. Relativism is a convenient approach to accommodate various ethical and cultural values but does not produce absolute values. Placing ethics, and thus human rights, on a relativistic non-ethical foundation, on the denial of human primordial nature, or on just individual morality to which conscience and ethics has been reduced in secular ethical discourse, does not seem to be ethically, intellectually, morally and spiritually satisfactory. We also face difficulties if we explain and justify ethics and human rights in descriptive ethical terms, as it seems to be the case with the UDHR. Descriptive ethics suggests that 'what is right' is what most people think and say it is right. But what most people think and say is right differs and has differed at different times and places. This is why comparative ethics has established itself. Islam, on the other hand, places morality and rights and responsibilities on solid spiritual and ethical foundation and suggests that there are principles such as justice, equality, truth, humanity, ethics, knowledge, human rights and so on which derive their value and authority from primordial human nature or *fitrah* and enjoy divine sanction and rewards. This is one way of saving these principles from ambiguity, misunderstanding and abuse.

There is a distinction between ideal ethics and mores. While all members of the human community throughout history distinguish in some way between virtue and vice, good and bad, right and wrong – mores – ethics *qua* ethics has not always been the foundation of these mores. Secular societies suffer more from this weakness. In secular societies individuals regard mores as arbitrary and organizations set their moral codes and framework. They are therefore subject to relativism. Ethical values and even mores have no solid, absolute or even rational basis and are thus subject to relativity and plurality and thus lead to conflict. This is why a number of recent Western moral philosophers have advanced the position that no philosophical theory can adequately explain and systematically relate all aspects of moral life, hence the need to base them on a solid spiritual and religious basis. Perhaps the most important discussion of this topic is to found in Bernard Williams's book, *Ethics and Limits of Philosophy*.[5] Although religions generally base their ethical system on an absolute foundation some may prescribe mores that may contradict ethics *qua* ethics because of the independent nature of both ethics and religion. Islam places its ethical philosophy on divine bases: human primordial nature, and absolute Islamic ideology. Mulla M. Fayd Kashani calls human primordial nature an interior prophet. Islamic traditions introduce human reason as an interior prophet too.[6] However, there are some forms and some interpretations of relativism and plurality that do not necessarily contradict Islamic ethical system. But there are some that Islam certainly rejects. The main point here is that moral issues and ethical values should be based on and judged according to the absolute principles of Islamic philosophy of ethics and Islamic doctrines. The Islamic ethical system has accommodated deontological, teleological, and virtue orientation of mores and value (precept, aims and objectives, and virtue) in its ethical system. In Islam God has revealed the moral code of behaviour for man (precept); He has described the divine position of and proper end of man (aim); and He has provided man with the incarnation of virtue in the lives of prophets.

Although the UDHR is presented as recommendations it is regarded as an international law which must be implemented. We know that there are quite a few definitions of both law and ethics. It is not easy to prefer one to the others, for they all have shortcomings. The main difference between law and ethics in contemporary secular society seems to be as follows. Law is the collection of rules based on will and power and deals with what must be done because of material gain and threat of punishment to establish order and civility. Ethics is based on the concept of good and evil, right and wrong and deals with what should be voluntarily done because of inner satisfaction, happiness and conscience in order to establish a descent society. In Islam these two sets of motives and gaols are united. The Shari'ah rules should be implemented for both sets of reasons and objectives. A Muslim believes in the rule of Shari'ah ethically and spiritually and regards them as the code of practice legally. He does not face any conflict of ethics and law. But the main problem with the UDHR is that it is based on a secular approach but presented as rules of law to be respected because they are ethically universal. There is thus an obvious conflict between the form of the UDHR as law and its philosophy of law. How can we have a universal absolute law in a secular relativist world based on a secular relativist philosophy and foundation? Human primordial nature (*fitrah*) and innate human reason and wisdom (*hikmah*), as the two main sources of universal law and natural law, are refused any role in a secular relativist world and outlook to make contribution to the philosophy of the UDHR. They are thus a set of rules without a solid ground on which to stand and from which to be derived.

Generally speaking, virtually all states and communities now subscribe officially to some doctrine of human rights. And in all these circumstances there is, more or less explicitly a general theory justifying the doctrine. The problem of fitting a doctrine of human rights into the general justificatory theory is different in different states and communities. There are many varieties of justificatory theories for human rights in the Western world today. They all tend to approximate to one of three types: the individualist–liberal theory, whose roots are generally traced to Locke; the socialist theory, whose roots are essentially in Marx's socialist theory; and the populist general theory, whose roots are in Rousseau. In each of these three types of theory there is a problem of fitting the modern notion of human rights into the general lines of the theory. The individualist–liberal theory has no difficulty accommodating the rights of life, liberty and property, for it was built largely on the assertion of these as the natural rights of the individual, but it finds some difficulty fitting in the modern ideas of economic, social justice and social rights. The Marxian and Rousseauian theories, on the other hand, find little difficulty with the social and economic rights, but do not find it so easy to accommodate the earlier trilogy of natural rights of life, liberty and property, which they have tended to mistrust on the ground that these are essentially bourgeois rights. We can thus see the conflict of theories concerning the doctrine of human rights.

The root of this conflict is in the lack of the actual theory of universal man with universal human primordial nature, universal innate reason and universal ethical values.

K. Dalacoura explains this as follows. 'The origins of the principles of human rights, as they are conceptualized in our time, can be traced, at least, to two strands of Western philosophical and political thought: secularized natural law and enlightenment secular rationalism.'[7] The outcome of this double secularization and materialization was Western liberalism and individualism. Individualism puts the individual at the centre of universe instead of God. It supports the belief in the human being as the ultimate locus of knowledge, power, rights and truth. Individual rights (sometimes introduced as natural rights of individuals), branded as human rights, replaced God's rights, society's rights and divine rights. How can we expect the followers of religions to accept this philosophy of human rights? Some rights introduced by liberals, such as the right to life, may be absolute. But does the absolute right to life also mean the right to give up life legally, e.g. euthanasia? But liberalism on the whole rejects the concept and philosophy of absolutism in the field of ethical values. This has created a contradiction. Individualism in its essence negates the concepts of absolute rights and universal moral values. This is why even the pioneers of liberalism and even of liberal democracy, who at the simple technical level strongly promoted individuals' natural rights, have been challenged. Their concept of natural right is so different from most ideas of natural right that their claim to be natural right men might be disallowed by a systematic classifier or modern supporter of human or natural right.

Islam and indeed all monotheistic (and even non-monotheistic) religions are both social and individual codes of life and practice. Individuals have responsibility towards community, without the fulfilment of which their individual potentials are not realized. A religion without social dimension and confined to the private sphere of the individual loses its hold even on individuals. In human society public and private, knowledge and truth, individuals and community cannot be separated.

In the Islamic, and indeed religious, understanding of man, man's reason, primordial nature and intellect, and in the traditional understanding of natural law, man is seen as endowed with reason by God. It is only as such that man is sacred and because of this his dignity and moral worth and natural and divine rights must be respected. One of the challenges to the secular philosophy of human rights is the belief that nothing is true, because truth as such does not exist. This is the inevitable progression of the Enlightenment. Once human rights became divorced from natural law, spiritual values and divine purpose they do not have any solid ground to stand on. Those who take this position cannot consistently and fundamentally defend and support universal human rights. Once we lose the possibility to resort to the transcendental (and we could, if we believe that we can formulate and discover the truth on our own and with our own resources), our appeal to reason as endowed by God collapses and we are left with relativistic human reason and rationality and thus with relativistic values and rights. When we start functioning on the basis that we can formulate and discover truth on our own and with our own resources, one possible argument would be that truth does not exist at all, that truth is purely a construct of our mind. In this case our appeal to human reason (as an absolute standard) and the belief in our cognitive capacities therefore ceases. Belief in human reason depends on its characteristics and benefits from self-evidence. When this self-evidence becomes a matter of dispute the belief in reason is questioned and the belief in human rights, which is based on this foundation, collapses. In this case there is no standard independent of us by means of which moral/ethical principles and norms can be judged, evaluated, justified and explained. [8]

If the enlightenment, secularization and desacredization of nature, man and the order of nature undermine belief in God, lead inevitably to God's death, and deprive natural law of its origin in divine law (and thus individualism is established as the only code of life), then how could the moral worth and the inalienable rights of man, nature and creation be defended? Ivan Karamazov in Dostoevsky's *The Brothers Karamazov* contends that if there is no God, then 'I am God,' in which case everything is permissible. Voltaire remarked that 'If God did not exist it would be necessary to invent Him.' Even some atheists have suggested that moral/ethical imperatives cannot be the subject of relativism, that they should be based on absolute solid ground and that there should be an inclusive relation between religion and morality, divine commands and moral imperatives. J.L. Mackie, as an admitted atheist, argues that the only way to make sense of the relation between facts and value is either through Hume's moral philosophy or through a religious theory.[9] He even confesses that if no variation on Hume's theory is ultimately defensible, we should be forced to seek a religious explanation to the manner in which values seem to supervene on natural properties. One of the challenges to the individualistic secularized philosophy of human rights is the belief that nothing is true, because truth as such does not exist. One of the outcomes of enlightenment (one of the twin pillars of the UDHR) is the positive distinction between fact and value as well as the idea of truth as representation or correspondence. Those who support this idea believe that the truth, facts and the world do not exist independent of us and that our minds are not mirrors of nature and that there is no standard independent of us against which things can be judged. This line of thought rejects the notion of reason and rationality advocated by the Enlightenment and thus creates another contradiction. If man is deprived of its rational potentials, and if the divine dimension of human reason is denied, then man no longer has any moral leg to stand on to be able to pass judgement on human rights. The only liberation offered to him is that of self-destruction. This line of thinking is self-annihilating and therefore profoundly anti-humanistic. If we do not believe that there is truth 'out there' that exists independently of us, all arguments and discussions stop. The implication of this position for morality and human rights is obvious. In this case we cannot discuss liberty and human rights at all. For it is vain to search for truth, certainty, rights and moral principles, because there is neither the truth nor a means to discover it. We have therefore two options: a leap of faith – faith in the sacredness of the human being – or dropping the discourse of human rights altogether. If we discard the belief that human beings have an inherent universal moral worth and standard which we can all agree upon and recognize we cannot proceed.[10]

This dilemma also exists in both cases of considering the non-existence of metaphysical questions and principles, as Rotry suggests, or limiting metaphysical, spiritual, moral and religious principles to the private sphere of life, as Rawls proposes. This is because a sharp distinction between private and public issues is not an easy position for anyone to maintain.[11]

Islam approaches life and its problems in their totality. Salvation and happiness in Islam are inclusive, multi-dimensional, and comprehensive. An individual can earn partial happiness and salvation in isolation. But full happiness is only available by working in the society. One's spiritual and religious potential is actualized in the community. There is no shortcut to salvation in Islam. It has to be earned through the continuous challenge of the whole life, which is only faced through living a full life in a community. The Prophet of Islam was not the Son of God. He was a father, a husband, a father-in-law, a grand father and a full member of society. In fact he created the Islamic society of *ummah.* His saying that 'He who starts the day without caring about the affairs of the community is not a Muslim' has become the maxim in Islamic literature and Muslim's code of practice. The Islamic moral system is in fact a behavioural and societal one. It regards sacrifice as a great virtue. This sacrifice itself is in many forms and varieties. These principles do not correspond with Western individualism and liberalism, which is the basis of the philosophy of the UDHR. Islam does not recognize any contradiction between individual rights and the other rights and between physical rights and other rights. Human rights in Islam are human privileges with divine sanction.

The starting point here is to discover and understand the conceptual and ideological resources and principles available in Islam for a programme of human rights in Islam. Islam has a full spectrum of potentials, symbols, traditions, principles, basis and concepts for human rights such as, for example, the concept of the divine vicegrency of man, the concept of human responsibility and guardianship towards all creatures and nature, the concept of respect for the entire creation, universe, animate and inanimate, life and human dignity, the concept of justice, equality etc. It is important to explore and examine these potentials within Islam for human rights. In the field of politics some Muslim scholars have associated and identified the principle of consultation in Islam (*shura*) with the concept of human rights and the rights of people to govern and administer their own affairs: 'The people being the vicegerents of Allah, have a general right to be in charge of their own affairs on the basis of the principle of consultation.' And this should and would now involve 'the formation of an assembly whose members are the real representatives or agents of the people"[12] Without a thorough discussion of these ideas, ideals and potentials it is not fair to judge Islam. It is certainly difficult to understand the position of Islam with regard to human rights without due consideration. The Western advocates of a Western model of human rights do not appreciate that peoples with a different culture, civilization, history, religion and traditions have different concepts of human rights. 'This is especially true of advocates of the style of democracy (and human rights) found in Western Europe and the USA, whose people believe themselves to be the true heirs to the only legitimate democratic tradition and thus view any other efforts to create democracies (and human rights) as false and regard others as perverse and lunatic.'[13] An effort to establish a cultural and conceptual monopoly of human rights and restrict it to only Western concepts can rightly be viewed as cultural imperialism, political hegemony and cultural globalization by those who have suffered in the past and are still suffering from all sorts of direct and indirect imperialism, exploitation, discrimination and disrespect. Western academics, politicians, and advocates of the Western concept of human rights present it as a universal concept, while denying the universal nature of man, the absolute universal philosophy of human rights and give the impression that there is no other alternate concept. Many Muslim and non-Muslim scholars and advocates of human rights are engaged in providing a more universally applicable definition of human rights without the contradictions associated with the Western philosophy of and the concept of human rights.

Reconceptualization of traditional ideas and institutions played a great role in the development of the Western concept of human rights and democracy. Likewise the Islamic concept of human rights should be allowed to be developed and formulated on the basis of Islamic traditions, history, culture, ideas and ideals. 'Because of its very nature, each experience will be different, since indigenous foundations are different. It is in this context that the special conditions (human rights) and democracy in the Muslim world should be viewed. It is especially important to identify crucial elements in the Islamic tradition that have been redefined and reenvisaged in ways that can strengthen the dynamics of democratization (and human rights) in Muslim societies.'[14] In Islam there are several very important concepts, images, and principles, traditions and foundations that shape the vision of what a just humane society should be. These are the basis for the Islamic perceptions of human rights and democracy, which must be taken into consideration in order to formulate a truly universal human rights. For example, perhaps the most important point to make is that, in Islam, rights belong first to Allah, then to the community and then to individuals. The second most important point is that in Islam rights cannot be divorced from responsibilities. In fact, rights are responsibilities. The third point is that in Islam rights enjoy divine blessings and sanction. They also enjoy spiritual, ethical and moral priority so that, for example, the right of life cannot be subordinate and secondary to the right of property.

Denial of the religious basis, the natural law, ethical absolutism, spiritual values and the primordial nature of man as the foundations for the UDHR renders it a contested concept. Acceptance of the contested nature of human rights, its diversity and development enables the recognition that there can be alternative and rival use of the term and flexibility of its concept, philosophy and basis. Thus human rights and democracy need not simply be the adoption of the Western version, concepts and forms but can also be the formulation of indigenously rooted cultures and traditions of peoples with different backgrounds. We must appreciate the fact that the formulation of legitimacy, democracy and human rights in the West was not something new but was also due to the contribution of mankind throughout history and was the product of a reinterpretation or reformulation of older concepts, beliefs and institutions. This belief opens up the possibility that other cultural and religious traditions have contributed, and must continue to do so, in generating and accommodating human rights and democratic forms and concepts. In short, the actual concept of universal human rights in general cannot be challenged, but there should be room for cultural and religious manoeuvre within the general concept.

In fact, there is among some Muslims an explicit attempt to compare the Islamic mode of political organization to Western-style pluralist democracy and human rights, usually with the intent of proving Islam's superiority to Western concepts in moral as well as practical terms. Inspired by the spirit of Islam, some Muslim scholars have tried to explain that Islam served as the source for human rights. They suggest that Islam set the model from which democratic principles of human rights such as the rule of law, the concept of the social contract, and the respect for creation, animate and inanimate, were taken by European thinkers of the Middle Ages and the Enlightenment.[15] There are, in fact, a sizeable number of studies and books by Muslims dealing with similar subjects. The fact that such studies are so numerous suggests that there are considerable resources in Islam for developing and promoting these concepts but within the spirit of Islam.

It is thus reasonable to suggest that the Islamic spiritual, philosophical values and the spirit of Islamic jurisprudence should be included as the means and the sources of evaluating the position of Islam with regard to the question of human rights. No one should expect to find the exact text and order of the UDHR, a relatively recent product of Western intellectual-liberalism, the history of which goes back only to the French revolution, in Islamic law, the foundations and principles of which enjoy long history. Even the early Western texts and concepts of human rights of the eighteenth century cannot and do not fully correspond with the later interpretations and recent criteria of human rights laid down in the UDHR. The concept of human rights has gone through changes, developments and amendments and this is why a few generations of human rights have been produced.[16] How then are we supposed to make literal comparison between Islam and the UDHR and expect them to fully correspond with each other without any reservation? This is the approach adopted by the incriminating Western critics of the position of human rights in Islam and also by some Muslim scholars. This approach fails to appreciate the spirit of Islam and Islamic law and fails to recognize the richness, potential and history of Islamic law, the variety within it and the scope for change, development in Islamic law and the provisions that Islam has made for the formulation of human rights.

An underlying theme is that the strength of human rights codes, covenants and legislation depends greatly on the political and cultural factors which surround their adoption. The value which the population attaches to a code of human rights will be adversely affected, for example, if it is seen as reflecting values of a different culture or as constituting a foreign imposition.

Human rights do need to be set within a universalistic concept and context: they concern the rights which human beings should have regardless of their ethnic, cultural or religious identities and other backgrounds. The language of human rights has, therefore, to transcend the concepts of any particular cultural grouping – and yet to draw from the inspirations found within particular cultural and religious traditions, and to cohere with the values held in those traditions. Contrary to what is publicized by secularists, religions and religious loyalty, tendencies and commitment are much more universal than secular ones. The majority of the world population still, even at this juncture of history, is more religiously committed and culturally based than otherwise. Human rights declarations therefore have to respect the feelings and aspiration of the majority of the world population. Secularism of states does not necessarily mean secularism of the citizens of the states. At least religious culture still is the basis of the culture of the majority of the world population. Being a universal religion, supporting the unity of man, transcending all the racial, cultural, geographical, historical, ethnic and other barriers, Islam fits this framework. This is not to say that Islam as a religion and because it is a religion suggests that human rights and moral values in their Western form necessarily correspond with it. We are simply saying that Islam sets the kind of moral framework, and suggests the concept of human rights, that corresponds with universal moral and spiritual principles and with human primordial nature and basic human rights.

The UDHR is not and cannot be regarded as universal and absolute in the true sense of the term, because it is not based on the universal aspiration and primordial nature of man. The initiators of it do not make such a claim either. Its declaration was made universal and not its contents. It is a universal declaration of human rights and not a declaration of universal human rights. A committee of fifteen experts from different countries drafted the UDHR. None of the members of this committee were nationally, culturally, socially or politically representative. In fact it was a specific term of their engagement that they did not represent any national or cultural interests. Nevertheless, the declaration was called 'universal' in order to give it an aura of authority and legitimacy. This of course does not mean that some individual rights expressed in it are not universally accepted or do not have universal legitimacy. When the term universal is attributed to it, it is meant simply to explain that it is approved unanimously or by the majority of the members of the United Nations at the time or that it should be enforced and complied with universally. However, if it is meant to be the declaration of universal human rights, then it has to draw its legitimacy from universal natural sources, from human primordial nature, from principles of universal standing and from absolute moral, ethical and ideological principles. In this case there is no fundamental contradiction and conflict between the UDHR and Islam. Islam certainly promotes the doctrine of universal moral, ethical, ideological principles and values and human primordial nature and natural order. Islam certainly supports the idea and concept of certain universal natural and universal human rights. For example, Islam suggests that nature, animate and inanimate, and natural laws enjoy sanctity and must be treated with responsibility. Islam certainly supports the dignity of man and the sanctity of human and animal life.

In Islam man is born free.[17] But his freedom is within the limits of 'his responsibility towards his Creator (rights of Allah (swt):Huqooq al-Allah), and his responsibility towards his fellow human beings (rights of people, Huqooq al-Nas).[18] His rights, the rights of his Creator and those of people are all divine, and they have been granted by God and not by kings, legislative assemblies or other means.[19] The concept of power and democracy in Islam is based on the principle of *tawhid*, which rejects the authority of anything but Allah (swt) (which in turn leads to the rejection of all forms and shades of human dictatorship and subjugation). In Islam man as such has some rights: *inter alia*, right to life, safety of life (sanctity of life),[20] the right to justice, the right to a basic standard of life, the right to respect, dignity and integrity, freedom, choice, equality, etc. Allah (swt) has the right to be obeyed, worshipped, dignified, worshipped and respected. [21] People have the rights to security of life, property, honour, privacy, freedom, choice, protest against oppression, freedom of association, freedom of conscience, freedom of movement, protection against imprisonment, the right of equality before the law and the right to participate in their own affairs and the affairs of state.[22] Man's fellow creatures have the right to mercy, justice, protection against cruelty, and the basic necessities of life. Human rights in Islam have to be viewed within a wider context than those declared by the UDHR. In Islam, government derives its legitimacy from the concept of representation and the rights of people to administer their own affairs and man's overall responsibility. The authority of the government is based on its responsibility to see that the rights of those it represents are fully respected and implemented. [23] These brief but well-substantiated principles suggest that Islam portrays man as basically the vicegerent of Allah (swt) with divine responsibility, sacred intention and holy purpose and with duty towards Allah (swt), towards him/herself, his or her family, community, humanity in particular and the entire creation in general. Islam enshrines the prime objective of man's quest as perfection (*takamul*), comprehensive happiness and salvation of mankind (*sa'adat*), fulfilment of inclusive responsibility towards Allah (swt) and the entire creation including nature, past, present and future. The foundation of rights in Islam is really responsibility. It was in the light of these principles that Ibn Taymiyyah wrote one of his major works subtitled *Fi Huqooq al-Ra'i wa al-Ra'iyyah* (*On the Rights of the Authority and the Subjects*) in which he speaks of civil individual rights over one's life and possessions and other rights.

It should be pointed out that some Muslim scholars suggest that according to the major Islamic principles, for a government to be Islamic it must protect the sanctity of human rights. This is a prerequisite of defending the sanctity of Islam, for defending the sanctity of Islam requires that man should be regarded as man first, with his/her rights, so that he/she is able to be the servant of God. Human rights enjoy priority over religious duties because religious duties are only implacable in the light of human rights. A religious society embraces religion in large part because it accords with the society's general sense of justice, which is a human right. Defending human rights is in fact defending religion, because a just understanding of Islam incorporates human rights. Observance of human rights guarantees observance of religion. Abrogation of human rights is in fact the abrogation of justice, which is the foundation of Islamic political system.[24]

The Case of the Constitution of the Islamic Republic of Iran

It is within the context of the above principles and explanation that the preamble to the Constitution of the Islamic Republic of Iran (CIRI) has been formulated. Article 2, paragraph 6 of CIRI corresponds and reflects, to a great extent, the preamble of the UDHR.[25] It emphasizes the commitment of the

CIRI to human rights, national integrity, independence, freedom, justice and equality (equality, fraternity and liberty, principles of the French Revolution, too) which are reflected in the first, second and third articles of the UDHR. Keeping the above discussion in mind, we can now proceed to compare some aspects and articles of the UDHR individually with the Islamic perspective and at the same time make references with the Constitution of the Islamic Republic of Iran as a constitution inspired by the spirit of Islam.

Article 1 of the UDHR is of special interest and deserves attention from the Islamic point of view. It insists on the liberty, equality of people, with respect to their rights, and fraternity amongst people, which are emphasized in Islam.[26] These principles are taken care of also in the CIRI.[27] These principles are also emphasized in the much-quoted tradition reported from the Prophet (puh) which is well-expressed by Sadra of Shiraz as follows.

All members of each other are mankinds,
Since all of one soul are refined.
One member's pain of body, hearts or mind
Means the rest no lasting peace can find.
Those who to share thy brother's pang declined
Their claim to share the name of man resigned.

Article 2 of the UDHR is also sanctioned by Islam and CIRI.[28] Article 3 is fully accepted and sanctioned by Islam and CIRI.[29] For example, Article 3 of the UDHR reads 'Everyone has the right to life, liberty and security of person.'[30] Article 22 of CIRI reads: 'Dignity, life, properties, rights and occupations of people are inviolable.'

Article 4 deals with the question of slavery. This article complies with the spirit of Islam. It should be emphasized that the modern form of slavery has not been dealt with here, but it has been taken care of in Islam and in CIRI.[31] Nevertheless, Article 4 needs explanation. Although it appears at first sight to be contrary to Islamic law, closer examination reveals that it complies fully with the spirit of Islam. Articles 5 to 11 conform fully to Islamic law and spirit.[32]

Article 12 is fully compatible with Islamic law and the spirit of Islam and the CIRI. People's private lives, residence and correspondence are fully respected in Islam and the CIRI.[33] This is reflected in the following anecdote. During the reign of the second Caliph 'Umar, either he or his police climbed on the roof to enforce a law. The resident replied to his objection of breaking the law by saying that 'maybe I have committed one sin; but think how many sins you have committed. You have committed:

1. spying, despite God's command, 'Thou shall not spy';[34]
2. breaking and entering – by coming in from the roof despite the order, 'Enter houses by the door';[35]
3. entering without permission, in defiance of God's order; the Qur'an declares 'Enter no house without the owner's permission;'[36] and
4. ignoring courtesy despite its being recommended.[37]

Article 13: not only has this right been recognized; it has been encouraged. The question of freedom of movement and emigration has been treated as a virtue by Islam and sanctioned by CIRI.[38] Article 14: Islam and article 24 of CIRI have taken care of this right.

Article 15: Islam suggests the brotherhood of believers and suggests internationalism. This however, does not challenge the concept of nationhood as the basic unit of the international community. This is why provisions have been made in the CIRI for this.[39]

Article 16 should be taken with reservations. As far as the right of marriage is concerned, Islam encourages and promotes the principle without reservation. Islam also suggests that family is the natural basic unit of human society. The sanctity of these two in Islam is beyond any question. Nevertheless, being a comprehensive way of life and legal system, Islam has formulated its own concept, rules, regulations and restrictions of marriage and family.[40] We know that religion and culture play the most important role in family law. We must allow room for flexibility and respect religious and cultural values especially in the field of personal and family law.

Article 17: Islam again fully sanctions this article. The sanctity of ownership is provided for both in Islam and in CIRI.[41] Again, as usual this article must be viewed within the framework of the Islamic legal system. Generally speaking Islam laid down the principles and the sanctity of right of ownership in a comprehensive and complete form with its own rules, regulations and restrictions.[42] There is a legal maxim and principle established in the Islamic jurisprudence, based on a tradition from Muhammad (puh)), the meaning of which is roughly, 'People have the exclusive authority over their property and life' (*al-naso musalattun 'ala amwalihim wa anfosihim*).

Articles 18, 19: these articles are largely accepted but not without reservations. Islam certainly rejects compulsion in faith. The Qur'an declares that 'there is no compulsion in religion'. The CIRI also has made provision for this principle within the Islamic concepts and framework.[43]

Article 20 is reflected in CIRI, Article 25. Article 21 is fully respected and all its sections are taken into consideration in the CIRI.[44]

Articles 22 and 23: all natural physical human needs of individuals and society have been taken care of in Islam. Islam is recognized by Muslims as a comprehensive way of life. It does not recognize the separation of religion and politics. It recognizes spiritual and physical needs and in fact introduces a strong balance between all aspects of human life and needs.[45]

Article 24 of the UDHR is fully supported by the Islamic code of life and work. There are many Muslims who recommend the division of twenty-four hours into three portions: eight hours for work, eight hours for rest, sleep and repose and eight for other things.[46]

Article 25: the contents of this article are provided for in the CIRI as a reflection of the Islamic attitude towards the matter.[47]

Articles 26 and 27 establish the right to education and the right to participate in cultural life. Islam beyond any doubt has encouraged the education of everyone. 'Acquisition of knowledge is the duty of every Muslim male and female' in Islam. The Qur'an has guaranteed this right on a few occasions. CIRI also includes the necessary provisions for this right.[48]

Article 28: Islam, unlike other religions, established its own social, political, economic etc. order. Prophet Mohammad (puh) established the first Islamic order and system as soon as it was possible for him to do so. Parts 2, 4, 5, 6, 8, 9, and 10 of the CIRI deal with the contents of Article 28 of the UDHR.

Article 29: the concept of part one of this article corresponds fully with the Islamic maxims: 'Everyone of you is responsible for his/her flock' and 'He who is not concerned with the state of affairs of the Muslim community is not truly a Muslim'. Part two is taken care of by article 40 of CIRI.[49]

Article 30 simply states that 'Nothing in the UDHR may be interpreted in a way to contradict with other parts and with the spirit of the UDHR or be misused by any means.'

Finally it should be pointed out that the UDHR deals mainly with the rights of individuals while CIRI deals with these and national rights as well; the responsibility of the executive and the judicial powers, the form of government, etc. CIRI thus covers a much larger area. But we can state that almost all the rights declared by the UDHR are taken care of by CIRI within a special political and socio-cultural framework and within the context of Islam as a comprehensive legal, political, social, economic, cultural and spiritual way of life.[50]

Notes

Chapter One

1. *Routledge Encyclopaedia of Philosophy*, 'Natural Law'.
2. Hart, H.L.A., *The Concept of Law*, Oxford, 1961, quoted in M.H. Kamali, 'Social Justice', *Islamica*, Vol. 3, No.1, 1999.
3. Introduction to Singer, P. (ed.), *Ethics*, O.U.P., 1994.
4. Rowe, C., *Plato*, pp. 9–11 (*Plato to Nato*)
5. Nicholson, P., *Aristotle*, pp. 18–30.
6. Nasr, S.H., *Religion and the Order of Nature*, pp. 87–95.
7. For further details about St. Thomas Aquinas see *Summa Theolooogica.*
8. Black, A., *St. Thomas Aquinas*, pp. 45–61.
9. Anglo, S., *Machiavelli*, pp. 61–73.
10. Tuck, R., *Thomas Hobbes*, pp. 85–96.
11. For a first account of Islamic philosophy, in this respect, see A. Leaman, *An Introduction to Medieval Islamic Philosophy*, Cambridge, C.U.P., 1985.
12. Nasr, S.H., *Religion and the Order of Nature*, pp. 103–7
13. Dunn, J., *John Locke*, pp. 96–108.
14. Locke, J., *Two Treaties of Government*, pp. 309–11.
15. Wokler, R., *Jean Jacques Rousseau*, pp. 108–20.
16. Finnis, John, *Natural Law and Natural Rights*, 1980.
17. For further details about the concept of justice see M.H. Kamali, 'Social Justice', *Islamica*, Vol. 3, No. 1, 1999.
18. For further details see James Rachels (ed.), *Ethical theory*, Oxford O.U.P., 1998.
19. Gray, John, *John Stuart Mill*, pp. 135–48.
20. For further details see Doyal L. and Harris R., *Empiricism, Explanation and Rationality*, London, Routledge, 1986.
21. Doyal, L. and Harris, R., *Empiricism, Explanation and Rationality*, London, Routledge, 1986.
22. Doyal, L. and Harris, R., *Empiricism, Explanation and Rationality*, London, Routledge, 1986.
23. See Al-Asi, M. *The West Record*...in *Crescent International*, August 16–31, 2000.
24. See Ian Graeme Barbour, *Issues in Science and Religion*, London, SCM Press, 1972, Ch. 3.
25. *Britannica*, 'Ethical Relativism'.
26. Ibid. 'Conscience'.
27. Gellner,Ernest, *Postmodernism, Reason and Religion*, 1997, p. 54.

28. For a critical analysis of relativism see Alasdair Macintyre, *Whose Justice? Which Rationality?* Notre Dame University Press, 1988.
29. For a thorough critical analysis of evolution and Darwinism see Harun Yahya, *The Evolution Deceit*, Ta Ha, 1999.
30. For the problems of liberalism and liberal democracy see C.B. Macpherson, *Democratic Theory*, Oxford, O.U.P., 1973.
31. *Qur'an*, 7:172. For the failure of materialism and relativism see H. Putnam, *Renewing Philosophy*, Cambridge, Harvard University Press, 1992, Ch. 4.
32. For further details see M. Legenhausen, *Contemporary Topics of Islamic Thought*, pp. 198–200.
33. Gellner, Ernest, *Postmodernism, Reason and Religion*, pp. 77–9.
34. For further details see Mary Midgley, *The Roots of Human Nature*, London, Methuen, 1978.
35. *Britannica*, 'Ethical Relativism'.
36. Gellner, E., *Postmodernism, Reason and Religion*, pp. 80–3.
37. Rachels, James, *Ethical Theory*, Oxford, O.U.P. 1998, pp. 26–9.
38. Gellner, E. *Postmodernism, Reason and Religion*, pp. 24–8.
39. Fazlur, Rahman, *Islam*, pp. 124–6.
40. *Britannica*, 'Existentialism'.
41. Legenhausen M., *Contemporary Topics in Islamic Thought*, pp. 41-47.
42. Ibid., pp. 81-89.
43. Qur'an, 49:13.
44. for further details see James Rachels (ed.), *Ethical Theory*, Oxford, O.U.P. 1998.
45. Ibid.
46. Heidegger, Martin, *A Letter on Humanism*, in D. F. Krell (ed.), *Martin Heidegger: Basic Writings*, trans. F.A. Capuzzi, New York, Harpers & Row, 1977.
47. Caputo, John, *D. Against Ethics*, Bloomington, Indiana U.P., 1993.
48. *Routledge Encyclopedia of Philosophy*, 'Philosophy of Law'.

Chapter Two

1. Kashani, M.M. Faid, *Tafsir al-safi*, Beirut, Vol. 5, p. 107.
2. al-Faruqi, Ismail, *The Challenge of Islam*, Ch. 5.
3. Qur'an, 42:13; 4:152; 43:6.
4. Qur'an, 3:19.
5. Qur'an, 2:213; 5:14.
6. Stoddart, W., *Sufism*, p. 23.
7. Brohi, A.K. *Human Rights in Islam. The Challenge of Islam* and *Islam in the contemporary Society.* published by the Islamic Council of Europe.
8. Qur'an, 14:31.
9. al-Attas, Naqib, S.M. *The Challenge of Islam* published by the Islamic Council of Europe, Ch. 3.
10. Kashani, M.M. Faid, *Tafsir al-Safi*, Beirut, Vol. 5, p. 107.
11. Nasr, S.H., *Religion and the Order of Nature*, pp. 62–3.
12. Shahristani, *Kitabo Nihayat al-Iqdam fi 'Ilm al-Kalam*, edit. and trans. by Alfred Guillaume, Oxford, O.U.P., 1934, pp. 90–1.
13. Donaldson, D. M. *Studies in Muslim Ethics*, London, SPCK, 1953, pp. 117–8.
14. Huxley, J., *Man in the Modern World*.

15. Qur'an, 30:30.
16. Ibid.
17. cf. Macdonald, *Religious attitude in Islam*, p. 243.
18. al-Faruqi, Ismail, *Islam in the Contemporary Society*, chapter on 'Islam as Culture'.
19. Legenhausen, M., 'Problems of Christian Theology', Tehran, Islamic Culture and Relations Organization, 1999, p. 22.
20. Legenhausen, M., *Contemporary Topics of Islamic Thought*, Tehran, Islamic Culture and Relations Organization, 1999, pp. 270–1
21. Schuon, F
22. Schuon, *Islam and the Perennial Philosophy*, p. 133.
23. Qur'an, 77:23; 41:10; 25:2; 65:3; 54:49.
24. Qur'an, 36:40.
25. Schimmel, A.M., *Deciphering the Signs of God*, Edinburgh U.P., 1994.
26. Stoddart, W., *Sufism*, p. 49.
27. Qur'an, 30:30; 17:77.
28. Nasr, S.H., *Science and Civilization in Islam*, p. 39.
29. *Britannica*, 'Ethical Relativism'.
30. *Futuhat al-M akkiyah* (*Meccan Revelations*), quoted by S.H. Nasr in *Science and Civilization in Islam*, p. 344.
31. *Britannica*, 'Rationalism'.
32. Hourani, G., *The Rational Ethics of 'Abd al-Jabbar*, Oxford, Clarendon, 1971.
33. Abd al-Jabbar, *Kitab al-Usul al-Khamsah*, translated by Richard C. Martin in Martin, R.C., Woodward, M.R. and Atmaja, D. S., *Defenders of Reason in Islam*, Oneworld, 1997, p. 12.
34. Ibid.
35. *Britannica*, 'John Locke'.
36. Ibid.
37. Moore, G.E., *Principia Ethica*, 1903.
38. Nasr, S.H., *Islam in the Contemporary Society*, chapter on 'Intellect and Intuition'.
39. see *Routledge Encyclopedia of Philosophy*, 'Philosophy of Law', 1998.
40. This treatise has been translated into English by the late George Hourani under the title *Islamic Rationality*.
41. Hovannisian, R.G., 'Ethics in Islamic traditionalist doctrine', pp. 48–49 in *Ethics in Islam*, Atlanta, Scholars press, 1985, pp. 48–9.
42. Tusi, K. Nasir al-Din, *Akhlaq-e-Naseri*, pp. 40–1.
43. Qur'an, 21:22.
44. Qur'an, 30:29.

Chapter Three

1. Nasr, S.H., *Islam*.
2. Islamic Council of Europe, *Islam and the Contemporary Society*, pp. 36–7.
3. Isfahani, Raghib, *Kitab al-Dhari'ah ila Makarim al-shari'ah*, Cairo, 1987.
4. The word *fitrah* and its derivatives have been used in the Qur'an at least in the following verses: 6:79; 30:30; 17:51; 20:72; 11:51; 36:22; 43:27; 21:56; 7:172. The word *hanif* and its derivatives have been used in the Qur'an in the following verses: 22:31; 58:5; 11:69; 2:135; 3:67, 95; 4:125; 6:79, 161; 10:105; 16:120, 123; 30:40.
5. Hanif, M. I.I., *Sahih Muslim, Bisharat al-Nawawi*, (*Book of Qadr*), Vol. 16, 1930, 1994, p. 207.

6. Mutahhari, M., *Fi trat, 'adl-e-Ilahy*, (*The Human Being in the Qur'an*), Tehran, I.P.O., 1983. The whole book of 100 pages deals with the question of *fitrah*.
7. Hanif, I.I.M. *Sahih Muslim*, op cit.
8. Mohamed, Yasien, *Fitrah: The Islamic Concept of Human Nature*, Ta Ha, 1996. The whole book makes very interesting reading on the question of *fitrah*.
9. Schultz, D. , *Theories of Personality*, 1994; *Nature*, 1987.
10. see, Stevenson, L. *Seven Theories of Human Nature*, Oxford, O.U.P., 1987.
11. see, Schultz, D, *Six Images of Human Nature*, 1990.
12. Kant, Immanuel, *Metaphysics of Morals*, trans. by Mary Gregor, Cambridge, C.U.P., pp. 159–62.
13. See Mohamed Y., *Fitrah*, pp. 150–155.
14. Mohamed, Y., *Fitrah*, Ta Ha Pub, 1996. pp. 101–105; Mustafa Achoui, pp. 71–97.
15. Ibid., pp. 150–159.
16. Donaldson, D. M., *Studies in Muslim Ethics*, pp. 108–9.
17. Farabi, A.N., *Fusul al-Muntaza'ah*, p. 81 (Aphorisms, 60). Cf. Enneads.1. 8, 3. p.85. Quoted in M., *Ethical Theories in Islam*, 2nd ed. , Leiden, New York, Brill, 1994.
18. Qur'an, 20:99, 113; 65:10.
19. Qur'an, 9:15; 21:50, 81. M.H. *Taba tabai, al-Mizan*. Commentary on Verse 2.
20. Finnis, J., *Natural Law and Natural Rights*, Oxford, Clarendon, 1980, pp. 33–6.
21. Qur'an, 30:30; 7:172; 2:209; 6:50; 30:8; 12:48; 2:31; 24:1 and many others.
22. Qur'an, 3:19; 2:83.
23. For further explanation of these terms and concepts, see M. Ajmal, 'Sufi Science of the Soul', in S.H. Nasr (ed.), *Islamic Spirituality*, Vol. 1, London: Routledge, 1987.
24. Kant, Immanuel, *Metaphysics of Morals*, trans. by Mary Gregor, Cambridge, C.U.P., pp. 159–62.
25. Newman, *Certain Difficulties felt by Anglicans in Catholic Teaching*, Vol. 11, p. 248.
26. Webb, C.C.J., *Religious Experience*, p. 44.
27. Pailin, David, A., *Philosophy of Religion*, pp. 211–13.

Chapter Four

1. Nietzsche, F., *Der Wille zur Macht* (*the Will to Power*), *Human All too Human*, see *Routledge Encyclopedia of Philosophy*, 'Nietzsche'.
2. Sabzevari, H., *Ghawali al-La'ali.*
3. Crow, Karim Douglas, 'The Role of 'Aql in Early Islamic Wisdom, with Reference to Imam Ja'far al-Sadiq', Ph.D thesis, McGill University, 1996. He produced an abridged version of it in an article 'Between Wisdom and Reason', *Islamica*, Vol. 3, No.1, 1999.
4. *Fusul al-Muntaz'ah*, p. 29. cf. English trans. by Dunlop, D. M. quoted by M.Fahkry in *Ethical theories in Islam*, pp. 76–80. Leiden. Brill. 1991
5. Legenhausen, M., *Contemporary Topics of Islamic Thought*, Tehran, Islamic Culture and Relations Organization, 1999, p. 87. For definition and concept of *'aql* see Karim Douglas Crow, 'Between Wisdom and Reason', *Islamica*, Vol. 3, No.1, 1999.
6. Crow, K.D. 'Between Wisdom and Reason', *Islamica*, Vol. 3, No.1, 1999.
7. Nasr, S.H., *Religion and the Order of Nature*, p. 171.
8. Ibid. p. 172.
9. Ibid. pp. 173–5.
10. Nasr, S.H., *Islam and the Contemporary Society*, pp. 36–7.
11. Watt, Montgomery, *Islamic Thought*, 1998, p. 180.

12. See Mulla Sadra, *Sharho Usul al-Kafi*. See also M. Al-Kulayni, *Al-Kafi*, Vol. 1, Part 1 *Kitab al-'aql wa al-Jahl*; Ibn 'Abd Rabbih, *Al-'Aqd al-Farid*, 11, 248 (this last quotation is a combination of Hadiths No. 1 and 14 of *Usul al-Kafi*. Vol. 1. Part 1.
13. The International Institute of Islamic Thought, 1981, pp. 42–5.
14. Martin, R.C., Woodward, M.R. and Atmaja, D. S., *Defenders of Reason in Islam*, Oneworld, 1997, pp. 16–18.
15. Guillaume, Alfred, *The Traditions of Islam*, Oxford, Clarendon, 1924, p. 71.
16. Martin, R.C., Woodward, M.R. and Atmaja, D. S., *Defenders of Reason in Islam*, Oneworld, 1997, pp. 16–19.
17. Ibid. pp. 7–15.
18. Nasr, S.H. *Islam and the Contemporary Society*, pp. 36–37
19. Ibid. p. 37
20. Warnock, 'Reason' in *Encyclopaedia of Philosophy*, N.Y., Macmillan.
21. Ewing, A.C., *Reason and Intuition*, 1968, p. 37.
22. Ewing, A.C., *Reason and Intuition*, pp. 41, 53, 55, 43, 53–60, 91. Quoted by David A. Pailin in *Philosophy of Religion*, London, 1986, p. 49.
23. Ibid.
24. Ibid.
25. Whitehead, *Process and Reality*, p. 39.
26. Warnock, 'Reason' in Encyclopaedia of Philosophy, New York.
27. Ewing, A.C., *Reason and Intuition*, pp. 41, 53, 55.

Chapter Five

1. Raghib, Isfahani, *Mufradat*, H.K.M. It seems as if *Hikmah* and *'aql* have the same literal meaning, for *'aql* also means to withhold, restrain and prevent, for it withholds and restrains its possessor from wrongdoing and binds him to the intellectual principles(*Hikmah*) and prevents him from misunderstanding mistakes and making wrong decisions. *'Iqal al-Jamal* is the rope used to tie camel legs to stop him going astray.
2. Farabi, quoted by Dr A. Fuad, *Ma'ani al-Falsafah*, p. 7.
3. *Encyclopaedia Of Islam*. 'Hikmah'.
4. Jurjani, *Mufradat, hikmah.*
5. Ibid.
6. See Farabi, *Tahsil al-S'adat.*
7. Avicenna, *Rasail, al-hikmaht* is the passage of the soul of man to the possible for him within two bounds and action.
8. Averroes, *Tahafut al-Tahafut.*
9. Ibn Taymiyyah, *Al-Radd 'ala al-Mantiqiyin*, 3, 4, 5, 6 are quoted from M. Afnan, *Philosophical Lexicon*, Iran, 1983, pp. 78–9.
10. See B. Radtke, *The Concept of Sainthood in Early Islamic Mysticism*, Curzon, 1996, pp. 1–3.
11. Raghib, Isfahani, *Mufradat, Shara'a.*
12. The Qur'an, 45: 18; 5:48.
13. Rahman, Fazlur, *Islam*, second ed. , University of Chicago Press, 1979, Chap. 6. 'The road to the watering place'; *Encyclopaedia of Islam, Shi'ah.*
14. al-Tahausoni, Muhammad, *Kashshaf Istilahat* p. 71; Raghib, *Mufradhat, Shara'a.* It is noteworthy that water has been used as the physical source of life in Arabic

literature. *shari'ah* has been compared to the road to water because it is the physical and spiritual source of life.

15. Qur'an, 5:4; 45:18.
16. Qur'an, 3:15; 3:19.
17. Rahman, Fazlur, *Islam*, Chapter 6.
18. *Al-tujih al-Tashrii fi al-Islam*, Cairo, 1972, Vol. 3, p. iii.
19. Rahman, Fazlur, *Islam*, pp. 117–19.
20. Qur'an, 3:15, 19.
21. Rahman, Fazlur, *Islam*, pp. 114–15.
22. Fakhry, M., *Averroes*, Beirut, 1960, p. 26.
23. Ibid.
24. Schuon, F., *Islam and the Perennial Philosophy*, p. 71.
25. The word *hikmah* has been used in the Qur'an in the following verses at least: 54:5; 3:81; 17:39; 16:125; 42:63; 2:231; 33:34; 2:209; 31:12; 38:20; 2:251,129; 4:48; 31:68; 4:54; 3:113; 5:110; 62:2.
26. Qur'an, 62:2.
27. It has been used many times, e.g. as follows: 11:1; 27:6; 41:42; 44:4; 3:58; 3:126; 10:1; 31:2; 39:1; 45:2; 40:2; 62:1.
28. Qur'an, 62:1, 4; 41:26; 31:8. *Hakim* here means the divine being whose works and will and commands are based on *hikmah*.
29. Qur'an, 31:11; 5:110; 3:48.
30. Qur'an, 31:1.
31. Qur'an, 10:1; 12:1.
32. Ibid.
33. Qur'an, 2:129, 151and 231; 3:48, 81 and 164; 4:54, 113; 5:110; 12:2. Al-Asi, Mohammed, 'Introducing the Importance of *Hikmah* (wisdom) for Understanding the Noble Scripture', *Crescent International*, 16–31 July 2000.
34. Qur'an, 2:209; 6:50; 30:8; 12:48; 2:31; 24:1, and many more.
35. For the terms *'aqala*, *'alama*, *taddabara*, *taffakara* and similar terms see *al-Ma'jam al-Mufahras* (the index to Qur'anic terms).
36. See the six great Sunni collections of Traditions (*al-Sehah al-Settah:* Bukhari, Hanbali, Awza'i, Malik, Dawood, Tirmidhi and the four great Shi'ite collections of traditions: *Tahdhib*, *Istibsar*, *Usul al-Kafi* and *Man La Yahdorho al-Faqih* and their later collections of traditions.
37. Qummi, Abu al-Qasim, M., *Qavanien al-Usul*, p. 260.
38. Mubashir Ibn Fatik, *Mukhtar al-Hikam*, F.H.I.P., p. 2.
39. Qur'an: 31, 12.
40. *Fi al-Huduth* in *Rasailo Ikhwan al-Safa*, pp. 67f. Mulla Sadra, *al-Asfar*, 11, *Fall*, 246f.
41. **Source of quote?**
42. Rahman, Fazlur, *Islam*, pp. 104–7.
43. Qur'an, 62:2.
44. see especially Avicenna's works.
45. Ibn Abi Usaiba'ah, '*Uyoon al-Anba'*, Vol. 2, p. 39; Al-Baïdawi, A. *Al-Turath al-Yonani*, p. 148; al-Nashar; *Nash'at al-Fikr*, p. 81.
46. Mubashir b. Fatik; *Mukhtar al-Hikam*, p. 2.
47. Qur'an, 2:129, 231; 3:81; 62:2.
48. Qur'an, 2:251–2; 38:20; 5:110; 43:63.

49. Averroes believes that all Prophets (pbt) are philosophers but not all the philosophers are Prophets (pbt). *Tahafut al-Tahafut.*
50. Al-Shahristani, *Milal wa Nihal*, Vol. 1, p. 237.
51. Rashid Rida, *Al-Manar*, vii, 292, cited in Adams, *Islam and Modernism*, p. 19; see also Goldziher, *Die Richtungen*, Leiden, 1920, pp. 352–3, quoted by M. Kerr, *Islamic Reform*, p. 129.
52. Ibn Taymiyyah, *Fatawa*, 20/496.
53. Ibn Taymiyyah, *al-Iradah wa al-Amr* in his *Rasa'il*, Cairo, 1323, pp.334–5.
54. Ibn Taymiyyah, *Fatawa*, 20/496. See Mohamed Yunis Ali, M. *Medieval Islamic Pragmatics*, Curzon Press, 2000, pp. 1–2.
55. Ibn Taymiyyah, *al-Iradah wa al-Amr* in his *Rasa'il*, pp. 334–5.
56. Ibn Taiymiyyah, *Minhaj*, 1.124. quoted from G. Makdisi, *Religion, Law and Learning in Classical Islam*, 1991, p. 60.
57. Ibn 'Aqil, *Kitab al-Funun*, p. 400,11.2 ff. Quoted by G. Makdisi, *Religion, Law and Learning in Classical Islam*, 1991, pp57–61. 58.Fazlur Rahman, *Islam*, pp. 122–3
59. Al-Kendi, *Rasa'il al-Falsafiyyah*, p. 97.
60. Ibid. pp. 355, 373.
61. Fakhry, Majid, *A History of Islamic Philosophy*, 2nd ed. , New York, Columbia University Press, 1983, pp. 63–4.
62. Ibid.
63. Al-Baihaqi, *Tatemato Sevan al-hikmah*, Lahore, AH1351, p. 25.
64. See his letter to Ahmad ibn Mu'Tasim, Egypt, AH1369, pp. 244–5
65. Al-Kendi, *Rasail*, p. 244 Egypt 1950
66. 'Abd al-Jabbar, *al-Mughni*, vi 64, translation by Hourani in *Islamic Rationality*, p.132.
67. Hourani, G. *Islamic Rationality*, Oxford, 1971, p. 136.
68. Imad al-din 'Abd al-Jabbar, *Sharh Usul al-Ahkam*.
69. 'Abd al-Jabbar, *al-Mughni*, vi 64, translation by Hourani in *Islamic Rationality*, p.132.
70. Ibi*d.* XVII, 101–2, C.H.I.R., Oxford, 1971, pp. 131–6.
71. Hourani, G. *Islamic Rationality*, p. 136
72. We have explained al-Jabbar's views in some detail because he seems to represent the *Mu'tazilites* at this crucial formative period. It should be pointed out that it has not been established that the book *Sharh al-Usul al-Khamsah* is by 'Abd al-Jabbar. It is suggested that the book is by a student of 'Abd al-Jabbar and represents his teacher's views.
73. Paul Kraus, (ed.) *Rasail al-Falsafiyyah/Opera Philosophia*, Cairo, 1939, pp. 17–18. Translated by Eric L.Ormsby. Quoted in *World Philosophy*, ed. by R.C. Solomon, pp. 122–4.
74. He is the author of an Arabic book outlining the principles of rationalism in Islam (*Risalaton fi al-'aql*) in which he deals with the human intellect for the first time exclusively.
75. Farabi, *Risalaton Fi al-'aql* (a treatise on intellect).
76. Farabi, *The Book of Religion*. p. 47; Muhsin Mahdi,*Kitab al-Millah wa Nususon ukhra.* Beirut, 1968.
77. Colmo, Christopher, in an article in *Review of Politics*, Notre Dame University, 1998.
78. Ahmad Amin, *Zuhar al-Islam*, Vol. 3, p. 233.
79. Sharif, M.M., *Short History of Muslim Philosophy*, Delhi, 1995, Vol. 1, p. 1376.
80. See Avicenna's books on philosophy, *Shafa* and *Isharat*, Chapter on *'aql*; Qummi, M.A., *Qavaneen*, chapter on *'aql;* al-Naraqi, *Jami' al-Sa'adah*, Vol. 1, p. 118.

81. See Farabi, *Madinat al-Fadilah*, p. 79, 1955 Beirut and Avicenna, *Al-Nejat*, p. 167.
82. *Al-Tujih al Tashri'i fi al-Islam*, Al-Azhar, Vol. 4. pp. 23–26.
83. Hakim, T. *al-Usul al-Ammah.*
84. Ghazzali, *al-Mustasfa*, Vol. 1. p. 127.
85. Fakhry, Majid, *A History of Islamic Philosophy*, 2nd ed. , New York, Columbia University Press, 1983, p. 100.
86. Legenhausen, M. *Contemporary Problems of Christian Theology in Islamic Thought*, Tehran, Islamic Culture and Relation Org., 1999, p. 20.
87. See Ghazzali, *al-Musta:fa*, pp. 63–64. Quoted by Kamali, M.H., *Principles of Islamic Jurisprudence*, p. 11.
88. Pernez Hoodboy, *Islam and Science*, London, Zed Books, 1991, p. 105.
89. Pervez Hoodbhoy, *Islam and Science*, London, Zed Books, 1991, p. 106.
90. al-Baihaqi, *Tatemmato Sevan al-hikmah*
91. Rahman, Fazlur, *Islam*, second ed. , University of Chicago Press, 1979,
92. Original was numbered 78 (out of sequence and already used) what is source?
93. Ghazzali, *Tahafut al-Falasafah*, pp. 16f: *M'iyar al-'Ilm* pp. 60f: Supra, pp. 249f., *F.H.I.*, Cambridge, C.U.P., 1970, p. 347.
94. Ghazzali, *Ihya al-'Ulum*, Vol. 1, pp. 76–8.
95. Ibid. Vol. 3, p. 7.
96. Fakhry, Majid, *A History of Islamic Philosophy*, 2nd ed. , New York, Columbia University Press, 1983, pp. 354–5.
97. Al-Shahristani, *al-Melal*, Vol. 1, p. 237–492.
98. This voluminous commentary on the Qur'an is also called *Mafatih al-Ghayb* (*The Keys to the Unknown*).
99. Ibn Tufayl, *Hayy ibn Yaqzan.*
100. Nasr, S.H. *Science and Civilization in Islam*, pp. 315–318. Also see M.M. Sharif, *Short History of Muslim Philiosophy*, Vol. 1, p. 1387.
101. Wren, *The World of Islam*, London, 1960.
102. Averroes, *Fasl al-Maqal.*
103. Ibid. pp. 3–5.
104. Averroes, *Fasl al-Maqal*, pp. 6–8.
105. Ibid. pp. 13–14.
106. Ibid. pp. 7, 15–16.
107. Ibid. pp. 13–14.
108. For this see the whole *Fasl al-Maqal* and *Tahafut al Tahafut.*
109. Ibid.
110. Ibn Rushd, *Fasl al-Maqal*, pp. 31–32
111. Ibid. p. 15 and a few other places in the book.
112. This point has been made in *Fasl al-Maqal* several times, e.g. pp. 27 and 17.
113. Tusi, *Akhlaq-e-Naseri* and *Tahdhib*, quoted by Fakhry, M. *Ethical Theories in Islam.*
114. Nasr, S.H., *Science and Civilization in Islam*, p. 35.
115. Ronan, Ernest, **op. cit,** p. 80 and Sharif, M. *Short History of Muslim Philiosophy*, Vol. 1, p. 1381.
116. Goddard, Hugh, *Christians and Muslems*, Curzon, 1995, p. 62.
117. Smart, Ninian, *World Philosophies*, London, 1999, p. 165.
118. Hedgson, M.G.C. *The Venture of Islam*. pp. 433–4

119. See *al-Mu'jam al-Mufahras* for the number of Qur'anic verses dealing with this subject (*the word Islam* and its derivatives in the Qur'an) (this doesn't seem to fit the text)
120. Sharif, M., *Short History of Muslim Philiosophy*, p. 1378.
121. Jalal al-din Rumi is a very well known example of this approach. This idea is clearly reflected quite a few times in his work *Mathnawi*. Mulla Sadra of Shiraz is another supporter of this doctrine. Like Sheikh al-Ishraque, Mulla Sadra believed in the unity of truth transmitted in unbroken chain from Adam to Muhammad and to the philosophers and Sufis of Islam.
122. O. Leaman, Can rights co-exist with religion? in *S.I.M.E.T.T*, Oxford, O.U.P., 2000, pp. 163,174.
123. It should be pointed out here that this Sheikh al-Ishraque is not the same as the other scholar with the same name who adopted a completely different approach and compiled a work against Greek philosophy, *A book of Refreshing Religious Advice and Uncovering of Greek Scandals.*
124. Fakhry, Majid, *A History of Islamic Philosophy*, 2nd ed. , New York, Columbia University Press, 1983, p. 339.
125. Nasr, S.H. Science and Civilization in Islam, p. 328.
126. Ibid, p. 294.
127. Mulla Sadra, *Al-Hikmat al-Muta'alliyyah fi al-Asfar al-Arba'ah*, Beirut, Vol. 1, p. 13, 1981.
128. Mclean, G.F., *Faith Reason and Philosophy*, US, Council of Research, 2000, p. 69.
129. He wrote a book on the *Islamic law of inheritance.*
130. See Mahdi, M., Ibn Khaldoon's *Philosophy of History*, p. 3; Fakhry, Majid, *A History of Islamic Philosophy*, 2nd ed. , New York, Columbia University Press, 1983, p. 361.
131. Fakhry, Majid, *A History of Islamic Philosophy*, 2nd ed. , New York, Columbia University Press, 1983, p. 361.
132. Ibn Khaldoon, *al-Muqadamah*, Carus N.D. , p. 519.
133. *Risalaton Fi al-Huduth* in *Rasail* by Akhund, pp. 67–69, 110f, cf. *al-Asfar al-Arba'ah* (*The four Journeys*, f., 246 f., quoted by Fakhry, Majid, *A History of Islamic Philosophy*, 2nd ed. , New York, Columbia University Press, 1983, p. 341–4.
134. Kerr, M.H. *Islamic Reform*; Lutf Allah Khan, *Jamal al-din*; Rashid Reia, *Tarikh.*
135. See '*Urwat al-Wuthqa*; *al-Manar*
136. Sadr al-din Shirazi, *al-Hikmat al-Muta'aliyyah fi al-Asfar al-Arba'ah*, Tehran 1387/1958, Vol. 1, Part 1, p. 20.
137. A paper presented by J. Lumbard to the International Conference on Mulla Sadra, London, 12–13 May 2000.
138. Jamal al-din, *al-Raddo 'ala al-Nituriyyah*, p. 375.
139. Fakhry, Majid, *A History of Islamic Philosophy*, 2nd ed. , New York, Columbia University Press, 1983, p. 373–5.
140. 'Abduh's systematic work *Risalatu al-Tawhid* can be regarded as text book which shared the same goal and approach as Averroes's *Fasl al-Maqal.*
141. 'Abduh, *Risalat al-Tawhid*, pp. 24–5.
142. Kerr, M. *Islamic Reform*, p. 105.
143. Ibid. p. 109.
144. Ibid, p. 109.
145. Rashid Reda, *Tarikh al-Ustad*, pp. 1, 11, 12.
146. *Risalat al-Tawhid*, pp. 6–8, translated by Kerr in *Islamic Reform* p. 110.

147. Ibid. pp. 5, 71, 72.
148. Ibid. pp. 51, 73.
149. Kerr, *Islamic Reform*, p. 126.
150. 'Abduh, *al-Islam wa al-Nasraniyyah*, Cairo, AH 1350, p. 56.
151. 'Abduh, *Resalat al-Tawhid*. p. 25.
152. For further details, see his work, *Tahdhib al-Akhlaq*.
153. Fazlur Rahman, *Islam*, pp. 215–17.
154. Legenhausen, M., *Contemporary Topics of Islamic Thought*, pp. 81–89.
155. Legenhausen, Muhammad, *Contemporary Topics of Islamic Thought*, pp. 81–88.
156. Al-Minar 29, 1928 :40; cited in Juynboll, *Authenticity*, p. 139.
157. Shibli, *Sirat al-Nu'man*, p. 194.
158. For further details, see his book, *The Spirit of Islam*, p. 371.
159. Fakhry, Majid, *A History of Islamic Philosophy*, 2nd ed. , New York, Columbia University Press, 1983, p. 388.
160. For further details, see his work, *Reconstruction of Religious Thought in Islam*. pp. 2, 4, 11, 30, 52, 54 and 66.
161. Ibid. pp. 123–125.
162. Fazlur Rahman, *Islam*. p. 225.
163. Ibid.
164. Ibid. pp. 119–120.
165. Madhkoor, Muhammad Salam, *Tarikh al-Tashri'*, Egypt, 1959, p. 188.
166. It is suggested that he rejected analogy and replaced it with syllogism, for he compiled a book supporting the latter: *Taqrib le Hiad al-Mantiq*.
167. Ibn Taymiyyah's book on *Refutation of Logicians* is as outstanding as Ibn Hazm's book on rejection of rational reasoning, and Ghazzali's book *Incoherence of Philosophers*. However, Ibn Taymiyyah's book *The Harmony of Precise and Absolute Reason with Authentic Scripture*, may make us think twice in regarding him as one of the opponents of the doctrine of harmony.
168. 'Abd al-Jabbar, *al-Mughni*, VI.-i, 64; XVII, 101. Also see Martin, R.C., Woodward, M.R. and Atmaja, D. S., *Defenders of Reason in Islam*, Oneworld, 1997.
169. Kerr, M. *Islamic Reform*, p. 107; Khalifah 'Abd al-Hakim, *The Natural Law in Muslim Traditions*, U.N.D. I.N. *Law Proceedings*, Vol. 1, 29, 65, 1951
170. Ibid. p. 127.
171. *Britannica*, 'Kant'.
172. 'Abduh, *Risalat al-Tawhid*, pp. 51–73; Kerr, *Islamic Reform*, p. 129.
173. It has been suggested that 'Abduh's theological discourse amounted implicitly to the revival of Mu'tazilism, quoted by Kerr in *Islamic Reform*, p. 105.
174. Montet, Edouard, *La Propagande Chrétienne et ses Adversaires Musulman*, Paris, 1890, pp. 17–18.
175. For this section see A. Ezzati, *Rabeteh-e Din wa Falsafeh dar Islam*, University of Tabriz Press, 1972.

Appendix

1. Dias, *Jurisprudence*, 67ff. n6.
2. *Britanica*, 'Natural Law'.
3. Imam Ali ibn al-Husein, *Risalat al-Huquq* (*treatise on rights*), translated into English by W.C. Chittick, Muhammadi Trust UK, 1987.

4. Donnelly, Jack, *Universal Human Rights in Theory and Practice*, Ithaca, Cornell, 1993. M. Legenhausen, *Contemporary Topics of Islamic Thought*, Islamic Culture and Relation Org., Iran, 1999.
5. Williams, Bernard, *Ethics and Limits of Philosophy*, in Edmund L. Pincoffs, *Quanderies and Virtues.*
6. Kashani, M.M.F., *Mahajat al-Bayda*, Vol. 1, p. 21 and *Ilm a-Yaqin*, Vol. 2, p. 1054.
7. Macpherson, C.B., *Democratic theory*, p. 224; Dalacoura, K., *Islam, Liberalism and Human Rights*, p. 6.
8. Ibid. p. 14.
9. Mackie, J.L., *The Miracle of Theism*, Oxford, O.U.P., 1982.
10. Macpherson, C.B., *Democratic theory*, p. 224; Dalacoura, K., *Islam, Liberalism and Human Rights*, p. 6. pp. 14–17.
11. Ibid. p. 19.
12. Sadr, M.B., *Islamic Political System*, pp. 81–2.
13. Esposito, John L. and Voll, John O., *Islam and Democracy*, Oxford, O.U.P., 1996.
14. Ibid. p. 23.
15. Fahmi Huwaidi, *Al-Islam wa al-Dimuqratiyyah*, pp. 5–37; Legenhausen, M., 'The Islamic Writing of Human Rights', in *Contemporary Topics of Islamic Thought*, Islamic Culture and Relation Org., Iran, 1999, p. 177.
16. *Britannica*, 'Human Rights'.
17. A tradition states: 'Do not submit to the authority of others as God has created you free.'
18. Qur'an, 5:32; 6:151.
19. Ibid. 5:32.
20. Ibid. 5:3; 5:8; 4:135.
21. Ibid. 51:12.
22. Ibid. 7:4, 93; 2:188; 49:11–12; 24:27; 4:58; 4:148; 9:71; 3:110; 6:164; 28:4; 42:38.
23. Ibid. 16:99; 4:13.
24. Vakili, Valla, *Debating Religion and Politics in Iran*, 1996.
25. We have left out the Article for the sake of brevity. See CIRI, Article 2, Paragraph 6.
26. Qur'an, 111:64; 49:13; 5:35; CIRI Articles 9, 19.
27. CIRI, Par. 6, Articles 9, 62.

Glossary

abad	everlasting
'adl	justice, balance, measure
adah	habit
ahkam	legal rules, regulations, precepts, decrees, commandments
akhbar	traditions, reports
akhbaris	the traditionalists
akhlaq	ethics
'aql	human reason/intellect
al-'aql al-'amali	practical intelligence
al-'aql bi al-fi'l	actual intelligence
al-'aql al-fa'al	active intelligence
al-'aql al-ilahi	divine intelligence
al-'aql al-muslafad	acquired intelligence
al-'aql al-nazari	speculative intelligence
al-insan al-kamil	perfect man
al-insan al-kulli	universal man
ayah	sign, verse
azal	eternal
dalil	proof, evidence, sign
din al-fitrah	ur-religion, religion naturalis
fadilah	virtue
faqih	jurist, legal scholar
fikr	thinking, contemplating
fiqh	Islamic law in practice
firqah	sect, school
fitrah	human primordial nature
gharizah	instinct
gubh	evilness, bad
hakim	wise, Muslim theosopher, all wise
haqiqah	the inner truth
haqq	truth
hikmah	Islamic philosophy, theosophy
hujiyyat	authority
husn	beauty, goodness, good
ijma'	consensus of opinions

ijtihad	qualified, credible legal research and reasoning to ascertain rules of law
ilham	inspiration
illiyyat	causality, causation
al-'ilm al-huduri	presential knowledge, intuition
iman	faith
iradah	will power
'irfan	gnosism
istidlal	deduction
istilah	usage, term
istinbat	inference, understanding, finding the legal rules
istiqra'	induction
jawhar	essence, substance
kamil	perfection
khalifah	vicegerent, guardian, successor
madhab	sect, school of law/thought
mahiyyah	essence, quiddity
mulazamah	harmony, correlation
nawamis	orders, secret laws
nihlah	philosophical group/school
qadir	all powerful
qalb	heart
al-qiyas al-fiqhi	analogy
al-qiyas al-manteqi	syllogism
ra'y	legal opinion, opinion, juristic speculation
ruh	soul, spirit
shar'	Islamic law in general
shari'	legislator, law giver, (in Islam Allah)
tab', tabi'at	mature
tabir	natural
tafsir	commentary on the Qur'an
taklif	obligation, duty
tawhid	monotheism
ta'wil	esoteric exegesis
tajalli	theophany
'urf	common law, custom
usul al-fiqh	Islamic jurisprudence
usulis	the Muslim lawyers who followed the methodology of Islamic law (usul)
wahdat al-wujud	oneness of being, monism
wahdat wajib al-wujud	unity of the cause of existence, monotheism
wahy	revelation
waqiyyah	reality
wujub	obligation, necessity
zahiris	literalists

Bibliography

'Abdul Latif, Dr Sayyed, 'The Concept of Society' in: Donaldson, D. M., *Studies in Muslim Ethics*, London, SPCK, 1953. (This book has to be read critically. The author tries hard and apologetically to attribute Islamic codes of ethics to non-Islamic sources.)

'Abd al-Jabbar, Abu al-Hasan, *Fadl al-Itizal wa Tabaqat al-Mu'tazilah.*

'Abduh, Muhammad, *Risalto al-Tawhid, Al-Islam wa al-Nasraniyyah.*

Aquinas, Thomas (d. 1274), *Summa Theologiae*, 1273.

Arberry, A.J., *Revelation and Reason in Islam*, London, Allen & Unwin, 1954.

Aristotle (d. 322 BC), *Laws; Ethics; Politics; Rhetoric.* For text of Aristotle's *Nicomachean Ethics* see Ryan, *Justice*, Oxford, O.U.P, 1993.

St. Augustine (d. 430), *On Christian Doctrine; The City of God.*

Averroes (Ibn Rushd), *Fasl al-Maqal fi ma bain al-Shariat wa al-hikmat men al-Ittisal.*

Bacon, Francis (d. 1626), *Essays* (1597); *New Atlantis* (1626).

Barbour, Ian Graeme, *Christianity and Scientist*, Association Press, 1960.

Barbour, Ian Graeme, *Issues in Science and Religion*, London, SCM Press, 1972.

Barbour, Ian Graeme, *Science and Secularity: the Ethics of Technology*, New York, Harper & Row, 1970.

Bentham, Jeremy (d. 1832), *Introduction to the Principles of Morals and Legislation.*

Calvin, John (d. 1564), *Institution of Christian Religion.*

Cicero (d. 43 BC), *De Oratore*; *De Republica*; *De Regibus.* For text of Cicero's *De Officiis* see Ryan, *Justice*, Oxford, O.U.P, 1993.

Crow, Karim Douglas, 'Between Wisdom and Reason', *Islamica*, Vol. 3, No. 1, 1999.

Crow, Karim Douglas, 'The Role of *'aql* in Early Islamic Wisdom', Ph.D thesis, McGill University, 1996.

Davidson, Herbert, *Alfarabi, Avicenna, and Averroes on Intellect*, Oxford, New York, O.U.P., 1992.

Donnelly, Jack, *Universal Human Rights in Theory and Practice*, Ithaca, Cornell, 1993.

Esposito, John L. and Voll, John O., *Islam and Democracy,* Oxford, O.U.P., 1996.

Ezzati, A., *The Harmony between Religion and Philosophy in Islam*, University of Tabriz, Iran, 1975.

Fakhry, Majid, *A History of Islamic Philosophy*, 2nd ed. , New York, Columbia University Press, 1983.

Fakhry, Majid, *Ethical theories in Islam*, 2nd ed., Leiden, New York, Brill, 1994.

Fakhry, Majid, *A Short Introduction to Islamic Philosophy and Theology*, 1998.

Farabi, Abu Nasr, *Risalaton fi Ma'ani al-'aql.*

Al-Faruqi, Ismail, *Humanism and the Law: the Case of the Shari'ah*, Lagos, NIALS, 1983.

Finnis, J., *Natural Law and Natural Rights,* Oxford, Clarendon Press, 1980. (A wide-ranging and fundamental treatment with some, but not exclusive, emphasis on legal philosophical issues; suitable, though difficult, for a first approach to the subject.)
Gellner, Ernest, *Postmodernism, Reason and Religion*, London, Routledge, 1993.
Grotius, Hugo (d. 1645), *De Jure Belli et Pacis.*
Haifa, Jawad, *The Rights of Women in Islam*, London, Macmillan,1998.
Hegel, G.W.F. (d. 1831) *The Philosophy of Right* (1821); *The Philosophy of History* (1837).
Heidegger, Martin, *A Letter on Humanism,* in D. F. Krell (ed.), *Martin Heidegger: Basic Writings*, trans. F.A. Capuzzi, New York, Harpers & Row, 1977.
Hobbes, Thomas (d. 1679), *Leviathan* (1651).
Hourani, G., *Islamic rationality*, Oxford, O.U.P.
Hourani, G., 'Islamic Rationalism: The ethics of Abd al-Jabbar', *Middle East Journal*, 25, 1971.
Hume, David (d. 1776), *Treatise of Human Nature* (1739–40); *Essays Moral and Political* (1742); *Political Discourses* (1753).
Iqbal, Muhammad, *The Reconstruction of Religious Thought in Islam*, Oxford, O.U.P., 1934.
Islamic Council of Europe, *The Challenge of Islam, Islam and the Contemporary Society*.
Islamic Council, *Universal Islamic Declaration of Human Rights,* London, 1982.
Legenhausen, M., 'The Islamic Writing of Human Rights', in *Contemporary Topics of Islamic Thought*, Islamic Culture and Relation Org., Iran, Dec.1999.
Little, David, Kelsay, John and Sachedina, Abdulaziz, A., *Human Rights and the Conflict of Cultures*, University of South Carolina Press,1988.
Locke, John (d. 1704) *Two Treatises of Government* (1690).
Luther, Martin, (d. 1546), *Temporal Authority* ; *Thiev ing Hordes of Peasants*; *Agains t the Murderous*; *Open Letter to Christian Nobility* (1520).
Machiavelli, N. (d. 1527), *The Prince* (1515); *The Art of War* (1520); *The Discourses* (1531).
Macintyre, Alasdair, *Whose Justice? Which Rationality?* Notre Dame University Press, 1988.
Madhkoor, M., *Tarikh al-Fikr al-Islami.*
Martin, R.C., Woodward, M.R. and Atmaja, D. S., *Defenders of Reason in Islam*, Oneworld, 1997.
Al-Marzouqi, A.A. Muhammad, 'Human Rights in Islamic Law', Ph.D dissertation, University of Exeter, 1991.
Mayer, Ann Elizabeth, *Islam and Human Rights*, Boulder, Westview Press, 1991.
Mill, James (d. 1836), *Essay on Government* (1820).
Mill, John Stuart (d. 1873), *On Liberty* (1859); *Considerations on Representative Government* (1861).
Mohamed, Yasien, *Fitrah: The Islamic Concept of Human Nature*, Ta Ha, 1996.
Mohamed, Yasien,; 'Fitrah and its Bearing on the Principles of Islamic Psychology', *AJISS* Vol.1, 12, pp.1–18.
Montesquieu, C. (d. 1755), *Persian Letters* (1721); *The Spirit of Laws* (1748).
Mughniyah, M., *Al-Islam wa al-'Aql wa al-Tashayyu'.*
Mutahhari, M., *Fi trat, 'adl-e-Ilahy*, (*The Human Being in the Qur'an*), Tehran, I.P.O., 1983.
Mutahhari, M., *Woman and Her Rights*, trans. M.A. Ansari, London, Al-Khoei Foundation, 1992.
Na'im, Abdullahi, *Towards an I slamic Reformation: Civil Liberties, Human Rights and International Law*, UK, 1996.
Nashshar, Ali, *Nash'at al-fikr al-Falsafi fi al-Islam*.
Nasr, S.H. *History of Islamic Philosophy*, Routledge, 1996.
Nasr, S.H., *Knowledge and the Sacred*, Edinburgh University, 1981.

Nasr, S.H. *Man and Nature, Religion and the Order of Nature.*
Pailin, David A., *Philosophy of Religion*, London, 1980.
Paine, Thomas (d. 1809), *Common Sense* (1776); *The Rights of Man* (1791–2); *The Age of Reason* (1795).
Peters, Ruud, 'Islamic Law and Human Rights', in *Islam and Christian-Muslim Relations*, Vol.10, No.1, 1999.
Piscatori, James, 'Human Rights in Islamic Political Culture', in Thompson, K.W. (ed.), *The Moral Imperatives of Human Rights*, Washington DC, University Press of America, 1980.
Plato (d. 347 BC), *Republic.* For text see Ryan, *Justice*, Oxford, O.U.P, 1993.
Putnam, H., *Renewing Philosophy*, Cambridge, Harvard University Press, 1992.
Rabbani Gulpayegani, Ali, *Fitrat wa Din* (*Human Primordial Nature and Religion*), Tehran, Canoon Andisheh Javan, 2001,
Rahman, Fazlur, *Islam*, second ed., University of Chicago Press, 1979.
Rahman, Fazlur, *Prophecy in Islam: Philosophy and Orthodox*, University of Chicago, 1979.
Rahman, Fazlur *Islam and Modernity*, University of Chicago Press, 1982.
Rahman, Fazlur, *Islamic Methodology in History*, Islamabad, Islamic Research Institute, 1984.
Renan, Ernest, *Averroes and Averroeism.*
Rispler-Chaim, V., 'Human Rights in Islam', in *Proceedings of the 1991 International Conference on Middle Eastern Studies*, Durham, BRISMES, pp.478–90.
Rommen, H., *The Natural Law: A Study in Legal and Social History and Philosophy*, St Louis and London, Herder, 1947.
Rousseau, J.J. (d. 1790), *Discourses* (1750, 1755); *Emile* (1762); *The Social Contract* (1762).
Routledge Encyclopedia of Philosophy, London, Routledge, 1998.
Rushdi, Muhammad, *Al-'aql 'ind al-Shi'ah.*
Russell, Bertrand (d. 1970) *The Principles of Social Reconstruction* (1916); *Power: A New Social Analysis* (1938).
Sadr, M.B., *Contemporary Man and the Social Problem*, Tehran, WOFIS, 1980.
Schimmel, A.M. *Mystical Dimension of Islam* Chapel Hill, University of North Carolina, 1975.
Schuon, F. *Understanding Islam*, London, 1976.
Sharif, M.M., *A Short History of Muslim Philosophy*, Delhi, 1995.
Shirazi, M.H., *Man's Dual Inclinations*, translated by M.J.Khalili, Tehran, International Publishing, 1997.
Singer, P. (ed.), *Ethics*, O.U.P., 1994.
Smith, Adam (d. 1778), *The Theory of Moral Sentiment* (1759).
Spinoza, B. (d. 1677), *Tractatus Theologico-politicus* (1670); *Tractatus Politicus* (1677).
Stevenson, Leslie, *Seven Theories of Human Nature*, Oxford, O.U.P., 1987.
Tabandeh, Sultanhussein, *A Muslim Commentary on the Universal Declaration of Human Rights*, trans. by Francis Goulding, Guildford, Goulding, 1970.
Tabataba'i, M.H., *Tafsir al-Mizan*, Tehran, 1342 AH.
Al-Tawil, Tufiq, *Al-Din wa al-Falsafah.*
Tuqan, Badri, *Maqamo al-'Aql 'ind al-Arab.*
Vincent, R.J., *Human Rights and International Relations*, Cambridge, C.U.P., 1986.
Zanjani, 'Abbas 'Ali Amid *Minority Rights* [in Islam], Tehran, International Pub, 1997.

Index